McDougal Littell

Grammar
for Writing

McDougal Littell
A HOUGHTON MIFFLIN COMPANY

McDougal Littell

Grammar for Writing

- GRAMMAR
- USAGE
- MECHANICS

McDougal Littell
A HOUGHTON MIFFLIN COMPANY

ISBN 13: 978-0-618-56622-8   ISBN 10: 0-618-56622-8

Printed in the United States of America.

Acknowledgments begin on page 345.

3 4 5 6 7 8 9–DCI–12 11 10 09 08

Contents Overview

10 Other Punctuation Marks

Quick-Fix Editing Machine

Special Features

Real World Grammar

Grammar in Literature

Quick-Fix Editing Machine

Student Resources

Grammar, Usage, and Mechanics

Making It Work

What makes an automobile run? How does a grandfather clock keep time? These machines may seem to work effortlessly, but beneath their outer shells lie gears and cams and switches—the mechanisms that do all the work. The mechanism behind language works the same way. The tools of grammar—parts of speech, punctuation marks, and usage rules— work together to make our language function.

LAST CHANCE
FULL SERVICE 24 HRS
GAS • WATER • FOOD
EIGHT PARTS OF SPEECH

As you reach the end of high school and drive toward your future, you may want to tune up your grammar skills. You will be needing those skills in whatever you do after high school. Just as you can't go anywhere without gas in your car, you can't use language well without understanding the eight parts of speech. If your brain has gotten a little rusty about those eight parts, take the self-check on the next page and see where you need a little oil!

Hey, with a tune-up and a clean

An **interjection** is a word or short phrase used to express emotion. (p. 22)

A **preposition** shows the relationship between a noun or pronoun and another word in the sentence. (p. 19)

A **conjunction** connects words, phrases, or clauses in a sentence. (p. 21)

An **adjective** modifies a noun or a pronoun. (p. 16)

Write the part of speech of each underlined word.

<u>Whoa!</u> You better pull over <u>fast,</u> chum. This is definitely your <u>last</u>
(1)   (2)   (3)

chance to give the <u>eight</u> parts <u>of</u> speech a final check. The <u>territory</u>
(4)   (5)   (6)

ahead could get rough, <u>you</u> know. No use <u>running</u> headlong <u>into</u>
(7)   (8)   (9)

clauses and <u>phrases</u> <u>or</u> whatnot, unless you have your eight parts of
(10)   (11)

speech well oiled <u>and</u> working in unison like pistons. So it's a <u>good</u>
(12)   (13)

thing you stopped <u>here,</u> even momentarily. Give <u>yourself</u> a
(14)   (15)

diagnostic right now. Then, if <u>it</u> turns out you're <u>still</u> grinding the
(16)   (17)

gears <u>on</u> grammar, this chapter can <u>provide</u> just the tune-up you
(18)   (19)

need. Take a look at the sentence <u>below</u> as a first step.
(20)

Self-Check Answers (upside down)

1. interjection	6. noun	11. conjunction	16. pronoun
2. adverb	7. pronoun	12. conjunction	17. adverb
3. adjective	8. verb	13. adjective	18. preposition
4. adjective	9. preposition	14. adverb	19. verb
5. preposition	10. noun	15. pronoun	20. adjective

windshield, I can see success ahead!

| A **pronoun** replaces a noun or another pronoun. (p. 9) | A **verb** expresses an action, a condition, or a state of being. (p. 13) | A **noun** names a person, thing, place, or idea. (p. 6) | An **adverb** modifies a verb, an adjective, or another adverb. (p. 17) |

❶ Review the Basics

▶ **A noun is a word that names a person, place, thing, or idea.**

PERSONS	**uncle, astronaut, Macbeth, Wynton Marsalis**
PLACES	**beach, arena, Tampa, Yellowstone National Park**
THINGS	**thermostat, lighthouse, volcano, Eiffel Tower**
IDEAS	**friendship, loyalty, hope, parenthood**

Common and Proper Nouns

A **common noun** is a general name for a person, place, thing, or idea. A **proper noun** is the name of a particular person, place, thing, or idea. Capitalize proper nouns.

Common and Proper Nouns	
Common nouns (general)	**Proper nouns (particular)**
woman	Jane Goodall, Amy Tan, Queen Noor
holiday	New Year's Eve, St. Patrick's Day, Labor Day
language	Urdu, Navajo, Chinese, English
city	Mexico City, Los Angeles, Dublin, Calcutta

Are you unsure which nouns to capitalize? See p. 198.

Singular and Plural Nouns

A **singular noun** names one person, place, thing, or idea. A **plural noun** names more than one. To make most nouns plural, add –s or –es to the singular form.

SINGULAR NOUNS	**cliff**	**leaf**	**cathedral**	**bus**
PLURAL NOUNS	**cliffs**	**leaves**	**cathedrals**	**buses**

For help in spelling singular or plural nouns, see p. 131.

Collective Nouns

A **collective noun** names a group—people or things that are regarded as a unit.

COLLECTIVE NOUNS	**congregation, team, club, board**

REVIEW

Abstract and Concrete Nouns

A **concrete noun** names an object that can be seen, heard, smelled, touched, or tasted. An **abstract noun** names something that cannot be perceived through the senses. An abstract noun names something that you can think about but cannot see or touch.

CONCRETE NOUNS **platform, steam, locomotive, street**

ABSTRACT NOUNS **envy, love, revenge, justice**

Compound Nouns

A **compound noun** is made up of two or more words. Compound nouns may be written as one word, as two words, or as a hyphenated word.

Compound Nouns		
As one word	**As two words**	**Hyphenated**
hilltop	steering wheel	flip-flop
beachcomber	surgeon general	self-portrait
tadpole	fishing pole	jack-of-all-trades

Possessive Nouns

A **possessive noun** shows ownership or belonging. Add –'s to form a singular possessive noun.

Dad's old car, *Sophie's Choice*

Add –s' to most plural possessive nouns.

parents' dilemma, the truckers' speed limit

For more about spelling rules for nouns, see p. 138.

For more about spelling rules for nouns, see p. 138.

Herman by Jim Unger

© 1986 Universal Press Syndicate

10-30   © 1982 Jim Unger

"Of course it's half eaten! You said
you wanted the Chef's salad."

PARTS OF SPEECH

❷ Nouns in Action

REVIEW

You can use both concrete and abstract nouns to add power to descriptions. Notice how Vera Brittain uses contrasting nouns to create a vivid description of what she sees and feels.

LITERARY MODEL

For a whole month in which off-duty time had been impossible, I had ceased to be aware of the visible world of the French countryside; my eyes had seen nothing but the **wards** and the **dying,** the **dirt** and dried **blood,** the obscene **wounds** of mangled **men** and the **lotions** and **lint** with which I had dressed them. Looking, now, at the pregnant **buds,** the green **veil** flung over the **trees** and the spilt **cream** of **primroses** in the bright, wet **grass,** I realized with a **pang** of **astonishment** that the **spring** had come.

> Nouns of death and destruction

> Nouns of beauty and life

I can look back more readily, I think, upon the War's tragedies—which at least had dignity—than upon those miserable weeks that followed my return from France. From a world in which **life** or **death, victory** or **defeat,** national **survival** or national **extinction,** had been the sole issues, I returned to a society where no one discussed anything but the price of butter....

> Paired nouns set up powerful contrasts.

—Vera Brittain, *Testament of Youth*

REVIEW: Nouns

The nouns in the following exercise are taken from the Literary Model. Use the following categories to identify each noun: concrete noun, proper noun, abstract noun, possessive noun, or compound noun. You will use two categories to identify some of the nouns.

1. War's	**6.** primroses
2. blood	**7.** death
3. astonishment	**8.** butter
4. dirt	**9.** tragedies
5. dignity	**10.** countryside

For more practice, see the EXERCISE BANK, p. 286.

REVIEW 2 · Pronouns

① Review the Basics

▶ **A pronoun is a word used in place of a noun or another pronoun.** The word that a pronoun stands for is called its antecedent. The **antecedent** may be found in the same sentence or in an earlier sentence.

The coach rejoiced at his good luck. He hugged his players.

♦ ANTECEDENT   ♦ PRONOUN   ♦ PRONOUNS ♦

Personal Pronouns

Personal pronouns refer to the first person (I), second person (you), and third person (he, she, it).

I think you should be nice to him.

♦ FIRST   ♦ SECOND   THIRD ♦
PERSON   PERSON   PERSON
(SPEAKER) (SPOKEN TO) (SPOKEN ABOUT)

A personal pronoun has three cases that indicate how it is used in a sentence.

• The nominative case is used for subjects and predicate nominatives.

• The objective case is used for the objects of verbs and prepositions.

• The possessive case is used to show ownership or belonging.

I warned you about her sense of humor.

♦ NOMINATIVE ♦ OBJECTIVE ♦ POSSESSIVE

Personal Pronouns			
	Nominative	**Objective**	**Possessive**
First person *(speaker)*	I, we	me, us	my, mine, our, ours
Second person *(person spoken to)*	you	you	your, yours
Third person *(person spoken about)*	he, she, it, they	him, her, it, them	his, her, hers, its, their, theirs

Gender Personal pronouns in third-person singular also have gender. These pronouns are masculine, feminine, or neuter depending on whether they refer to a male, a female, or a thing.

PARTS OF SPEECH

Possessive Pronouns

A **possessive pronoun** shows ownership or belonging. The following possessive pronouns are used to replace possessive nouns: mine, yours, his, hers, its, ours, theirs.

One more goal and victory is ours!

The following possessive pronouns are used as modifiers before nouns: my, your, his, her, its, our, their.

MODIFIES   MODIFIES

Is that a picture of your grandparents on their wedding day?

The possessive pronoun *his* can be used both ways.

His uniform really isn't his to keep.

Reflexive and Intensive Pronouns

Both reflexive and intensive pronouns are formed by adding *–self* or *–selves* to forms of the personal pronouns. Although these two types of pronouns look identical, they are used in different ways. A **reflexive pronoun** reflects an action back on the subject.

REFLECTS BACK

Ouch! I stuck myself with the pin.

An **intensive pronoun** adds emphasis to another noun or pronoun in the same sentence.

EMPHASIZES

The President himself urged Congress to act quickly.

Reflexive and Intensive Pronouns	
First person	myself, ourselves
Second person	yourself, yourselves
Third person	himself, herself, itself, themselves

Is it a reflexive or an intensive pronoun? If it can be removed without changing the meaning of the sentence, then it's an intensive pronoun.

Interrogative Pronouns

An **interrogative pronoun** asks a question.

who   whom   which   what   whose

Whose car is blocking the drive?
What would you have me do instead?

Demonstrative Pronouns

A **demonstrative pronoun** points out specific persons, places, things, or ideas. *This* and *these* point out persons or things that are relatively nearby in space or time. *That* and *those* point out persons or things that are farther away in space or time.

POINTS OUT
These are not my plates and forks.

POINTS OUT
That is a movie I'd like to see!

Relative Pronouns

A **relative pronoun** introduces a subordinate clause.

who   whose   whom   which   that

SUBORDINATE CLAUSE
He arrived late for the performance, which infuriated the whole cast.

For more on subordinate clauses, see p. 76.

Indefinite Pronouns

An **indefinite pronoun** does not refer to a specific person or thing. An indefinite pronoun usually does not have an antecedent.

Something tells me our secret is out.

Common Indefinite Pronouns	
Singular	another, anyone, anything, each, either, everybody, everyone, everything, much, neither, no one, nothing, one, somebody, someone, something
Plural	both, few, many, several
Singular or plural	all, any, more, most, none, some

For more on using pronouns correctly, see p. 133.

Calvin and Hobbes by Bill Watterson

PARTS OF SPEECH

❷ Pronouns in Action

In the model below, a young narrator observes a couple in love who are visiting a museum. Several pronouns in the passage refer to people or things mentioned earlier in the story. This use of pronouns keeps the writing both tight and unified by keeping relationships clear.

LITERARY MODEL

> **They** were talking, though **I** couldn't hear **what they** were saying because **they** were on the far side of the gallery. **They** stopped in front of a case and **I** could see **their** faces quite clearly. **They** stood there looking at **each** other, not talking any more, and **I** realized **I** hadn't made a mistake after all. Absolutely not. **They** didn't touch **each** other, **they** just stood and looked; **it** seemed like ages. **I** don't imagine **they** knew **I** was there.
>
> And that time **I** was shocked. Really shocked. **I** don't mind telling you, **I** thought **it** was disgusting. **He** was an ordinary-looking person—**he** might have been a schoolmaster or **something**, he wore **those** kind of clothes, old trousers and sweater, and **he** had greyish hair, a bit long. And there was **she**, and as **I've** said **she** wasn't pretty, not at all, but **she** had this marvelous look about **her**, and **she** was years and years younger.
>
> **It** was because of **him**, **I** realized, that **she** had that look.
>
> —Penelope Lively, "At the Pitt-Rivers"

REVIEW: Pronouns

Refer to Penelope Lively's passage above to complete these exercises.

1. Find an example of each of these kinds of pronouns in the passage: personal, possessive, relative, and indefinite.
2. Identify the nominative pronouns and the objective pronoun in this sentence: "<u>It</u> was because of <u>him,</u> <u>I</u> realized, that <u>she</u> had that look."
3. Identify the persons—first, second, or third—in the sentence, "<u>I</u> don't mind telling <u>you,</u> <u>I</u> thought <u>it</u> was disgusting."

For more practice, see the EXERCISE BANK, p. 286.

Verps

REVIEW 3

❶ Review the Basics

▶ **A verb is a word used to express an action, a condition, or a state of being.** The two main categories of verbs are action verbs and linking verbs.

Action Verbs

An **action verb** expresses an action. The action may be physical or mental.

PHYSICAL ACTION	**sing**	**run**	**sneeze**	**throw**
MENTAL ACTION	**brood**	**trust**	**consider**	**analyze**

Transitive and Intransitive Verbs Action verbs may be transitive or intransitive. A **transitive verb** transfers the action from the subject toward a **direct object.**

ACTS ON

The referee penalized the Tigers five yards.

An **intransitive verb** does not transfer action, so it does not have an object.

The crowd objected angrily.

Linking Verbs

A **linking verb** connects the subject with a word or words that identify or describe the subject. It can connect the subject with a noun, the predicate nominative.

LINKS TO

The queen's diamond tiara is a national treasure.

A linking verb can also connect the subject to a pronoun or an adjective in the predicate.

LINKS TO

The judge became impatient with the mumbling witness.

LINKS TO

The responsibility is hers.

Linking verbs can be divided into two groups: forms of *be* and verbs that express conditions.

Linking Verbs			
Forms of *be*	am	can be	has been
	is	may be	have been
	are	might be	had been
	was	will be	shall have been
	were	could be	could have been
	being	would be	would have been
	be	must be	will have been
Express Condition	appear	look	sound
	become	remain	stay
	feel	seem	taste
	grow	smell	turn

Most linking verbs express a state of being.

Grandpa was handsome back then, don't you think?

Some linking verbs express condition.

The restaurant looked deserted, so we kept going.

Some verbs can function as both action and linking verbs.

The cab driver turned into a dark alley. (ACTION)

The weather turned nasty. (LINKING)

LINKS

 Is it a linking verb or an action verb? It's a linking verb if it can be replaced by a form of the verb *be* and still make sense.

It sounds loud. It is loud. *SOUNDS* = LINKING VERB

Auxiliary Verbs

Auxiliary verbs, also called **helping verbs,** help the main verb express action or make a statement. Auxiliary verbs also help indicate voice, mood, or tense. A **verb phrase** is made up of a main verb and one or more helping verbs.

We should have called for directions first.

AUXILIARY VERBS   MAIN VERB

Common Auxiliary Verbs					
be	is	should	does	have	can
were	being	am	will	did	could
had	been	are	has	was	may
shall	do	must	might	would	

For more on using verbs correctly, see p. 130.

❷ Verbs in Action

Well-chosen verbs can make your writing more vigorous and interesting. Notice how both action and linking verbs in the following passage vividly capture sounds and movements in nature.

PROFESSIONAL MODEL

Our headlights **made** a tunnel of light, the sides shifting constantly as trees and shrubs **cast** flickering shadows ahead. . . . An elephant suddenly **burst** out of the trees, **rushed** across the roadway, and **disappeared.** It **ran** madly with its trunk thrown up, and it **screamed** in a wavering, high-pitched voice. That hysterical shriek **bespoke** the creature's terror; it also **inspired** terror. It **was** incongruous that such a huge, powerful animal **could be frightened** witless merely by the lights of an automobile.

As we **paused** to listen to the fading sounds of the elephant, we **became** conscious of other night noises. Small nameless creatures **rustled** in the dead grass. A leopard **coughed,** a short, harsh sound repeated several times. . . . This **was followed** by insane cackles from several throats—hyenas around a lion's kill.

—Victor H. Cahalane, "African Discovery"

REVIEW: Verbs

Refer to the passage above to complete these exercises.

1. Write the sentence from the last paragraph that contains a linking verb. Underline the two words that are connected by the linking verb.
2. Write a verb phrase from the passage. Underline the auxiliary verbs.
3. Find examples of two transitive verbs in the first paragraph. Write the transitive verbs and the direct objects that receive their actions. Example: <u>made</u> a <u>tunnel</u>
4. Write three action verbs from the passage that describe sounds. Then write three action verbs of your own that describe other sounds in nature.
5. Find examples of two intransitive verbs in the second paragraph. Write the intransitive verb and its subject. Example: <u>we</u> <u>paused</u>

For more practice, see the EXERCISE BANK, p. 287.

(REVIEW 4) Adjectives and Adverbs

❶ Review the Basics

Adjectives and adverbs are modifiers—they describe other words in a sentence.

▶ **An adjective is a word that modifies a noun or a pronoun.**

MODIFIES NOUN   **The map says there's a scenic outlook ahead.**

MODIFIES PRONOUN   **Let's stop at scenic outlooks! They can be spectacular.**

▶ **An adverb modifies a verb, an adjective, or another adverb.**

MODIFIES ADVERB   **That knife cuts really well.**

MODIFIES VERB   **It slices through bread easily.**

MODIFIES ADJECTIVE   **You'll find it's especially useful for peeling apples.**

Adjectives

An adjective qualifies or specifies the meaning of the noun or pronoun it modifies. It answers one of these questions:

WHAT KIND? **gold watch, enormous earrings, silky dress**

WHICH ONE? **this ring, another wedding, these gifts**

HOW MANY? **several guests, some cake, most bands**

HOW MUCH? **enough delays, more vacation**

There are four main categories of adjectives: articles, nouns used as adjectives, proper adjectives, and predicate adjectives.

Articles The articles a, an, and the are considered adjectives because they modify the nouns they precede.

   an uncle   **a boast**   **the reward for patience**

Nouns as Adjectives Sometimes nouns are used as adjectives.

   beach towel   **palm trees**   **suntan oil**

Proper Adjectives Proper adjectives are formed from proper nouns and are always capitalized, just as proper nouns are.

Proper Adjectives	
Proper Nouns	**Proper Adjectives**
America	American
France	French
Jefferson	Jeffersonian

Predicate Adjectives Predicate adjectives follow linking verbs and modify the subject of a sentence. Unlike most adjectives, predicate adjectives are separated from the words they modify.

MODIFIES

That painting is amateurish.

MODIFIES

Barbeque sauce with molasses tastes smoky.

For guidelines on capitalizing proper adjectives, see p. 201.

Adverbs

An adverb modifies a verb, an adjective, or another adverb. Most adverbs end in -ly. They answer the questions *how, where, when,* and *to what extent.*

Adverbs	
How?	whispered **urgently**, peeked **carefully**, closed **slowly**
Where?	drove **away**, headed **west**, climbed **upward**
When?	left **suddenly**, telephoned **constantly**, wrote **daily**
To what extent?	**very** happy, **exceptionally** pleased, **so** relieved

The word *not* is an adverb that tells to what extent. Though it often appears between the parts of the verb, it is not part of the verb. Example: could not go; verb = could go

For more information on using adverbs, see p. 178.

❷ Adjectives and Adverbs in Action

Notice how adjectives and adverbs help create the landscape faced by a mountain climber.

PROFESSIONAL MODEL

Nothing prepared me for that first unforgettable view. As I rounded a slope overlooking Tibet's great Kangshung Glacier, I suddenly faced an immense mass of ice and rock thrusting toward the vault of the sky. For many moments I stood motionless at the majesty of the scene—the virtually unknown East Face of Mount Everest.

As I watched, an avalanche silently began from somewhere on the mountain's height about a dozen miles away. Gathering size and speed as it descended the face, the slide spilled down and over the great buttresses of rock, exploding in a cloud of atomized ice on the surface of Kangshung Glacier, two miles below the mountain's summit. A long minute later the delayed rumble of the avalanche reached me in the stillness.

It was not a good omen.

—Andrew Harvard, "The Forgotten Face of Everest"

> **FEELING OF POWER AND SIZE**
>
> **FOCUS ON STILLNESS**
>
> **SPECIFIC DETAILS**

REVIEW: Adjectives and Adverbs

Tell whether each highlighted word in the preceding passage is an adjective or an adverb. Then locate the word that each one modifies. Write that word and its part of speech.

Example: immense—adjective;
modifies mass, a noun

For more practice in identifying adjectives and adverbs, see the EXERCISE BANK, p. 288.

❶ Review the Basics

A **preposition** shows the relationship between a noun or pronoun and another word in a sentence.

Each preposition below relates *slid* to *first base,* but a change of preposition means a change of action.

He slid into first base.

He slid over first base.

He slid toward first base.

He slid past first base.

Common Prepositions				
about	before	during	off	toward
above	behind	except	on	under
across	below	for	out	underneath
after	beneath	from	outside	until
against	beside	in	over	unto
along	between	inside	past	up
among	beyond	into	since	upon
around	but	like	through	with
as	by	near	throughout	within
at	down	of	to	without

Prepositional Phrases

A preposition always introduces a **prepositional phrase.** A prepositional phrase ends in a noun or pronoun called the **object of the preposition.** If the object has modifiers, they also are part of the prepositional phrase.

PREPOSITIONAL PHRASE

Throw the ball to second base.

PREPOSITION ⬆ MODIFIER ⬆ OBJECT OF PREPOSITION

Prepositional phrases can function as adjectives or adverbs.

PARTS OF SPEECH

Compound Prepositions and Objects

A **compound preposition** is a preposition that consists of more than one word.

Compound Prepositions	
according to	in place of
in addition to	in spite of
prior to	aside from
by means of	

The director praised the cast **prior to** the performance.

↑ COMPOUND PREPOSITION

A **compound object** is two or more objects of a single preposition.

Special seats were reserved for **parents, reviewers, and friends.**

↑   ↑   ↑
COMPOUND OBJECTS

❷ Prepositions in Action

You can use the short, simple preposition to clarify complex relationships. Here, W. Somerset Maugham uses prepositions to clarify location, time, gesture, and action.

LITERARY MODEL

    We walked back **through** St. James's Park. The night was so lovely that we sat down **on** a bench. **In** the starlight Rosie's face and her fair hair glowed softly. She was suffused, as it were (I express it awkwardly, but I do not know how to describe the emotion she gave me) **with** a friendliness **at** once candid and tender. She was **like** a silvery flower **of** the night that only gave its perfume **to** the moonbeams. I slipped my arm **round** her waist and she turned her face **to** mine.

    —W. Somerset Maugham, *Cakes and Ale*

REVIEW: Prepositions

For each colored preposition in the first two sentences above, write the entire prepositional phrase. Label the preposition with *P,* the object of preposition with *OP,* and any modifiers with *M.*

For more practice, see the EXERCISE BANK, p. 288.

Conjunctions and Interjections

❶ Review the Basics

▶ **A conjunction is a word used to join words or groups of words.**

Coordinating Conjunctions

A **coordinating conjunction** connects words or groups of words that have equal importance in a sentence.

> **and   but   or   for   so   yet   nor**

> **I added parsley, sage, rosemary, and thyme to the spaghetti sauce.**

> **Mom suggested a pinch of nutmeg, but we didn't have any.**

Conjunctive Adverbs A conjunctive adverb is an adverb used as a coordinating conjunction to clarify the relationship between clauses of equal weight in a sentence.

> **Keep the flame low; otherwise, the sauce will taste bland.**

When a conjunctive adverb is used within a clause instead of between a clause, use commas to set it off.

> **If you are in a hurry, however, turn up the heat and stir the sauce.**

Conjunctive Adverbs			
accordingly	finally	indeed	still
also	furthermore	moreover	then
besides	hence	nevertheless	therefore
consequently	however	otherwise	

Correlative Conjunctions

Correlative conjunctions are pairs of conjunctions that connect words or groups of words. Always used in pairs, they correlate with one another.

> **Put either olive oil or butter on pasta after it has been cooked.**

> **Both garlic bread and a salad go well with spaghetti.**

Correlative Conjunctions	
both . . . and	not only . . . but also
either . . . or	whether . . . or
neither . . . nor	

Subordinating Conjunctions

Subordinating conjunctions introduce subordinate clauses—clauses that cannot stand alone—and join them to independent clauses.

SUBORDINATE CLAUSE   INDEPENDENT CLAUSE

Even if you follow a recipe, mistakes can happen.

Subordinating Conjunctions

after	because	since	when
although	before	so that	whenever
as if	even if	than	where
as long as	even though	though	wherever
as much as	in order that	unless	while
as soon as	provided that	until	

Interjections

▶ **An interjection is a word or short phrase used to express emotion.** It has no grammatical connection to other words in a sentence. Interjections are usually set off from the rest of a sentence by a comma or by an exclamation mark.

Gosh! That was close!
Boy, there's something to be proud of.

© The New Yorker Collection 1998 Charles Barsotti

❷ Conjunctions in Action

You can use conjunctions to connect actions and ideas.

LITERARY MODEL

When at table, he was totally absorbed in the business of the moment; his looks seemed riveted to his plate; **nor** would he, **unless** when in very high company, say one word, **or** even pay the least attention to what was said by others, till he had satisfied his appetite, which was so fierce, and indulged with such intenseness, that while in the act of eating, the veins of his forehead swelled, and generally a strong perspiration was visible. To those whose sensations were delicate, this could not **but** be disgusting; . . .

—James Boswell, *The Life of Samuel Johnson*

LIMITS ACTIONS

COORDINATES ACTIONS

SHOWS CONTRAST

REVIEW: Conjunctions

Find these examples in the preceding passage:
- two coordinating conjunctions and the words they link
- two subordinating conjunctions

For more practice, see the EXERCISE BANK, p. 289.

Here's How Which Part of Speech Is It?

Many English words are used for more than one part of speech. To determine a word's part of speech, you need to look at how it's used.

Noun or verb?

The **slide** is fun.	**noun** (serves as subject)
Can you **slide?**	**verb** (serves as action)

Preposition or adverb?

She walked **down** the stairs.	**preposition** (has an object, *stairs*)
She fell **down!**	**adverb** (modifies verb *fell*)

Adjective or pronoun?

They hold **few** dances.	**adjective** (modifies noun, *dances*)
Few were invited.	**pronoun** (serves as subject)

Conjunction or preposition?

Call her **after** you rehearse.	**conjunction** (connects clauses)
Call her **after** the play.	**preposition** (has an object, *play*)

Chapter 1

The Parts of a Sentence

Instructions for returning Mr. Hyde to the form of Dr. Jekyll, penned by the doctor himself!

Use at my own risk. Incomplete or wrongful
transformations may occur! Side effects are common!
Boil one head of red cabbage in a large pot
Wait until liquid turns blood
Decant liquid into a seco
~~Save cabbage for sou~~
Add one cup of vine
Add one teaspoon of baking soda
Laugh maniacally. Repeat — higher this time.
Liquid will turn bright blue and fizz!

Oh, no!

An overturned beaker has sealed the fate of Dr. Jekyll!

Theme: Transformations and Changes

Nowhere to Hyde!

A real dilemma faces Dr. Jekyll. The spilled beaker has turned his instructions into fragments. Without a complete set of instructions, he is unable to change from the horrible Edward Hyde back into a well-respected physician. Will he find a way out of his predicament? Never has the importance of a complete sentence been more clear!

Write Away: Another You
Write about a time that you didn't seem like yourself. What made you seem different? How did friends react to you? Place your description in your ⬜ **Working Portfolio.**

Choose the letter of the term that correctly identifies each numbered part of this passage.

> On the dark streets of London, innocent people were being terrorized nightly. <u>By a sinister figure known as Edward Hyde</u>. <u>The life of this</u>
> (1)   (2)
> <u>criminal, Hyde,</u> was somehow linked to the life of Dr. Jekyll. Much to his attorney's dismay, Jekyll <u>had named Edward Hyde as his beneficiary</u>. Dr.
> (3)
> Jekyll's conservative <u>friends</u> disliked the youthful, arrogant Hyde.
> (4)
> However, they were unaware that Hyde was the result of one of Jekyll's experiments. <u>Friends and the household staff</u> were unaware of the
> (5)
> changes the doctor could force upon himself. They never <u>realized or</u>
> (6)
> <u>witnessed</u> the doctor's obsession with his identity-changing experiments.
> <u>What a transformation it was</u>! <u>Only by gaslight appeared the leering</u>
> (7)   (8)
> <u>Hyde</u>. Dr. Jekyll gave <u>terror</u> a new face. He was a doomed <u>genius</u>.
> (9)   (10)

1. A. inverted sentence
   B. exclamatory sentence
   C. fragment
   D. complete subject

2. A. complete predicate
   B. complete subject
   C. simple subject
   D. simple predicate

3. A. simple predicate
   B. complete predicate
   C. subject complement
   D. predicate nominative

4. A. simple subject
   B. simple predicate
   C. predicate nominative
   D. predicate adjective

5. A. direct object
   B. compound subject
   C. indirect object
   D. predicate adjective

6. A. compound verb
   B. compound subject
   C. compound noun
   D. compound adjective

7. A. declarative sentence
   B. interrogative sentence
   C. exclamatory sentence
   D. imperative sentence

8. A. interrogative sentence
   B. imperative sentence
   C. complete predicate
   D. inverted sentence

9. A. predicate adjective
   B. predicate nominative
   C. indirect object
   D. direct object

10. A. indirect object
    B. predicate adjective
    C. complete subject
    D. predicate nominative

Subjects and Predicates

❶ Here's the Idea

▶ **A sentence is a group of words used to express a complete thought. A complete sentence has a subject and predicate.**

- The **subject** tells whom or what the sentence is about.
- The **predicate** tells what the subject is or does, or what happens to the subject.

Robert Louis Stevenson	wrote *Dr. Jekyll and Mr. Hyde.*
SUBJECT	PREDICATE

Simple Subjects and Predicates

The most basic parts of a sentence are the simple subject and predicate.

▶ **The simple subject tells who or what performs the action in a sentence.**

By day, the compassionate **doctor** served the London community with great dedication.

▶ **The simple predicate tells what the subject did or what happened to the subject.**

Mr. Poole, Dr. Jekyll's butler, *expressed* concern about the mental state of his employer.

The doctor's erratic behaviors *did alarm* his staff.

> **Here's How** Finding the Simple Subject and Predicate
>
> - To find the **simple subject**, ask *who* or *what* is doing or being something.
> - To find the *simple predicate*, ask what the subject *does* or what *happens* to the subject.
>
>   Henry Jekyll *hid* his obsession from friends.

Complete Subjects and Predicates

▶ **The complete subject includes all the words that identify the person, place, thing, or idea a sentence is about.**

By day, the compassionate doctor served the London community with great dedication.

▶ **The complete predicate includes all the words that tell what the subject did or what happened to the subject.**

> **Mr. Poole, Dr. Jekyll's butler,** expressed concern about the mental state of his employer.

If either the subject or the predicate is missing from the sentence, the group of words is a **sentence fragment**.

> **Sentence Fragment:**
> Poured **the mixture into a glass beaker.** (MISSING SUBJECT)
>
> **Sentence:**
> **Dr. Jekyll** poured **the mixture into a glass beaker.**
>
> **Sentence Fragment:**
> **The** sight **of the frothing mixture.** (MISSING PREDICATE)
>
> **Sentence:**
> **The** sight **of the frothing mixture** frightened **Dr. Jekyll.**

Conversation frequently includes parts of sentences or fragments. In formal writing, however, you need to be sure that every sentence is a complete thought and includes a subject and predicate.

For more on fragments, see p. 89.

For more on fragments, see p. 89.

❷ **Why It Matters in Writing** ....

Both the subject and predicate are necessary for the meaning of the sentence to be clear. If you cannot find the subject or predicate in a group of words, the sentence is probably missing important information.

> **Mixed a potent concoction in his lonely laboratory.**
> (Who mixed a potent concoction? *Dr. Jekyll,* the subject, is missing.)
>
> **The twisted personality of Mr. Hyde.**
> (The twisted personality of Mr. Hyde did what? *Emerged* would make a good predicate to fix this fragment.)

❸ Practice and Apply

A. CONCEPT CHECK: Subjects and Predicates

Copy each sentence. Draw a line between the complete subject and the complete predicate. Underline the simple subject once and the simple predicate twice.

Answer: Kindly <u>Mr. Utterson</u> / <u>worried</u> about his troubled friend, Henry Jekyll.

Dr. Jekyll Unleashes Hyde
1. Jekyll's butler alerted the doctor's friends.
2. Hyde visited Jekyll nightly.
3. Mr. Utterson, an attorney and long-time friend of Dr. Jekyll's, suspected Hyde of blackmail.
4. Ironically, Jekyll willingly supplied his evil half with cash.
5. Hyde drew money from his own special bank account.
6. As Hyde, Jekyll slanted his handwriting.
7. Jekyll's former business associates were bewildered.
8. Hyde had some kind of weird power over the doctor.
9. Uncontrolled weeping often awakened the household.
10. Clearly, Jekyll was in the grip of something awful.

➡ **For a SELF-CHECK and more practice, see the EXERCISE BANK, p. 290.**

B. EDITING: Identifying What's Missing

Identify each word group as a complete sentence or a fragment. If it is a fragment, rewrite it to form a complete sentence.

Example: Wrote thrilling tales of adventure.
Answer: fragment;
  R. L. Stevenson wrote thrilling tales of adventure.

Profile of an Author
(1) In 1886, Robert Louis Stevenson penned the novella *The Strange Case of Dr. Jekyll and Mr. Hyde.* (2) Stevenson himself many transformations in his life. (3) As a child, his health was poor. (4) Didn't attend school regularly. (5) He studied engineering at Edinburgh University in Scotland. (6) But was unable to physically perform an engineer's tasks. (7) He tried law school, gaining entrance to the bar in 1875. (8) Not much to his liking, either. (9) Finally, after years of travel, began writing. (10) In a last attempt to regain his health, he retired to one of the Samoan islands, where he died at 44.

Compound Sentence Parts

❶ Here's the Idea

▶ **A compound sentence has more than one subject and verb, but neither is compound.** A sentence part containing more than one of these elements is called a compound part.

A **compound subject** consists of two or more simple subjects that share a verb. The subjects are joined by a conjunction, or connecting word, such as *and, or,* or *but.*

COMPOUND SUBJECT ↘   ↙ VERB

Some distant lamp or lighted window gleamed below me.

—James Joyce, "Araby"

A **compound verb** consists of two or more verbs or verb phrases that are joined by a conjunction and have the same subject.

The candle flame flutters **and** glows.

A **compound predicate** is made up of a compound verb and all the words that go with each verb.

I mounted the staircase **and** gained the upper part of the house.

—James Joyce, "Araby"

In the model below, the narrator has just asked a girl if she will go to the bazaar. The author makes actions flow by using compound subjects and verbs.

LITERARY MODEL

Her **brother** and two other **boys** were fighting for their caps and I was alone at the railings. She held one of the spikes, bowing her head towards me. The light from the lamp opposite our door caught the white curve of her neck, lit up her hair that rested there and, falling, lit up the hand upon the railing. It fell over one side of her dress and caught the white border of a petticoat, just visible as she stood at ease.

—James Joyce, "Araby"

> Compound subject

> Compound verbs

📁 **Working Portfolio** In your portfolio, find your **Write Away** assignment from page 24. Revise your description using compound subjects and verbs to tighten up your writing.

❷ Why It Matters in Writing

Often in your writing, you will use compound subjects or verbs to express your ideas more effectively. Be sure that compound subjects agree with the verb, and that compound verbs agree with the subject.

STUDENT MODEL

In the myth of Pygmalion, a sculptor designs and ~~craft~~ *crafts* a lovely ivory statue. He admires his creation and eventually ~~fall~~ *falls* in love with it. The goddess Venus ~~intervene~~ *intervenes* and transforms the statue into a beautiful, living woman. The sculptor and his creation ~~falls~~ *fall* in love. Venus blesses their marriage and they are wed.

❸ Practice and Apply

A. CONCEPT CHECK: Compound Sentence Parts

On a separate sheet of paper, write the compound subject or compound verb of each sentence.

Example: Ceres and Proserpine had a close mother-daughter relationship. *Answer:* Compound Subject: Ceres and Proserpine

Changes Caused by Love
1. Cupid and his mother, Venus, targeted Pluto, the god of the underworld, for their next victim.
2. Cupid shot Pluto with his arrow and transformed him into a lovesick youth.
3. From his chariot, Pluto saw Proserpine in a field of flowers and carried her off.
4. In fury and distress, Ceres sought revenge and stripped the land of its fertility.
5. After much wrangling, Pluto and Ceres reached a compromise.

➜ For a SELF-CHECK and more practice, see the EXERCISE BANK, p. 290.

B. WRITING: Creating Your Own Myth

Write your own myth. Create 10 sentences with compound subjects and verbs.

Kinds of Sentences

LESSON 3

❶ Here's the Idea

▶ **A sentence can be used to make a statement, ask a question, give a command, or show feelings.**

Kinds of Sentences

Declarative Expresses a statement of fact, wish, intent, or feeling
You have never jumped in a pile of leaves.

Interrogative Asks a question
Have you ever jumped in a pile of leaves?

Imperative Gives a command, request, or direction
Never jump in a pile of leaves.

Exclamatory Expresses strong feeling
What a great jump!

❷ Why It Matters in Writing

If your writing contains only declarative sentences, you will quickly lose your readers' interest. By adding an interrogative, imperative, or exclamatory sentence to the mix, you can recapture their attention.

❸ Practice and Apply

CONCEPT CHECK: Identifying Kinds of Sentences

Identify the following sentences as declarative, imperative, interrogative, or exclamatory.

There's Gold in Those Leaves!
1. New Englanders brag about the fall colors in their region.
2. Isn't the Great Lakes region being overlooked?
3. Michigan's fall colors are exceptional!
4. Take a ride through Michigan in October.
5. Michigan takes in a third of its tourist income in autumn.
6. Travel the eastern shore of Lake Michigan on back roads.
7. How lovely the beaches and state parks are!
8. Have you ever camped at Sleeping Bear Dunes?
9. You have to carry in all your gear!
10. Don't forget to bring your camera and lots of film.

➜ For a SELF-CHECK and more practice, see the EXERCISE BANK, p. 291.

Subjects in Unusual Positions

① Here's the Idea

Usually the subject is placed before the verb in a sentence. Sometimes, however, the subject appears after the verb.

Inverted Sentences

▶ **In an inverted sentence, the verb or part of the verb phrase is stated before the subject.** An inverted sentence can be used for emphasis or variety.

Usual Order: A leafless oak stood in the yard.

Inverted Order: In the yard stood a leafless oak.

Sentences Beginning with *Here* or *There*

▶ **When a sentence begins with *here* or *there*, the subject usually follows the verb.** Remember that *here* and *there* are almost never the subjects of a sentence.

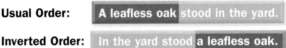

Here comes **the first sign of fall.** There was **a frost last night.**
         SUBJECT ↗   SUBJECT ↗

Subjects in Questions

In most questions, the subject appears between the words that make up the verb phrase.

Were **the leaves** scattered? Did **you** see **them?**

In questions that begin with the interrogative words *what, how many,* or *who,* the subject often falls between the parts of a verb.

How many piles did **all those** leaves make?

In some questions, however, the interrogative word functions as the subject and comes before the verb.

Who raked **them up?** What happened?

Subjects in Commands

The subject of an imperative sentence is usually *you.* When the subject is not stated, *you* is understood to be the subject.

Request: (You) Please remember to write me this fall.

Command: (You) Don't forget! We're going to wish on the moon.

❷ Why It Matters in Writing

Writing that consists only of declarative sentences structured with traditional subject-verb order can be boring to read. Using different types of sentences allows you to engage your readers and call attention to certain words and ideas.

PROFESSIONAL MODEL

Have **you** ever climbed an Adirondack Mountain? (**You**) Imagine that view painted a breathtaking array of colors. This **is** **autumn** in the Adirondacks.

QUESTION CAPTURES READERS' ATTENTION.

COMMAND ENGAGES THE READER.

INVERTED SENTENCE EMPHASIZES *AUTUMN.*

❸ Practice and Apply

A. CONCEPT CHECK: Subjects in Unusual Positions

Write the subjects and the verbs from the following sentences.

Example: Why do leaves change colors in the autumn?
Answer: subject: leaves; verb: do change

Why Leaves Change
1. There are new, brilliant shades of color on the trees.
2. At the base of each leaf's stalk forms a dense cell layer.
3. In the leaf, food production gradually decreases.
4. Obstructed are the cells and veins in the leaf.
5. Check the leaf for chlorophyll production.
6. Without chlorophyll, the green color is no longer visible.
7. Hidden by the green are the other hues of the leaf.
8. Contained in all leaves are yellow pigments.
9. Also present are red and purple pigments.
10. Will the trees in your area display brilliant colors this autumn?

➡ For a SELF-CHECK and more practice, see the EXERCISE BANK, p. 291.

B. REVISING: Creating Sentence Variety

Rewrite the following sentences to achieve variety.

Burning leaves used to be a fall ritual. The smell scented the autumn air. Concerns about the environment led to laws prohibiting leaf burning. Baking a pumpkin pie is an enjoyable alternative, and it smells wonderful too.

Subject Complements

LESSON 5

❶ Here's the Idea

> **A complement is a word or a group of words that completes the meaning of a verb.** There are two kinds of complements: subject complements and object complements.

A **subject complement** follows a linking verb and describes or renames the subject. Subject complements often come after a form of the verb *be*. There are two kinds of subject complements: **predicate adjectives** and **predicate nominatives**.

Do you remember the linking verbs? If not, see p. 14.

Predicate Adjective

Predicate adjectives follow linking verbs and describe subjects.

MODIFIES

A petrified tree's stone rings appear interesting.

MODIFIES

Scientists feel confident about the rings' meaning.

MODIFIES

Living and petrified redwoods seem similar.

Predicate Nominative

Predicate nominatives are nouns and pronouns that follow linking verbs and rename, identify, or define subjects.

SAME AS

In petrified trees, crystals are the remainder of iron oxide.

SAME AS

Chalcedony is a translucent pale-blue or gray quartz.

This sample of petrified wood is mine.

❷ Why It Matters in Writing

Subject complements allow you to further define your subject by providing additional information or explanation.

RENAMES

The sediments in petrified trees are often minerals. (*MINERALS* IS A PREDICATE NOMINATIVE THAT RENAMES THE SUBJECT.)

❸ Practice and Apply

CONCEPT CHECK: Identifying Subject Complements

Identify the predicate adjective or the predicate nominative in each sentence.

Example: Dr. Jane Carson is the lead paleontologist.
Answer: paleontologist = predicate nominative

What Fossils Are
1. Fossils are the preserved remains of once living organisms.
2. The fascinating science of fossils is paleontology.
3. Paleontology seems mysterious to some people.
4. Excellent sources of fossils are foundations of buildings, stone quarries, and coal mines.
5. Deposits of sediment are the best sources of fossils.
6. Long ago, conditions in Europe were prime for fossilization.
7. Fossils such as animal teeth, bones, and shells are typical.
8. Krems, Austria, is famous for its mammoth bone fossils.
9. An inclusion fossil is an embedded plant, insect, or flower.
10. Fossilized prints of fish, leaves, and blossoms look delicate.
11. Within shells, the changes appear artistic.
12. Silicon dioxide is the reason.
13. Stone core fossils, the result of shells filling with sand and calcifying, look remarkable.
14. A pseudofossil is only a mineral deposit.
15. Fossils are a valuable avenue for understanding history.

➡ **For a SELF-CHECK and more practice, see the EXERCISE BANK, p. 292.**

Objects of Verbs

❶ Here's the Idea

Many action verbs require complements called direct objects and indirect objects to complete their meaning.

Direct and Indirect Objects

▶ **A direct object is a noun or pronoun that receives the action of an action verb.** It answers the question *what?* or *whom?*

Eastern Arizona contains fascinating **displays** of petrified wood.

The petrified trees amaze **visitors.**

The direct object can be just one word, or it can consist of a phrase or clause.

Archaeology students practice **identifying fossils.**

Geologists understand **how the transformation occurred.**

▶ **An indirect object is a word or a group of words that tells *to whom* or *for whom* the action of the verb is being performed.**

These forests offer **scientists** a glimpse into the past.
　　　　　　　　　↑INDIRECT OBJECT ↑DIRECT OBJECT

Verbs that often take indirect objects include *bring, give, hand, lend, make, offer, send, show, teach, tell,* and *write.*

Objective Complements

▶ **An objective complement is a noun or adjective that follows the direct object and identifies or describes it.** Objective complements are usually paired with verbs such as *appoint, call, choose, consider, elect, find, make, name, render,* and *think.* These objective complements answer the question *what?*

Collectors find **fossils fascinating.**
　　DIRECT OBJECT ↗　　　↖OBJECTIVE COMPLEMENT

Geologists consider **a stone quarry prime fossil territory.**
                          DIRECT OBJECT   OBJECTIVE COMPLEMENT

❷ Why It Matters in Writing

Well-chosen complements can improve the clarity and precision of a sentence. Look at how changing the objects makes a difference in this sentence.
                                    visitors   glimpse
The petrified forest offers ~~people~~ a startling ~~look~~ at the past.
                              INDIRECT OBJECT   DIRECT OBJECT

❸ Practice and Apply

CONCEPT CHECK: Objects of Verbs

Each sentence below has at least one object. Write each object and identify it as a direct object, indirect object, or objective complement.

Example: Fossils bring people pleasure.
Answer: people, indirect object; pleasure, direct object

"Petrified Charlie," the Amateur Geologist
1. Calistoga, California, attracts thousands of visitors.
2. Geologists call the fossil forest there exemplary.
3. Layers of volcanic mud gave the trees a protective coating.
4. "Petrified Charlie" made the site famous.
5. In his pasture, he found a huge petrified redwood.
6. The process of petrifaction gives trees a stone-like aspect.
7. Neighbors thought Charlie crazy for digging up the giants alone.
8. His cow pasture contained dozens of buried petrified redwoods.
9. Charlie charged visitors a quarter to take a self-guided tour.
10. Robert Louis Stevenson, a visitor, called Charlie brave.

➜ For a **SELF-CHECK** and more practice, see the **EXERCISE BANK, p. 292.**

SENTENCE PARTS

Sentence Diagramming

❶ Here's the Idea

Watch me for diagramming tips!

A sentence diagram is really a graphic organizer.

- It gives you a visual representation of the sentence.
- It helps you understand how the parts of a sentence are connected.

When you diagram a sentence, you analyze its components, classify its parts, and observe how its parts are related.

Simple Subjects and Verbs

The simple subject and the verb are written on one line and are separated by a vertical line that crosses the main line.

Scientists | study   Researchers | discover

Compound Subjects and Verbs

For a compound subject or verb, split the main line. Write the conjunction on a dotted line connecting the compound parts.

Compound Subject: Scientists and researchers study.

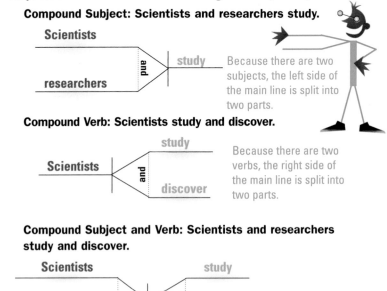

Scientists

and study

researchers

Because there are two subjects, the left side of the main line is split into two parts.

Compound Verb: Scientists study and discover.

study

Scientists

and

discover

Because there are two verbs, the right side of the main line is split into two parts.

Compound Subject and Verb: Scientists and researchers study and discover.

Scientists   study

and   and

researchers   discover

A. CONCEPT CHECK: Subjects and Verbs

Diagram these sentences, using what you learned above.

1. Archaeologists analyzed.
2. Archaeologists analyzed and examined.
3. Archaeologists and paleontologists analyzed and examined.

Adjectives and Adverbs

Because adjectives and adverbs modify, or tell more about, other words in a sentence, they are written on slanted lines below the words they modify.

The unsuccessful excavation ended suddenly.

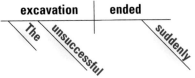

B. CONCEPT CHECK: Adjectives and Adverbs

Diagram these sentences, using what you learned above.

1. The weary scientists rejoiced happily.
2. A new specimen and an ancient artifact finally surfaced.
3. The proud researchers and their students celebrated and gratefully rested.

Subject Complements: Predicate Nominatives & Predicate Adjectives

Write a predicate nominative or a predicate adjective on the main line after the verb. Separate the subject complement from the verb with a slanted line that does not cross the main line.

Dr. Jones is the expedition leader. (PREDICATE NOMINATIVE)

Dr. Jones | is \ leader

The fossil site looks worthless. (PREDICATE ADJECTIVE)

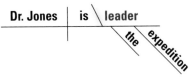

The slanted line separating a subject complement from a verb does not cross the main line.

C. CONCEPT CHECK: Subject Complements

Diagram these sentences using what you have learned.

1. The expedition was totally unsuccessful.
2. The costly trip was an unhappy experience.
3. The largest treasure is still valuable.

Direct Objects

A direct object follows the verb on the same line.

Fossil hunters use delicate instruments.

The vertical line between a verb and its direct object does not cross the main line.

Direct objects can also be compound. Like all compound parts, they go on parallel lines that branch from the main line.

These scientists use tiny tools and dental drills.

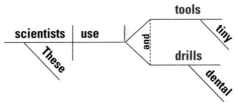

To show a compound predicate, split the line and show both parts of the predicate on parallel lines.

Workers preserve the fossils and transport the shipment.

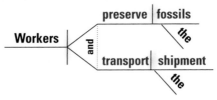

Indirect Objects

Write an indirect object below the verb, on a horizontal line connected to the verb by a slanted line.

Researchers gave the fossils a final inspection.

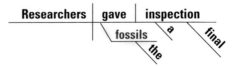

They faxed the museum staff their fossil data.

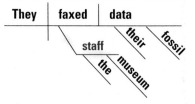

Objective Complements

An objective complement is written on the main line after the direct object and is separated from it by a slanted line.

A fossil discovery makes people happy.

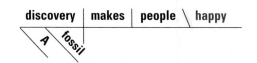

Scientists consider the mammoth bones an important find.

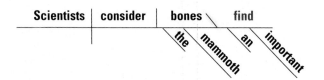

D. MIXED REVIEW: Diagramming

Use what you have learned about parts of a sentence to diagram the following sentences.

1. Rock formations change gradually.
2. Sedimentary rocks appear dusty.
3. Sandstone is a common sedimentary rock.
4. Weight and pressure layer metamorphic rock.
5. Treasure hunters gather specimens and examine them.
6. Fiery magma material formed igneous rocks.
7. Tremendous pressure gives bituminous coal a hard quality.
8. Geologists painstakingly classify rocks and minerals.
9. Scientists study geologic transformations and publish their results.
10. Rock collectors consider specimens valuable.

Real World Grammar

Feature Article

Any written article or report usually begins in note form. To transform notes into a well-written article, the writer must fix fragments, add details, and create paragraphs. Tamara Bentley, a reporter for the school newspaper, took notes for a story about the drama club's production of *The Strange Case of Dr. Jekyll and Mr. Hyde*. She then began planning how she would transform her notes into a finished piece of writing.

Transforming Dr. Jekyll into Mr. Hyde

Brant Wilson, senior, plays Jekyll and Hyde
goes from conservative doctor to hideous Hyde
used makeup and body language
Heather Mikes, junior, makeup artist
heavy foundation
• make Hyde scary with dark eyebrow pencil
and small toothbrush for eyebrows
brush brown makeup for ruddy complexion
add muted red color on cheeks
Hyde is arrogant but smaller than Jekyll
body language for transformation
audience reacts well—effect complete

make sure to use complete sentences

start new paragraph

start new paragraph

add details

Using Grammar in Writing	
Tips	**Technique**
Avoid choppy sentences	Use compound sentence parts to combine ideas.
Don't bore your readers	Provide a mix of the four kinds of sentences.
Emphasize key ideas	Invert sentence order, when appropriate.
Avoid fragments	Make sure your sentences have subjects and predicates.

CHAPTER 1

REVISED DESCRIPTION

This is the way Tamara's article appeared, rewritten from her notes.

Transforming Dr. Jekyll into Mr. Hyde

The drama club faced a challenge in presenting that classic spine-tingler, *The Strange Case of Dr. Jekyll and Mr. Hyde.* What could transform a nice-looking, conservative doctor, played by Brant Wilson, into the hideous creature known as Edward Hyde? The answer, of course, is the creative application of makeup. Skillful use of makeup and ingenious use of body language can drastically change a character's appearance.

To make Brant's transformation realistic, makeup artist Heather Mikes, a junior, applied a heavy foundation. Brant's Hyde character repulsed and intimidated people. To make him look scary, Heather used a dark eyebrow pencil and a small toothbrush on his eyebrows. Next, she brushed on brown makeup for a ruddy complexion. Finally, she streaked Brant's cheeks with a muted red color.

Mr. Hyde was much more arrogant than Dr. Jekyll, but he was much smaller in stature. Brant slouched and affected a swagger for a complete transformation. Many playgoers felt that his terrible alteration, achieved through the use of makeup and body language, was very effective.

PRACTICE AND APPLY: Revising

Jorge Ocampo helped Heather do the makeup for the production of *The Strange Case of Dr. Jekyll and Mr. Hyde.* Here are the notes he took about applying stage makeup. Use the writing tips in the chart, "Using Grammar in Writing," to write an instructional paragraph from his notes.

STUDENT MODEL

How to Apply Stage Makeup

assemble tools—begin with foundation—get damp sponge—apply base for even coating—actor looks up when you paint under the eyes—flatten makeup brush for thick line—fine strokes create feathering—shade with intense hues of color—blend—damp sponge for smooth finish—vivid colors are good

A. Subjects, Predicates, and Kinds of Sentences Read the passage. Then write the answers to the questions below it.

(1) Charles Dickens, one of the greatest writers of the nineteenth century, experienced many changes in his personal life. (2) During his childhood, he suffered bouts of great poverty and even stayed in the Marshalsea Prison for a time. (3) Did you know that the young Charles Dickens once worked in a warehouse? (4) His mother and father, although loving, did not know how to manage their finances. (5) Dickens based the character of the financially strapped, eternally optimistic Mr. Micawber in *David Copperfield* on his own father. (6) His inspiration grew out of his own unhappy childhood. (7) Editors purchased Dickens's works. They serialized them. (8) In his later life, Dickens's wealth and fame grew. (9) A very dramatic person, Dickens loved theater and acted in plays himself. (10) Have you read that Dickens once toured and lectured in America?

1. What are the simple subject and predicate in sentence 1?
2. What is the compound verb in sentence 2?
3. What kind of sentence is sentence 3?
4. What are the compound parts in sentence 4?
5. What is the simple predicate of sentence 5?
6. Revise sentence 6 so that it is an inverted sentence.
7. Combine the sentences. Use a compound verb in the new sentence.
8. What is the compound subject in sentence 8?
9. What is the compound verb in sentence 9?
10. What kind of sentence is sentence 10?

B. Subject and Object Complements Identify each underlined word in the following passage as a direct object, an indirect object, a predicate nominative, or a predicate adjective.

In 1795, William Smith was an <u>engineer</u> in England. A routine
   (1)
project made <u>him</u> a self-taught geologist instead. While supervising
   (2)
the digging of the Somersetshire Canal, he discovered an

extraordinary <u>fact</u>. Fossils were a chronological <u>record</u> in
   (3)   (4)
sedimentary rock from top to bottom. The identical order appeared

<u>consistent</u> everywhere. When the project ended, Smith gave <u>himself</u>
   (5)   (6)
an ambitious <u>goal.</u> For fifteen years, he painstakingly created a
   (7)
geologic <u>map</u> of England. He felt <u>unappreciated</u> by the scientific
   (8)   (9)
community. Finally, in 1831, the Geological Society of London

awarded the humble <u>engineer</u> its highest honor.
   (10)

CHAPTER 1

Choose the letter of the term that correctly identifies each numbered part of this passage.

Which holiday classic was penned in three weeks in 1843? Why, the
(1)
classic is none other than the famed *A Christmas Carol!* Dickens found
(2)
the little book's popularity astonishing.
(3)

At the beginning of the tale, Ebenezer Scrooge has a vision of his dead
(4)
partner, Jacob Marley. Marley, who was once as miserly as Scrooge, warns
him to change. Three spirits visit Scrooge and reveal the dire costs of his
(5)
selfishness.

Scrooge is a changed man. He gives his loyal, overworked clerk, Bob
(6)   (7)
Cratchit, a higher salary. He purchases an enormous turkey for the
(8)
Cratchit family. The man who was "solitary as an oyster" becomes a
(9)
"second father" to Tiny Tim! This is the power of a change of heart.
(10)

---

1. A. exclamatory sentence
   B. interrogative sentence
   C. imperative sentence
   D. declarative sentence

2. A. simple subject
   B. predicate nominative
   C. predicate adjective
   D. indirect object

3. A. predicate adjective
   B. objective complement
   C. simple predicate
   D. direct object

4. A. simple predicate
   B. predicate adjective
   C. indirect object
   D. direct object

5. A. simple predicate
   B. predicate adjective
   C. complete predicate
   D. direct object

6. A. direct object
   B. predicate adjective
   C. predicate nominative
   D. objective complement

7. A. indirect object
   B. direct object
   C. predicate adjective
   D. simple subject

8. A. indirect object
   B. direct object
   C. simple subject
   D. predicate adjective

9. A. declarative sentence
   B. interrogative sentence
   C. imperative sentence
   D. exclamatory sentence

10. A. simple subject
    B. predicate nominative
    C. predicate adjective
    D. direct object

SENTENCE PARTS

Student Help Desk

The Sentence at a Glance

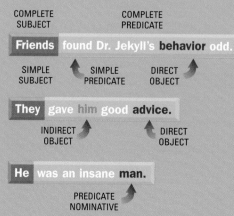

COMPLETE SUBJECT   COMPLETE PREDICATE

Friends found Dr. Jekyll's **behavior** odd.

SIMPLE SUBJECT   SIMPLE PREDICATE   DIRECT OBJECT

They gave him good **advice.**

INDIRECT OBJECT   DIRECT OBJECT

He was an insane **man.**

PREDICATE NOMINATIVE

Subjects and Predicates   Watch the Sentence Grow

Simple Subject	**Dr. Jekyll** was a man.
Compound Subject	**Dr. Jekyll** and **Mr. Hyde** were the same man.
Simple Predicate	Dr. Jekyll and Mr. Hyde fought for control.
Compound Subject and Compound Verb	**Dr. Jekyll** and **Mr. Hyde fought** and **died** for control.

Complements (not compliments)

Term or Concept	Example	Tips and Techniques
Predicate nominative	So this is **Hyde.**	Renames the subject
Predicate adjective	You, sir, are **repugnant.**	Describes the subject
Direct object	You abuse **people.**	Receives the verb's action. Ask, *Does what?*
Indirect object	You should give **us** a reason for your behavior.	Tells to or for whom the action is done. Ask, *Does what to whom?*

Subject in Unusual Positions

Toying with the Recipe

Inverted Sentence

In an inverted sentence, the verb is stated before the subject.
Normal: A **light** shone from Jekyll's laboratory.
Inverted: From Jekyll's laboratory shone a **light.**

Sentences beginning with *here* or *there*

When sentences begin with *here* and *there,* the subject usually follows the verb.
Here: Here is the **butler** to help us.
There: There lies Jekyll's **notebook.**

Subjects in questions

Find the subject by changing the question to a statement.
Question: Is **he** going to regret this?
Statement: **He** is going to regret this.

Subject in commands

The subject in a command is *you.*
(You) Get me the police immediately!
(You) Leave me alone—I insist!

The Bottom Line

Sentence Completeness Checklist

Do my sentences have . . .

____ subjects and predicates?

____ specific information and descriptive details?

____ word order that creates emphasis?

____ compound subjects or verbs to make my meaning clearer?

____ subjects and verbs that agree?

Using Phrases

E-mail

New Memo   Delete   File   Forward   Reply

To: Bigfoot/Sasquatch Database   **Subject:** I saw. . . Bigfoot?
Submitted by: (Confidential)   **Date:** September 15, 2000
When Sighted: February or March 2000
Where: Chemult, Oregon, Amtrak station
Observed: While waiting for the train, we noticed something on the opposite side of the tracks—maybe 200 ft. south of us. It was on the east side of the tracks, walking away in a lurching manner. At first, we thought it was someone in costume but soon realized that this big, brown hairy creature was a real "thing." At that point, one of the boys ran after it, but the creature moved at a surprisingly swift pace and disappeared.

Theme: Eyewitness Accounts

Why Do Phrases Matter?

Have you ever seen anything as incredible as a Bigfoot? If so, were you able to recount your experience as clearly as this eyewitness does? Phrases can help you clarify precisely what happened, where, and in what order—if you know how to use them. For example, the writer of this account uses phrases such as "on the opposite side of the tracks" to pinpoint the locations of the people—and "creature"—as well as to describe exactly what each does and when.

Write Away: Extraordinary Experiences
Describe an event you experienced firsthand. This might even be something startling. Be sure to make clear what you saw and precisely where you saw it. Save it in your 📁 **Working Portfolio.**

Choose the letter of the description that identifies the function of each underlined group of words.

You might think it's like making a downhill ski run <u>on a vertical cliff</u>.
(1)
This cliff, however, is moving <u>under your feet</u>. You are a surfer riding
(2)
"Jaws," <u>the enormous waves of Hawaii</u>. <u>Occurring about twelve times a</u>
(3)   (4)
<u>year</u>, Jaws' huge waves are caused by Pacific storm winds that break in a

deep reef off the north shore of Maui, <u>Hawaii's second largest island</u>.
(5)
<u>That having been said</u>, would you like <u>to meet some of the surfers who</u>
(6)   (7)
<u>think of Jaws as fun</u>? Dave Kalama describes <u>being "wiped out" by Jaws</u>,
(8)
saying, "You're doing cartwheels and flips and somersaults all at the same

time." <u>To reach shore safely</u> is Mike Waltze's goal, but he never misses a
(9)
chance <u>to ride Jaws again</u>. Why? He's consumed by the thrill.
(10)

---

1. A. participial phrase
   B. appositive phrase
   C. prepositional phrase
   D. gerund phrase

2. A. adverb prepositional phrase
   B. adjective prepositional phrase
   C. infinitive phrase
   D. dangling participle

3. A. gerund phrase
   B. prepositional phrase
   C. participial phrase
   D. appositive phrase

4. A. prepositional phrase
   B. participial phrase
   C. appositive phrase
   D. infinitive phrase

5. A. essential appositive phrase
   B. nonessential appositive phrase
   C. absolute phrase
   D. participial phrase

6. A. prepositional phrase
   B. appositive phrase
   C. gerund phrase
   D. absolute phrase

7. A. infinitive phrase used as adjective
   B. infinitive phrase used as noun
   C. infinitive phrase used as adverb
   D. prepositional phrase

8. A. gerund phrase used as subject
   B. gerund phrase used as indirect object
   C. gerund phrase used as direct object
   D. gerund phrase used as object of preposition

9. A. prepositional phrase
   B. infinitive phrase
   C. appositive phrase
   D. gerund phrase

10. A. infinitive phrase used as adjective
    B. infinitive phrase used as noun
    C. infinitive phrase used as adverb
    D. infinitive phrase used as appositive

PHRASES

Prepositional Phrases

▶ **A phrase is a group of related words that does not have a subject or a predicate.** A phrase functions as a single part of speech.

You can use phrases to add important details and information to your writing. This lesson shows you how to use prepositional phrases.

❶ Here's the Idea

▶ **A prepositional phrase consists of a preposition, its object, and any modifiers of the object.**

Captain Æneas Mackintosh sailed to the Antarctic.
                              PREPOSITION ↗

Notice how Captain Mackintosh uses prepositional phrases to make vividly clear some of the hardships he suffered at night.

LITERARY MODEL

...I shiver **in a frozen sleeping-bag**. The inside fur is a mass **of ice**, congealed **from** my breath. One creeps **into the bag**, toggles [zips] up **with half-frozen fingers**, and hears the crackling **of the ice**. Presently drops **of thawing ice** are falling **on** one's head. Then comes a fit **of shivers**.
—Æneas Mackintosh, quoted in *South* by Ernest Shackleton

PREPOSITIONAL PHRASES

For a list of prepositions, see p. 19.

You can use prepositional phrases as adjectives or adverbs.

Adjective Phrases

▶ **An adjective phrase is a prepositional phrase that modifies a noun or a pronoun.**

You can use an adjective phrase to answer the question "Which one?" or "What kind?" In the sentence below, the phrase "of shivers" answers the question "What kind of fit?"

                    MODIFIES
Then comes a fit of shivers.

Adverb Phrases

▶ **An adverb phrase is a prepositional phrase that modifies a verb, an adjective, or an adverb.**

You can use an adverb phrase to tell *when, where, how, why,* or *to what extent.*

Modifying a Verb:
Mackintosh shivered in a frozen sleeping-bag.
MODIFIES

Modifying an Adjective:
The fur lining was icy from his breath.
MODIFIES

Modifying an Adverb:
Still, he crept out of the bag reluctantly.
MODIFIES

To avoid confusing readers, position a prepositional phrase as close as possible to the word it modifies.

Confusing:
Scott reported the dark clouds to his captain in the east.

Revised:
Scott reported the dark clouds in the east to his captain.

② Why It Matters in Writing

You can use prepositional phrases to clarify such things as the order of events and the location of events, people, and objects.

> **LITERARY MODEL**
>
> **After** days **of** continuous heavy duty and scamped [hurried], inadequate meals, our nerves were none too reliable, and I don't suppose I was the only member **of** the staff whose teeth chattered **with** sheer terror as we groped our way **to** our individual huts **in** response **to** the order to scatter.
>
> —Vera Brittain, *Testament of Youth*

PREPOSITIONAL PHRASES

PHRASES

❸ Practice and Apply

A. CONCEPT CHECK: Prepositional Phrases

You may know Michael Palin from the television series *Monty Python's Flying Circus,* "Python" films, or other movies. He has also written many books—several about travel adventures. As you read the following sentences about the 50,000-mile journey he describes in *Full Circle,* write each prepositional phrase and tell whether it is an adjective phrase **(Adj.)** or an adverb phrase **(Adv.).**

Palin Puts You at the Pacific Rim
1. It is day 175 of Michael Palin's 1997 journey.
2. Palin is traveling around the Pacific Rim.
3. *Full Circle* makes you his companion on the adventure.
4. Today before dawn you left San Pedro de Atacama, Chile.
5. Soon you arrive at the El Tatio geyser field.
6. This is the highest-altitude geyser field on earth.
7. Here steam from the geysers condenses and freezes fast.
8. Tiny ice crystals sparkle in the early morning sunlight.
9. To your delight, a geyser's blow-hole produces heat.
10. You use the heat for cooking your breakfast eggs.

➜ For a SELF-CHECK and more practice, see the EXERCISE BANK, p. 293.

B. REVISING: Adding Clarity

Clarify locations of people and things by adding a prepositional phrase to each sentence that answers the question following it.

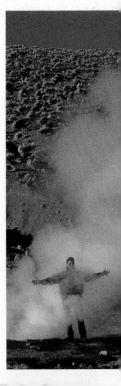

Picture This
1. Palin stands. (He stands where?)
2. The steam gushes. (Gushes from what?)
3. It billows like big clouds. (It billows where?)
4. Palin's crew takes pictures. (From where?)
5. This is just one amazing sight they capture. (They capture where?)

C. REVISING: Picturing a Place

In your 🗀 **Working Portfolio,** find your **Write Away** account from page 48. Add prepositional phrases to make it possible for someone unfamiliar with the setting to picture it. Then ask a classmate to illustrate the setting from your description.

ⓛ Appositive Phrases

❶ Here's the Idea

▶ **An appositive is a noun or pronoun that identifies or renames another noun or pronoun in a sentence.** An **appositive phrase** is made up of an appositive plus its modifiers.

Appositives and appositive phrases usually identify or give further information about the noun or pronoun they follow.

APPOSITIVE
The English biologist Dian Fossey wrote eyewitness accounts of gorillas.

APPOSITIVE PHRASE
Fossey was a primatologist, a scientist who studies such animals as gorillas and chimpanzees.

The appositive "Dian Fossey" gives you information you need to answer the question "Which one?" Such appositives are called **essential** or **restrictive** because they provide information that is essential to make the meaning of the sentence clear. Essential appositives are not set off by commas.

The appositive phrase "a scientist who studies such animals as gorillas and chimpanzees" is **nonessential** or **nonrestrictive**—that is, it is not necessary to clearly identify the noun to which it adds information. Nonessential appositives are set off by commas.

❷ Why It Matters in Writing

You can use appositive phrases to supply a name, a description, or even a definition.

PROFESSIONAL MODEL

   A young adult male, Ziz, succeeds in   **NAME**
eliciting a roughhouse play session from
his old father, Beethoven, during a day-   **NAME**
resting period, a time when social
interactions between group members   **DESCRIPTION**
are at their highest.

—Dian Fossey, *Gorillas in the Mist*

PHRASES

❸ Practice and Apply

A. CONCEPT CHECK: Appositive Phrases

Write the appositives and appositive phrases in these sentences.

A Look at *Gorillas in the Mist*

1. Fossey studied the mountain gorilla, an endangered species.

2. Icarus, one of the gorillas Fossey studied, was the only member of his group who was not afraid of her at first.

3. The group included two silverbacks, elder males whose back fur has turned a silver color.

4. The silverback Beethoven weighed about 350 pounds and was probably around 40 years old.

5. Fossey wrote about Beethoven and the other gorillas in her only book, *Gorillas in the Mist.*

➜ **For a SELF-CHECK and more practice, see the EXERCISE BANK, p. 293.**

For each essential appositive, write a brief explanation of why the appositive is essential.

B. REVISING: Adding Information

Rewrite each sentence, adding an appositive or an appositive phrase to include the information in parentheses. Use commas where you think they are needed.

Name Calling

1. Just as pet owners name their pets, Fossey named the gorillas in the band she studied. (A *band* is a group.)

2. Fossey probably named Beethoven after Ludwig van Beethoven. (Ludwig van Beethoven was a great composer.)

3. She gave the playful name to Beethoven's baby. (She gave it the name Puck.)

4. Fossey chose the name of the composer for the younger silverback. (The composer's name was Bela Bartok.)

5. She named an acrobatic gorilla after the Greek hero. (The Greek hero's name was Icarus.)

... AND THE WORLD RECORD IS HELD BY LIZZIE O'GARA, A BLACK LAB FROM ST. LOUIS, WHO RETRIEVED THIS BALL FIVE HUNDRED TIMES UNTIL HER OWNER COLLAPSED...OK, LET'S MOVE ON TO THE INTERACTIVE DROOL DISPLAY.

The Retriever Hall of Fame, Boise, Idaho.

Verbals: Participial Phrases

LESSON 3

▶ **A verbal is a verb form that acts as a noun, an adjective, or an adverb.** A **verbal phrase** consists of a verbal plus its modifiers and complements.

There are three kinds of verbals: **participles, gerunds,** and **infinitives.**

❶ Here's the Idea

▶ **A participle is a verb form that functions as an adjective.** A **participial phrase** consists of a participle plus any modifiers and complements. The participle may be in the present or past tense.

MODIFIES

Circling the moon, the astronauts broadcast their message.
PARTICIPIAL PHRASE

MODIFIES

Televised live, this telecast amazed viewers.
PARTICIPIAL PHRASE

Just as you would do with any adjective, you should place a participial phrase as near as you can to the noun or pronoun it modifies.

> **PROFESSIONAL MODEL**
>
> So it was on the day before Christmas in 1968 that three astronauts, Frank Borman, William Anders and James Lovell, cruising 69 miles over the slate-rubbled surface of the back side of the Moon, having ventured farther from home than any humans in history, looked up and saw their home world, again, for the first time, as a planet, a blue oasis in the void, rising over the dead gray moonscape.
>
> —Dennis Overbye, "A Blue Oasis, Seen from Space"

Astronauts is modified by two **participial phrases.**

Surface is modified by one 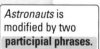participle.

Planet is modified by one **participial phrase.**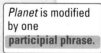

Don't confuse participial phrases with verbs. Participles are verb forms, but they act as adjectives.

Absolute Phrases An absolute phrase consists of a participle and the noun or pronoun it modifies. An absolute phrase has no grammatical connection to the rest of the sentence.

ABSOLUTE PHRASE

Apollo 8 **having orbited the moon ten times,** the astronauts headed back to earth.

You can use absolute phrases to add information about time, reasons, and circumstances to a sentence.

Don't confuse absolute phrases with dangling participles. An absolute phrase contains a subject. A dangling participle has no subject and does not logically modify any of the words in the sentence in which it appears—that's why it's dangling.

❷ Why It Matters in Writing

You can combine two ideas in one sentence by expressing one of the ideas in a participial phrase. Doing that makes your writing more concise and focuses your reader's attention on whichever idea you consider to be more important.

Notice how this student uses participial phrases to focus readers on the key ideas in her writing.

STUDENT MODEL

DRAFT

We were watching a meteor shower. We couldn't believe its beauty. Thousands of tiny lights were streaking through the night. They made the sky look like a cosmic fireworks display.

REVISION

Watching the meteor shower, we couldn't believe its beauty. Thousands of tiny lights **streaking through the night** made the sky look like a cosmic fireworks display.

❸ Practice and Apply

A. CONCEPT CHECK: Participial Phrases

Identify the participles and participial phrases in the following sentences. If the participle or participial phrase modifies a noun or pronoun in the main part of the sentence, write that word in parentheses after the participle or participial phrase.

Our Eyes on the Skies
1. Launched in 1957, *Sputnik 1* opened the space era.
2. Ever since then, millions have followed space news appearing in their newspapers and on television.
3. In the 1960s, their eyes glued to their TVs, they watched Neil Armstrong step onto the moon.
4. In the 1990s, they wondered whether the *Mir* station was still a safe destination for visiting space shuttle astronauts.
5. Most of all, they cheered the triumphs of the space program and mourned its tragedies, such as the exploding *Challenger*.

➡ For a SELF-CHECK and more practice, see the EXERCISE BANK, p. 294.

B. REVISING: Combining Sentences

Combine each pair of sentences into one, expressing the less important idea in a participial phrase. The less important idea is underlined.

Example: *Mir experienced many malfunctions.* *Mir* no longer seemed safe.
Answer: Experiencing many malfunctions, *Mir* no longer seemed safe.

The International Space Station
1. The International Space Station replaced the old Russian space station *Mir*. The new station is staffed by Russian and American astronauts.
2. A series of experiments will be performed. The astronauts will study the effects of long-duration spaceflights on the human body.
3. Capsules will be launched from Kazakhstan. The capsules will return the astronauts to Earth.
4. An Automated Transfer Vehicle will deliver food, water, air, equipment, and supplies. The Automated Transfer Vehicle is equipped with its own propulsion and navigation systems.
5. One of the astronauts participated in the Boston Marathon while aboard the space station. She did so by running on a treadmill.

PHRASES

Verbals: Gerund Phrases

❶ Here's the Idea

▶ **A gerund is a verb form that ends in -ing and acts as a noun.**
A **gerund phrase** consists of a gerund plus its modifiers and complements.

Just like a noun, the gerund can function in different ways.

Six Uses of Gerunds

Function in Sentence	Example
subject	**Sightseeing** is a real adventure.
predicate nominative	In fact, my favorite hobby is **sightseeing.**
direct object	I go **sightseeing** on foot with a guide book.
indirect object	I first gave **sightseeing** a try in Seattle.
object of a preposition	Before **sightseeing,** I asked friends for advice.
appositive	My great conversation-starter, **sightseeing** in Seattle, even prompted strangers to offer tips.

You can usually determine whether a verb form is a gerund by substituting a noun or pronoun for the gerund—or gerund phrase—and seeing if the sentence still makes sense.

I love sightseeing. ➡ **I love it.**
(HERE, THE SECOND SENTENCE STILL MAKES SENSE.)

❷ Why It Matters in Writing

You can use gerunds to make your writing more lively and vivid. For example, "I like traveling" emphasizes the actual experience of traveling more than does the statement "I like to travel." Notice how gerunds enhance this account.

> **PROFESSIONAL MODEL**
>
> Before each match, the two opposing [Sumo] wrestlers always perform an ancient traditional ritual involving **clapping** their hands, **throwing** some salt into the ring, **squatting,** and **raising** their legs sideways one at a time, then **stomping** them down, as though **killing** ancient traditional cockroaches.
> —Dave Barry, *Dave Barry Does Japan*

③ Practice and Apply

A. CONCEPT CHECK: Gerund Phrases

For each sentence, write the gerund or gerund phrase and its function: *subject, predicate nominative, direct object, indirect object, object of a preposition,* or *appositive.*

Two Travelers Tell Tales of "Real" United States
1. Traveling across the country with his poodle, Charley, was the focus of John Steinbeck's book *Travels with Charley.*
2. According to Steinbeck, the best thing about the trip was talking to the people he met along the way.
3. He particularly liked stopping at truck stops because the food and the conversation were good.
4. About twenty years later, William Least Heat-Moon began by exploring the country in a similar expedition.
5. As he noted in *Blue Highways,* Least Heat-Moon placed great importance on visiting places such as Nameless, Tennessee, rather than big cities.

➡ For a SELF-CHECK and more practice, see the EXERCISE BANK, p. 294.

B. REVISING: Enlivening Captions with Gerunds

Rewrite the caption to the photograph below, replacing the underlined words and phrases with gerunds to enliven the text.

Driving Passion
Kylie loves <u>to drive</u> on the open road. <u>To see</u> what's around that next corner, <u>to feel</u> the wind in her hair, <u>to sing</u> at the top of her lungs—these are the experiences that make this feel like the ultimate freedom. <u>To snap</u> a photograph like this one is just an added bonus.

Verbals: Infinitive Phrases

LESSON 5

❶ Here's the Idea

▶ **An infinitive is a verb form usually beginning with the word *to* that can act as a noun, an adjective, or an adverb.** An **infinitive phrase** consists of an infinitive plus its modifiers and complements. An infinitive phrase can function as a subject, object, predicate nominative, adjective, or adverb.

MODIFIES

Douglas Adams and Mark Carwardine journeyed the world **to glimpse exotic, endangered creatures.** USED AS AN ADVERB

IDENTIFIES

Besides planning their trips, Carwardine's job was **to teach Adams about the animals.** USED AS A PREDICATE NOMINATIVE

MODIFIES

Adams had the job of being the one **to write down what they saw.** USED AS AN ADJECTIVE

Until recently, most people considered it wrong ever to split an infinitive—that is, to insert words between the word *to* and the verb. Now, most experts agree that a split infinitive is acceptable if the sentence reads more smoothly and clearly because of it.

To distinguish an infinitive from a prepositional phrase, remember the following:

to + verb = infinitive   to + noun = prepositional phrase

To see unusual creatures, he went **to unusual places.**
INFINITIVE   PREPOSITIONAL PHRASE

❷ Why It Matters in Writing

You can use infinitives and infinitive phrases to make a clearer connection between an action and its purpose.

Related Sentences:
Adams met with an expert on poisonous snakes.
Adams prepared himself for the dangers of Komodo island.

Combined:
Adams met with an expert on poisonous snakes to prepare himself for the dangers of Komodo island.

Practice and Apply ....

A. CONCEPT CHECK: Infinitive Phrases

Write each infinitive or infinitive phrase. In the phrases, underline the infinitive. Then tell whether the infinitive acts as a *subject, object, predicate nominative, adjective,* or *adverb.*

A Last Chance to See Kakapos?

1. Douglas Adams and Mark Carwardine teamed up to seek rare and exotic creatures.
2. A rare creature to find in New Zealand is the kakapo, a flightless bird.
3. To search for these rare birds was one of the twosome's goals.
4. To track the kakapos, Adams and Carwardine hired a guide.
5. The guide's job was basically to lead their expedition.

➜ **For a SELF-CHECK and more practice, see the EXERCISE BANK, p. 295.**

B. REVISING: Combining Sentences with Infinitives

Combine each pair of sentences, using an infinitive to connect the action with its purpose.

Example: New Zealand has established a refuge. Kakapos are protected there.

Answer: New Zealand has established a refuge to protect kakapos.

More About the Kakapo Caper

1. Adams and Carwardine contacted New Zealand authorities. They needed government permission to visit the kakapo refuge.
2. The government protects its kakapos. This protection prevents the kakapos from disappearing.
3. The team of explorers trudged through the wet, cold forest. They looked for kakapos.
4. Adams stopped often. He freed himself from undergrowth.
5. Eventually Adams witnessed a kakapo making eerie grunting noises that travel for miles. The kakapo's grunts attract a mate.

PHRASES

Problems with Phrases

❶ Here's the Idea

A **misplaced modifier** is a word or phrase that is placed so far away from the word it modifies that the meaning of the sentence is unclear or incorrect. A **dangling modifier** is a word or phrase that does not clearly modify any noun or pronoun in a sentence.

Misplaced Modifiers

Misleading Headline: MISPLACED MODIFIER
   Fire Accidentally Started by Two Students in Waste Basket

Unless the two students were in the waste basket when the fire broke out, the headline above is incorrect.

Clearer Headline:
   Fire Accidentally Started in Waste Basket by Two Students

Can you spot the misplaced phrase in the sentence below?

Misleading Sentence:
   Whirling by his house, Mr. Rigby saw the tornado.

Clearer Sentence:
   Mr. Rigby saw the tornado whirling by his house.

Dangling Modifiers

Readers expect the subject modified by a verbal phrase to follow or to precede the phrase. If the subject is missing, the meaning of the sentence may be unclear or even absurd. To fix the problem, include the subject that's modified by the phrase—or eliminate the phrase.

Dangling:
   Barking loudly, the burglar was stopped at the door. (WAS THE BURGLAR BARKING LOUDLY?)

   Hoping to catch him, a search was conducted. (WHO WAS HOPING?)

Revised:
   Barking loudly, Buster stopped the burglar at the door.

   Hoping to catch him, the police conducted a search.

❷ Why It Matters in Writing

If you misplace phrases, you can wind up expressing some pretty silly ideas—or, at the very least, misleading your readers.

Misleading Headline:
   Twins Meet After 30-Year Search in Airport

❸ Practice and Apply

A. CONCEPT CHECK: Problems with Phrases

Rewrite each sentence to correct a misplaced or dangling modifier, changing words or word order as necessary.

> **Witness Keeps Her Wits and Wallet**
> **1.** After getting cash at an ATM near her home, muggers attacked Donna Shalala.
> **2.** Making a scene, the muggers were frightened away.
> **3.** They jumped without her purse into their car.
> **4.** Describing the muggers and their getaway car for the police, the police considered Shalala an excellent witness.
> **5.** Using this information, the alleged muggers were caught.

➜ **For a SELF-CHECK and more practice, see the EXERCISE BANK, p. 295.**

B. EDITING AND PROOFREADING: Correcting Problems With Modifiers

Revise the paragraph below to correct all phrase problems.

STUDENT MODEL

Captain Spots Something Fishy at Sea
   Accused of murder, Scotland Yard wanted Dr. Crippen and his accomplice, Ethel Le Neve. Disguised as a father and son, Crippen and Le Neve's plan was to escape across the ocean to Canada. However, the ship's alert captain noticed that the "father" had recently shaved a mustache traveling under the name Mr. Robinson. He also had indentations from wearing glasses on his nose, although he was not wearing any. Suspecting who "the Robinsons" really were, a wire to Scotland Yard foiled their plan.

Choose a draft from your 📁 **Working Portfolio** and check it for misplaced and dangling modifiers.

Sentence Diagramming

Mad Mapper

❶ Here's the Idea

Diagramming is a tool you can use to figure out the role a phrase plays in a sentence.

Prepositional Phrases

Watch me for diagramming tips!

- Write the preposition on a slanted line below the word the prepositional phrase modifies.
- Write the object of the preposition on a horizontal line attached to the slanted line and parallel to the main line.
- Write words that modify the object of the preposition on slanted lines below the object.

Adjective Phrase

Michael Palin enjoyed the heat of the geyser's steam.

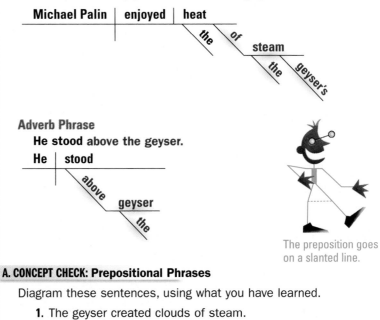

Adverb Phrase

He stood above the geyser.

The preposition goes on a slanted line.

A. CONCEPT CHECK: Prepositional Phrases

Diagram these sentences, using what you have learned.

1. The geyser created clouds of steam.
2. He was surrounded by these clouds.

Appositive Phrases

Write the appositive in parentheses after the word it identifies or renames. Attach words that modify the appositive to it in the usual way.

Appositive attitude!

The primatologist Dian Fossey studied mountain gorillas.

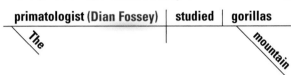

B. CONCEPT CHECK: Appositive Phrases

Diagram the following sentence, using what you have learned.

The gorilla Beethoven was a silverback.

Participial Phrases

Write the participle on an angled line below the word it modifies.

Present Participle

The new space station being built will replace *Mir*.

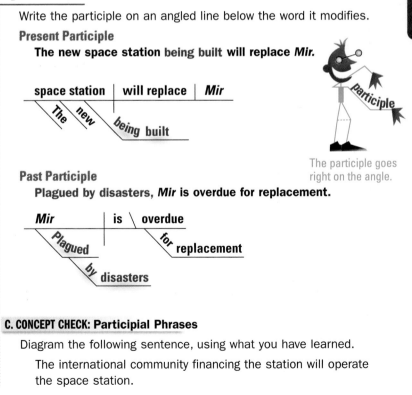

The participle goes right on the angle.

Past Participle

Plagued by disasters, *Mir* is overdue for replacement.

C. CONCEPT CHECK: Participial Phrases

Diagram the following sentence, using what you have learned.

The international community financing the station will operate the space station.

Gerund Phrases

- The gerund curves over a line that looks like a step.
- With a vertical forked line, connect the step to the part of the diagram that corresponds to the role of the gerund phrase in the sentence.
- Complements and modifiers are diagrammed in the usual way.

Gerund Phrase as Subject
Driving across the United States is a unique experience.

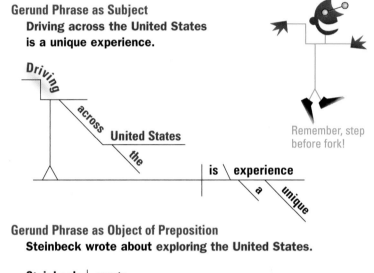

Remember, step before fork!

Gerund Phrase as Object of Preposition
Steinbeck wrote about exploring the United States.

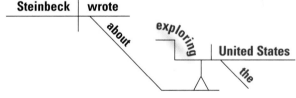

D. CONCEPT CHECK: Gerund Phrases

Diagram these sentences, using what you have learned.

1. Visiting small towns was the author's favorite pastime.
2. He wrote about visiting a town named Nameless.

Infinitive Phrases

- Write the infinitive on a bent line, with the word *to* on the slanted part and the verb on the horizontal part.
- When the infinitive or infinitive phrase functions as a noun, use a vertical forked line to connect the infinitive to the part of the diagram that corresponds to its role in the sentence.
- When the phrase functions as a modifier, place the bent line below the word it modifies.

Infinitive Phrase as Object
Adams and Carwardine wanted to find the kakapo.

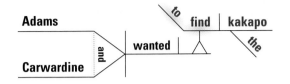

Infinitive Phrase as Subject
To see the endangered kakapo was their goal.

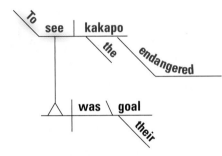

This one has a
fork, but no step.

PHRASES

E. CONCEPT CHECK: Infinitive Phrases
Diagram these sentences, using what you have learned.

1. To reach its habitat required hiking through forests.
2. A kakapo grunts to attract a mate.

F. MIXED REVIEW: Sentence Diagramming
Diagram the following sentences. Look for all types of phrases.

1. Annie Dillard is a close observer of nature.
2. She writes about her observations.
3. Dillard wrote the book *Pilgrim at Tinker Creek*.
4. The book focuses on one place, a creek in Virginia.
5. Standing on a hill, Dillard saw a flock of birds.
6. The birds, seen from the hill, were beautiful.
7. Observing a praying mantis fascinated Dillard.
8. She concentrated on learning about its habits.
9. She watched a green heron wading in the creek.
10. To observe nature closely requires deep concentration.

Real World Grammar

Accident Report

The need for good grammar skills will come up in all sorts of situations throughout your life. Even if you were to get into a car accident, you would need these skills. Why? On an accident report for the department of motor vehicles, you would need to be able to write a clear and accurate description of what happened.

The student who filled out this accident report has already discovered how essential good grammar is. Luckily, before submitting his report, he asked a classmate to review it.

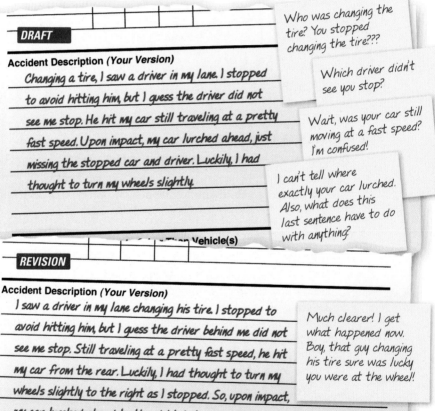

DRAFT

Accident Description (Your Version)

Changing a tire, I saw a driver in my lane. I stopped to avoid hitting him, but I guess the driver did not see me stop. He hit my car still traveling at a pretty fast speed. Upon impact, my car lurched ahead, just missing the stopped car and driver. Luckily, I had thought to turn my wheels slightly.

Who was changing the tire? You stopped changing the tire???

Which driver didn't see you stop?

Wait, was your car still moving at a fast speed? I'm confused!

I can't tell where exactly your car lurched. Also, what does this last sentence have to do with anything?

Vehicle(s)

REVISION

Accident Description (Your Version)

I saw a driver in my lane changing his tire. I stopped to avoid hitting him, but I guess the driver behind me did not see me stop. Still traveling at a pretty fast speed, he hit my car from the rear. Luckily, I had thought to turn my wheels slightly to the right as I stopped. So, upon impact, my car lurched ahead to the right, just missing the stopped car and driver ahead of me.

Much clearer! I get what happened now. Boy, that guy changing his tire sure was lucky you were at the wheel!

Identify Damaged Property Other Than Vehicle(s)

Using Phrases Correctly in Writing

Avoid misplacing modifiers	When you use a phrase as a modifier, position it as close to the word it modifies as possible.
Avoid dangling modifiers	When you use a phrase in a sentence, be sure you also include in the sentence the word or words the phrase modifies. When you begin a sentence with a phrase, be sure the subject the phrase modifies follows the phrase.

PRACTICE AND APPLY: Revising

A friend of yours has written the following description to submit on an accident report. Now she's asked you to look it over for her. Use the writing tips above to revise her description so that it presents a clear and accurate description of what happened.

STUDENT MODEL

Waiting to make a lefthand turn, a car was coming at a high speed towards me. Honking his horn, I watched with concern as he began weaving to pass cars. I had to wait like a sitting duck still unable to turn in the intersection. I waited until yellow. Then I went. Unfortunately, before turning red, he sped up instead of stopping. He hit the rear bumper of my car flying at top speed and sent my car spinning. By the time my car stopped turning, he was gone.

Other car

My car was here when I was hit.

Damage to my car from accident.

PHRASES

Mixed Review

A. Prepositional, Appositive, and Participial Phrases Élisabeth Vigée-Lebrun painted portraits of French royalty in the late 1700s. Read this passage from her diary and identify each underlined group of words as an *adverb prepositional phrase, adjective prepositional phrase, appositive phrase,* or *participial phrase.*

> **LITERARY MODEL**
>
> Toward the end **(1)** <u>of the exhibition</u> a little piece was given at the Vaudeville Theater, bearing the title, I think, "The Assembling of the Arts." Brongniart, **(2)** <u>the architect</u>, and his wife, whom the author had taken **(3)** <u>into his confidence</u>, had taken a box on the first tier, and called for me on the day of the first performance. As I had no suspicion **(4)** <u>of the surprise in store for me</u>, judge of my emotion when Painting appeared on the scene and I saw the actress **(5)** <u>representing that art</u> copy me in the act of painting a portrait of the Queen.
>
> —Élisabeth Vigée-Lebrun, *The Memoirs of Madame Vigée-Lebrun*

B. Prepositional, Gerund, and Infinitive Phrases After reading this section of Vigée-Lebrun's memoir, answer the questions that follow.

(1) I was so fortunate as to be on very pleasant terms with the Queen. **(2)** When she heard that I had something of a voice we rarely had a sitting without singing some duets by Grétry together, for she was exceedingly fond of music, although she did not sing very true. **(3)** As for her conversation, it would be difficult for me to convey all its charm, all its affability. **(4)** I do not think that Queen Marie Antoinette ever missed an opportunity of saying something pleasant to those who had the honor of being presented to her, and the kindness she always bestowed upon me has ever been one of my sweetest memories.

(5) One day I happened to miss the appointment she had given me for a sitting; I had suddenly become unwell. **(6)** The next day I hastened to Versailles to offer my excuses.

1. What is the infinitive in sentence 1?
2. What type of phrase is "with the Queen" in sentence 1?
3. What are the two gerunds in sentence 2?
4. Which gerund in sentence 2 is the object of a preposition?
5. What is the infinitive in sentence 3?
6. Does the infinitive act as a noun, an adverb, or an adjective?
7. What kind of phrase is "saying something pleasant" in sentence 4?
8. What word does the prepositional phrase "of being presented to her" modify in sentence 4?
9. What is the function of the gerund in sentence 5?
10. What type of phrase is "to offer my excuses" in sentence 6?

Choose the letter of the description that identifies the function of each underlined group of words.

Kent Weeks and his team were not typical visitors <u>to Egypt's Valley of</u>
<u>the Kings</u>. Most come <u>to view the tombs there</u> or to help excavate them. He
$$(1)$$
$$(2)$$
and his crew came <u>to map the tombs</u>, <u>an important preservation project</u>.
$$(3)$$
$$(4)$$
However, <u>mapping the tombs in Thebes from the ground alone</u> would
$$(5)$$
have taken them dozens of years. <u>Taking aerial photographs</u> would
$$(6)$$
shorten this time considerably. So, <u>at sunrise</u>, <u>dazzled by the sparkling</u>
$$(7)$$
$$(8)$$
<u>landscape</u>, team members snapped pictures from a hot-air balloon a
thousand feet above the city. In so doing, they not only shortened the
duration of their task, <u>still a lengthy job anyway</u>, but they also became the
$$(9)$$
first group ever <u>to make such a flight there</u>.
$$(10)$$

PHRASES

1. A. adverb prepositional phrase
   B. adjective prepositional phrase
   C. essential appositive phrase
   D. infinitive phrase

2. A. adverb prepositional phrase
   B. adjective prepositional phrase
   C. participial phrase
   D. infinitive phrase

3. A. infinitive phrase used as
      direct object
   B. infinitive phrase used as
      adverb
   C. adverb prepositional phrase
   D. participial phrase

4. A. essential appositive phrase
   B. nonessential appositive phrase
   C. present participial phrase
   D. past participial phrase

5. A. gerund phrase used as subject
   B. present participial phrase
   C. gerund phrase used as direct
      object
   D. past participial phrase

6. A. present participial phrase
   B. past participial phrase
   C. gerund phrase used as subject
   D. absolute phrase

7. A. appositive phrase
   B. absolute phrase
   C. adverb prepositional phrase
   D. adjective prepositional phrase

8. A. essential appositive phrase
   B. participial phrase
   C. adjective prepositional phrase
   D. gerund phrase

9. A. absolute phrase
   B. participial phrase
   C. essential appositive phrase
   D. nonessential appositive phrase

10. A. adverb prepositional phrase
    B. infinitive phrase used as
       adjective
    C. infinitive phrase used as
       direct object
    D. adjective prepositional phrase

Student Help Desk

Phrases at a Glance

Examples of each type of phrase are highlighted.

A **prepositional phrase** is one that begins with a preposition.

An **appositive phrase,** an identifier or clarifier, renames, defines, or describes the subject immediately before it.

Modifying a noun or a pronoun, a **participial phrase** always contains a participle and serves as an adjective.

Serving as a noun is the role of a **gerund phrase.**

You can use an **infinitive phrase,** a phrase that begins with *to* and the base form of a verb, to serve as the subject, object, predicate nominative, adjective, or adverb in a sentence.

Punctuating Phrases

When to "Capture" Them in Commas

Tip	Example
If the phrase is **essential or restrictive**—that is, it's necessary to identify which noun or pronoun you mean—then ***don't* use commas.**	We have nine eyewitnesses to the Bigfoot sighting. That eyewitness Jennifer can tell you more than the others. (*Jennifer* is necessary to clarify which of the nine you mean.)
If the **phrase is nonessential or nonrestrictive**—that is, it's *not* necessary to identify or clarify which noun or pronoun you mean—then ***do* use commas.**	The creature, a huge and hairy-looking thing, scared most of the other kids. (Here, the phrase adds information but isn't necessary to clarify which creature.)

Using Phrases in Writing

Type	Can Help You . . .	Examples
Prepositional Phrase	To clarify the order of events in time and the locations of events, people, and objects.	At sunset in the woods near the school, we saw something moving behind the big elm tree.
Appositive Phrase	To tell more about a subject and to define unfamiliar words.	Rachel said it was a Bigfoot, a large, hairy, humanlike creature that supposedly lives in the Pacific Northwest and Canada.
Participial Phrase	To combine two ideas in one sentence and, at the same time, focus your reader's attention on the more important of the two ideas.	We kept our distance. We watched the trees. *can become . . .* Keeping our distance, we watched the trees.
Gerund Phrase	To make your writing more lively and engaging.	Even staring into the trees is a thrill when you think a Bigfoot is out there.
Infinitive Phrase	To show the connection between an action and the reason for it.	To make the creature think we were gone, we stayed very quiet.

PHRASES

The Bottom Line

Checklist for Phrases

Have I . . .

____ placed all phrases that act as adverbs or adjectives as close as possible to the words they modify?

____ used phrases to add details and clarity to my writing?

____ omitted commas around all my essential appositive and participial phrases?

____ used commas with all my nonessential appositive and participial phrases?

Using Clauses

NO SWIMMING
IS ALLOWED
• if there has been an oil spill
• when an ozone warning is in effect
• before trash has been removed
  from the beach

Theme: Troubles with Travels

Playing by the Rules

These two swimmers were all ready for a nice day at the beach, but they didn't know about the pollution clauses. In this chapter, you will see that clauses—groups of words containing a subject and a verb—add important information to a sentence.

Write Away: We're Not in Kansas Anymore!
Whether they meet a giant squid on a submarine or miss their train at the subway station, travelers can experience all kinds of mishaps and go on to tell about them. Write a paragraph about a trip that went wrong for you, whether it was a vacation or the bus ride to school. Save it in your 📁 **Working Portfolio.**

For each numbered item choose the letter that correctly identifies it.

> Reading and driving don't mix, <u>as journalist Mark Abley learned the</u>
> <u>hard way</u>. He should have expected something to go wrong; <u>after all, he</u>
>   (1)   (2)
> <u>had dreamed about driving the night before his trip</u>. Abley, <u>who was</u>
>   (3)
> <u>anxious to arrive in Saskatoon</u>, started out the day behind schedule, so he
> was making up for lost time. He didn't know <u>where the turn-off was to go</u>
>   (4)
> <u>south to The Pas</u>. <u>As a singer wailed at him on the radio</u>, Abley grabbed
>   (5)
> the map. <u>Unfortunately, it was upside-down</u>. <u>Turning the map around, he</u>
>   (6)   (7)
> <u>glanced up in time to see that he was heading off the road</u>. <u>The car veered</u>
>   (8)
> <u>sharply, and then it flipped over before it landed in a ditch</u>. Abley felt
> sheepish. <u>Even though he was alive and in good condition</u>. <u>The car was a</u>
>   (9)   (10)
> <u>wreck, fortunately, a truck driver stopped to help</u>.

1. A. independent clause
   B. subordinate clause
   C. simple sentence
   D. complex sentence

2. A. independent clause
   B. subordinate clause
   C. simple sentence
   D. complex sentence

3. A. independent clause
   B. essential adjective clause
   C. nonessential adjective clause
   D. noun clause

4. A. essential adjective clause
   B. nonessential adjective clause
   C. adverb clause
   D. noun clause

5. A. essential adjective clause
   B. nonessential adjective clause
   C. adverb clause
   D. noun clause

6. A. compound-complex sentence
   B. complex sentence
   C. compound sentence
   D. simple sentence

7. A. compound-complex sentence
   B. complex sentence
   C. compound sentence
   D. simple sentence

8. A. compound-complex sentence
   B. complex sentence
   C. compound sentence
   D. simple sentence

9. A. phrase fragment
   B. run-on
   C. clause fragment
   D. simple sentence

10. A. phrase fragment
    B. run-on
    C. clause fragment
    D. complex sentence

Kinds of Clauses

❶ Here's the Idea

▶ **A clause is a group of words that contains a subject and a verb.**

There are two kinds of clauses: independent clauses and subordinate clauses.

Independent Clauses

▶ **An independent clause expresses a complete thought and can stand alone as a complete sentence.**

Many people travel.

SUBJECT   VERB

Subordinate Clauses

▶ **A subordinate clause does not express a complete thought and cannot stand alone as a sentence.**

Because they crave excitement

SUBJECT   VERB

Subordinate clauses are also called **dependent clauses,** because they depend on an independent clause for their complete meanings. A subordinate clause must be combined with or be a part of an independent clause to form a complete sentence.

Many people travel because they crave excitement.

INDEPENDENT CLAUSE   SUBORDINATE CLAUSE

Words That Introduce Clauses

A conjunction is a word or phrase that joins together words, phrases, clauses, or sentences.

A **coordinating conjunction** links two independent clauses. Examples include *and, but, or, for, so, yet,* or *nor.*

Hemingway was an adventurer, so he traveled extensively.

COORDINATING CONJUNCTION

A **subordinating conjunction** usually introduces a subordinate clause. Examples include:

although	since	even if	than
unless	whenever	as	until
after	that	wherever	before

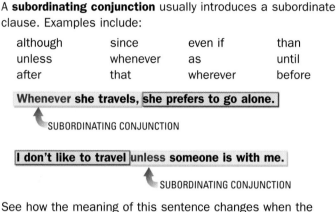

Whenever she travels, she prefers to go alone.

⬆ SUBORDINATING CONJUNCTION

I don't like to travel unless someone is with me.

⬆ SUBORDINATING CONJUNCTION

See how the meaning of this sentence changes when the conjunction changes.

I don't like to travel even if someone is with me.

⬆ SUBORDINATING CONJUNCTION

❷ Why It Matters in Writing

We think in complex ways. In order to express complex ideas, we need to use subordinate clauses. Try writing without them!

We like to go camping.
INDEPENDENT

After it rains, we like to go camping.
SUBORDINATE   INDEPENDENT

If we have a choice in the matter, we like to go camping.
SUBORDINATE   INDEPENDENT

As long as there are no bears around, we like to go camping.
SUBORDINATE   INDEPENDENT

Try rewriting these sentences without subordinate clauses. Is the meaning the same?

❸ Practice and Apply

A. CONCEPT CHECK: Kinds of Clauses

For each sentence below, identify the italicized words as an independent clause or a subordinate clause.

Read Before You Sign
1. *Before you sign up for a vacation trip,* read the fine print.
2. *Most tour companies are responsible operators.*
3. However, *travelers must agree to their terms and conditions.*
4. Whenever you see the word "liability," *read the text carefully.*
5. Pay attention to the details *as you read.*
6. Tour companies hire outside services, but *they aren't responsible for mishaps with those services.*
7. *If the airline loses your luggage,* the tour company isn't accountable.
8. When there's no heat in the mountain lodge, *the tour guide can only sympathize.*
9. In fact, he or she will probably complain *as much as you will.*
10. Of course, no one is responsible *if Mother Nature rains on your vacation.*

➡ **For a SELF-CHECK and more practice, see the EXERCISE BANK, p. 296.**

Rewrite sentences 4–8 by connecting the clauses with a different coordinating or subordinating conjunction. Briefly explain how the change affects the sentence's meaning.

B. IDENTIFYING: Finding Subordinate Clauses

There are five subordinate clauses in the following passage. Write each subordinate clause and its sentence number.

Learning the Hard Way
(1) Joe Bonds thought that he was in good shape. **(2)** When he signed up for a multisport vacation, he looked forward to hiking, biking, and kayaking in Colorado. **(3)** Unfortunately, he didn't read the trip ratings, so he chose a "moderate" trip. **(4)** Moderate trips were for people who exercised between five and seven hours a day. **(5)** Joe didn't. **(6)** The first day, the group hiked 13 miles up a mountain trail. **(7)** The second day, after Joe rode a mountain bike for 35 miles, he was a wreck. **(8)** The third day, Joe stayed in camp until a van arrived, and he went to a comfortable hotel. **(9)** A much wiser Joe now reads every description very carefully.

Adjective and Adverb Clauses

❶ Here's the Idea

There are three kinds of subordinate clauses: adjective, adverb, and noun clauses. Adjective clauses and adverb clauses, like adjectives and adverbs, modify nouns or pronouns in a sentence.

Adjective Clauses

▶ **An adjective clause is a subordinate clause used as an adjective to modify a noun or a pronoun.**

These clauses are sometimes called **relative clauses,** because they relate, or connect, the adjective clauses to the words they modify.

MODIFIES NOUN

Scientists who explore the sea face many hazards.

MODIFIES PRONOUN

Exploration is not for someone whose nerves are weak.

Words Used to Introduce Adjective Clauses	
Relative pronouns	who, whom, whose, that, which
Relative adverbs	after, before, when, where, why

MODIFIES NOUN

The waves, which pounded the shore, were 12 feet tall.

MODIFIES NOUN

The day before the storm hit was clear and calm.

MODIFIES NOUN

The crow's nest, where the lookout usually stood, was empty.

MODIFIES NOUN

Those were the days when no one expected to survive such a storm.

Essential and Nonessential Adjective Clauses

Adjective clauses can be **essential** or **nonessential** (also referred to as **restrictive** or **nonrestrictive**), depending on how important they are to the meaning of the sentence.

These sentences look similar, but their meanings are somewhat different:

MODIFIES NOUN

Sang Mee took the boat that has no anchor.

ESSENTIAL CLAUSE

(Which boat did she take? She took the one without an anchor.)

MODIFIES NOUN

Sang Mee took the boat, which has no anchor.

NONESSENTIAL CLAUSE

(Which boat did she take? She took the only boat there is.
By the way, that boat has no anchor.)

The nonessential clause is separated from the independent clause by a comma and begins with *which* instead of *that*. Removing the nonessential clause does not change the meaning of the sentence.

Essential clauses contain information that is necessary to identify the preceding noun or pronoun. Nonessential clauses add information about the preceding noun or pronoun that is nice to have but is not necessary.

When you write a sentence with an adjective clause, only you know whether the clause contains information that is essential to the sentence. Your punctuation and choice of *that* or *which* are the only things that will tell the reader whether the clause is essential or nonessential.

Adverb Clauses

▶ **An adverb clause is a subordinate clause that modifies a verb, an adjective, or another adverb.**

MODIFIES VERB

Whenever I have the chance, I travel.

MODIFIES ADJECTIVE

Spaceships are bigger than I thought they were.

MODIFIES ADVERB

Planes move faster than boats ever will.

Note that in the first of the three preceding sample sentences, the adverb clause goes before the independent clause, and the two clauses are separated by a comma.

Words Used to Introduce Adverb Clauses	
Subordinating conjunctions	when, because, than, although, as if, wherever

For a longer list of subordinating conjunctions, see p. 22.

Elliptical Clauses One or more words may be left out of an adverb clause when there is no possibility that the reader will misunderstand its meaning. Such a clause is called an **elliptical clause.**

> **While (she was) diving in Round Lake, the biologist collected samples.**

> **She did field work more often than her colleagues (did).**

❷ Why It Matters in Writing

CLAUSES

Adjective and adverb clauses allow your sentences to answer such questions as *what kind? how? to what extent? where? when?* and *why?*

STUDENT MODEL

DRAFT

Researchers often travel to exotic locations. They do field work. In the field they are exposed to dangers. They may prepare for problems. They can't anticipate every situation. The U.S. State Department is a source of help. It issues travel warnings. The warnings are posted. Sometimes a health or safety danger exists.

REVISION

Researchers **who do field work** often travel to exotic locations **where they are exposed to many dangers. Although they prepare for some problems,** they cannot anticipate every situation. One source of help is the U.S. State Department, **which issues travel warnings whenever a health or safety danger arises.**

❸ Practice and Apply

A. CONCEPT CHECK: Adjective and Adverb Clauses

For each sentence below, write the adjective or adverb clause and underline the introductory word or words. Then write the word or words modified by the clause.

Example: Robert Ballard, whom many greatly respect, is an oceanographer.
Answer: <u>whom</u> many greatly respect; Robert Ballard

Under the Sea

1. Robert Ballard, whose achievements include finding the *Titanic,* has explored the world's oceans.
2. Ballard was nervous because he was making his first dive in *Alvin,* a small research submarine.
3. The Gulf of Maine, where Ballard was gathering rock samples, was choppy that day.
4. The trip was more dangerous than Ballard imagined.
5. The submarine, which had sunk in 1968, made the trip safely that day.

➡ **For a SELF-CHECK and more practice, see the EXERCISE BANK, p. 297.**

Using sentences 1–5 as a guide, write five new sentences with adjective or adverb clauses.

B. REVISING: Using Clauses to Combine Sentences

Combine each of the following sentence pairs to form a single sentence. Using the introductory word or words in parentheses, change one sentence into an adjective or adverb clause.

Example: In 1973 Ballard went on an expedition. The expedition almost killed him. (that)
Answer: In 1973 Ballard went on an expedition that almost killed him.

Terror Beneath the Waves

1. French and American teams were exploring the Mid-Atlantic Ridge. The teams had never worked together before. (which)
2. They were a mile below the surface. The power failed. (when)
3. They solved that problem. An electrical fire started. (after)
4. Ballard put on his oxygen mask. He was still breathing smoke. (even though)
5. He struggled. Someone turned on the oxygen valve. (until)

Noun Clauses

LESSON 3

❶ Here's the Idea

▶ **A noun clause is a subordinate clause that is used as a noun in a sentence.**

In a sentence, a noun clause can be the subject, a direct object, an indirect object, a predicate nominative, or the object of a preposition. It can also function as the direct object of a verbal or as an appositive.

Whatever doesn't kill us makes us stronger.
      SUBJECT

Travel tests **how we cope with problems.**
          DIRECT OBJECT

It gives **whoever wants it** practice with flexibility.
      INDIRECT OBJECT

New experiences are **what we crave.**
            PREDICATE NOMINATIVE

Think about **where you'd like to go.**
        OBJECT OF A PREPOSITION

Turning **whichever corner we find** brings new excitement.
      DIRECT OBJECT OF A GERUND

To go **where we have never been before** is true adventure.
     DIRECT OBJECT OF AN INFINITIVE

The destination, **wherever we may stop,** is really unimportant.
          APPOSITIVE

HOT TIP

You can usually identify a noun clause by substituting the word *someone, something,* or *somewhere* for the clause.

Words Used to Introduce Noun Clauses

Relative pronouns	what, whatever, who, whoever, whom, which, whichever, wherever
Subordinating conjunctions	how, that, when, where, whether, why

Who we are determines our ability to face obstacles.

Do you ever wonder why we travel?

The introductory word *that* in a noun clause is sometimes dropped.

We all know (that) travel is educational.

❷ Why It Matters in Writing

Using noun clauses allows you to express a complex idea more succinctly. Imagine the following paragraph without noun clauses:

> **LITERARY MODEL**
>
> Psychologically as well as physically, there are no longer any remote places on earth. When a friend leaves for **what was once a far country,** even if he has no intention of returning, we cannot feel that same sense of irrevocable separation that saddened our forefathers. We know **that he is only hours away by jet liner, and that we have merely to reach for the telephone to hear his voice.**
>
> —Arthur C. Clarke, "We'll Never Conquer Space"

Noun clause gives information about the friend's destination.

Direct objects: both noun clauses convey two complex ideas in a single sentence.

Find three noun clauses in the following cartoon:

Calvin and Hobbes by Bill Watterson

❸ Practice and Apply

A. CONCEPT CHECK: Noun Clauses

Write the noun clause in each sentence. Label its function as a subject, direct object, indirect object, predicate nominative, object of a preposition, direct object of a gerund or of an infinitive, or appositive.

Example: She came from what I consider a great distance.
Answer: what I consider a great distance; object of a preposition

> **Travels Through Time**
> 1. Many people have wondered whether time travel is possible.
> 2. How one man travels to the future is the subject of the novel *The Time Machine* by H. G. Wells.
> 3. The Time Machine gives whoever drives it a trip through time.
> 4. A machine with a metal frame and two levers is what transports the Time Traveller to the distant future.
> 5. To know how people will live in the future is a common wish.
> 6. The Time Traveller finds that all workers live underground in the year 802,701.
> 7. The Morlocks, whoever they are, hide the Time Machine in the pedestal of the White Sphinx.
> 8. Discovering where his Time Machine is hidden becomes the Time Traveller's biggest problem.
> 9. Will he ever get back to where he belongs?
> 10. Back in the present, no one believes that he's telling the truth.

➔ **For a SELF-CHECK and more practice, see the EXERCISE BANK, p. 297.**

Using sentences 1–5 as a guide, write five new sentences with noun clauses.

B. REVISING: Using Noun Clauses to Improve Sentences

Replace the underlined word in each sentence with a noun clause to improve the meaning.

> **An Ordeal in the Desert**
> 1. While crossing the desert, a person might think <u>something</u>.
> 2. <u>Someone</u> must be willing to tempt fate.
> 3. In order to continue, a person must summon <u>something</u>.
> 4. The traveler's greatest fear is probably <u>something</u>.
> 5. He or she would gladly give all of his or her possessions to <u>someone</u>.

Sentence Structure

❶ Here's the Idea

A sentence's structure is determined by the number and kind of clauses it contains.

▶ **There are four basic sentence structures: simple, compound, complex, and compound-complex.**

Simple Sentences

A **simple sentence** contains one independent clause but no subordinate clauses.

> **Most maps of Borneo are useless.**

A simple sentence may have a compound subject, a compound verb, or both.

> **Dense forests and heavy rains** impede **and** challenge **hikers.**
> ⬆ COMPOUND SUBJECT ⬆   ⬆ COMPOUND VERB ⬆

Compound Sentences

In a **compound sentence,** two or more independent clauses are joined together.

> Some hikers seek adventure , but others search for knowledge.
> INDEPENDENT CLAUSE   INDEPENDENT CLAUSE

The clauses in the preceding compound sentence are linked by a comma and the coordinating conjunction *but.* Independent clauses also can be linked by a semicolon, or by a semicolon followed by a conjunctive adverb and a comma.

> Some hikers seek adventure ; others search for knowledge.

> Some hikers seek adventure ; however, others search for knowledge.

For more about coordinating conjunctions and conjunctive adverbs, see p. 21.

Complex Sentences

A **complex sentence** contains one independent clause and one or more subordinate clauses.

Before the hikers rested, they removed leeches from their legs.

SUBORDINATE ADVERB CLAUSE   INDEPENDENT CLAUSE

If a noun clause is part of the independent clause, the sentence is complex. In the following sentence, the subordinate noun clause functions as the subject.

SUBORDINATE NOUN CLAUSE

Whoever treks through the uncharted rain forest faces danger.

Compound-Complex Sentences

A **compound-complex sentence** contains two or more independent clauses and one or more subordinate clauses.

SUBORDINATE ADVERB CLAUSE   INDEPENDENT CLAUSE

When you're thirsty, you may want to drink the river water, but it's really not a good idea.

INDEPENDENT CLAUSE

➋ Why It Matters in Writing

Using different sentence structures makes your writing more interesting and sophisticated.

STUDENT MODEL

> A hike through the rain forest sounded like fun. **SIMPLE SENTENCE**
> The guides were friendly, and my fellow hikers were in good spirits as we entered the dense jungle along the Amazon River. **COMPOUND-COMPLEX SENTENCE** Within half an hour, I felt an uncontrollable panic that left me drenched and panting. **COMPLEX SENTENCE** I was surrounded by vegetation, and I couldn't see the sky. **COMPOUND SENTENCE** Was this claustrophobia?

CLAUSES

❸ Practice and Apply

A. CONCEPT CHECK: Sentence Structure

Identify each of the following sentences as simple, compound, complex, or compound-complex.

A Slippery Lesson

1. The rain forest is a dangerous place, but Karen Catchpole discovered that during the monsoon season, it is even more treacherous.
2. Catchpole had climbed mountains, and she had trekked across snowy plateaus, but she was not prepared for Borneo.
3. She wondered why she had ever started this 250-mile hike.
4. She and her fellow hikers should have known better.
5. In the rainy season, the forest floor was slippery muck.
6. They couldn't trust their senses, because distances were impossible to measure.
7. She and her guides could see only 12 feet ahead.
8. Plants snared her clothes and skin as she stumbled along, and rushing streams made the trail more treacherous.
9. For days she could only stare at her feet; however, she soon began to notice the abundant wildlife.
10. She saw a Kelabit longhouse that was home to ten families.

➜ **For a SELF-CHECK and more practice, see the EXERCISE BANK, p. 298.**

Combine sentences 4 and 5 to form a single complex sentence.

B. REVISING: Combining Sentences

The following passage contains simple sentences. Rewrite the paragraph by combining sentences. Write at least one compound sentence, one complex sentence, and one compound-complex sentence.

Respite in a Village
(1) Catchpole flailed through the jungle. (2) She ducked under vines. (3) This area was home to the Penan. (4) These people were once masters of the jungle. (5) Loggers and missionaries changed their way of life. (6) Catchpole was exhausted. (7) She arrived at a Penan village. (8) Still, she observed local custom and greeted the leader. (9) She got some rest. (10) It was time to go on.

🗐 **Working Portfolio:** Choose a draft from your portfolio. How can you improve it by varying the sentence structures?

Fragments and Run-Ons

LESSON 5

① Here's the Idea

In the rush to put ideas in writing, it is easy to leave out elements of a sentence or to forget punctuation. These omissions often result in fragments or run-on sentences.

Sentence Fragments

A sentence must have a subject and a verb. A fragment is missing one or both of these elements and does not express a complete thought.

▶ **A sentence fragment is only part of a sentence.**

Phrase Fragments A phrase has neither a subject nor a verb and does not express a complete thought.

> Incorrect: **In 1865 Western Union needed a telegraph cable. To link America and Europe.**
>
> Correct: **In 1865 Western Union needed a telegraph cable to link America and Europe.**

Clause Fragments A subordinate clause has a subject and a verb, but it does not express a complete thought.

> Incorrect: **Before they could lay the cable across Siberia. Someone needed to survey the land.**
>
> Correct: **Before they could lay the cable across Siberia, someone needed to survey the land.**

Other Kinds of Fragments Fragments also occur when a writer forgets to include the subject or a verb in a sentence.

> Incorrect: **The task of surveying to George Kennan, an accomplished telegrapher.**
>
> Correct: **The task of surveying went to George Kennan, an accomplished telegrapher.**

It is natural to use sentence fragments in casual speech; however, fragments can cause confusion in your writing.

Run-On Sentences

▶ **A run-on sentence is made up of two or more sentences that are written as though they were one sentence.**

The most common run-on sentence is the **comma splice,** or comma fault. Instead of the correct end punctuation, the writer uses a comma between two sentences.

> **Kennan was not a linguist, he thought Russian was impossible to learn.**

You can correct this run-on sentence in five different ways:

Ways to Correct Run-On Sentences	
Form two sentences	Kennan was not a linguist. **He** thought Russian was impossible to learn.
Add a comma and a coordinating conjunction	Kennan was not a linguist, **so** he thought Russian was impossible to learn.
Add a semicolon	Kennan was not a linguist**; he** thought Russian was impossible to learn.
Add a semicolon followed by a conjunctive adverb	Kennan was not a linguist**; consequently,** he thought Russian was impossible to learn.
Change one sentence into a subordinate clause	**Since** Kennan was not a linguist, he thought Russian was impossible to learn.

Remember to vary sentence structure when you fix run-ons, or your writing may sound monotonous. Use complex sentences as well as simple and compound sentences.

❷ Why It Matters in Writing

Fragments express incomplete thoughts and often don't make sense. Run-ons don't separate thoughts correctly, and they can be hard to follow.

STUDENT MODEL

The Kamchadal people lived in the southern part of the Kamchatka Peninsula. They lived in isolation, on rare occasions they held great celebrations. When someone would come to visit.

> The comma splice and clause fragment make this hard to understand.

❸ Practice and Apply

A. CONCEPT CHECK: Fragments and Run-Ons

Rewrite each sentence below by correcting the phrase fragment, clause fragment, or run-on sentence.

Example: As Kennan traveled through Kamchatka. He and his team used many different kinds of transportation.

Answer: As Kennan traveled through Kamchatka, he and his team used many different kinds of transportation.

Terrors of Travel

1. Kamchadal canoes were precarious. Because they capsized so easily.
2. One team member told Kennan to part his hair in the middle. To preserve perfect balance.
3. After winter arrived, the team had to travel by sled or by snowshoes. In order to avoid sinking in the deep snow.
4. Kennan was disillusioned, the reindeer pulling his sled did not measure up to those of his boyhood imagination.
5. As they ventured northward. They lodged with Korak people.
6. Their houses were 20 feet high they had no doors or windows.

➡ **For a SELF-CHECK and more practice, see the EXERCISE BANK, p. 298.**

B. REVISING: Correcting Fragments and Run-Ons

Correct the above fragments and run-on sentences by writing another revision of each sentence.

In your 🗀 **Working Portfolio,** find your paragraph from the **Write Away** on page 74. Fix any sentence fragments or run-on sentences.

Dilbert by Scott Adams

LESSON 6 Sentence Diagramming

❶ Here's the Idea

Diagramming is a way to show the structure of a sentence graphically. It helps you understand how a sentence is put together and how the parts relate to one another. Before learning how to diagram compound, complex, and compound-complex sentences, review the lesson on diagramming simple sentences on pages 38–41.

Watch me for diagramming tips!

Compound Sentences

- Diagram the independent clauses on parallel horizontal lines.
- Connect the verbs in the two clauses by a broken line with a step.

Steve McCurry takes exciting photographs, and each picture tells a story.

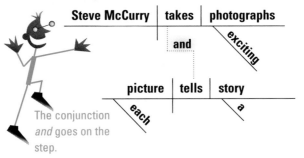

The conjunction *and* goes on the step.

A. CONCEPT CHECK: Simple and Compound Sentences

Use what you have learned to diagram these sentences.

Photographing War
1. The pictures sometimes shock us, but they always intrigue us.
2. War zones and foreign cultures are Steve's specialties.
3. Interpreters help Steve, and they solve many of his problems.

Complex Sentences

- Diagram an adjective or adverb clause on its own horizontal line below the main line, as if it were a sentence.
- Use a broken line to connect the word introducing the clause to the word it modifies.

Adjective Clause Introduced by a Relative Pronoun

His photos, which have won awards, bring world events into our homes.

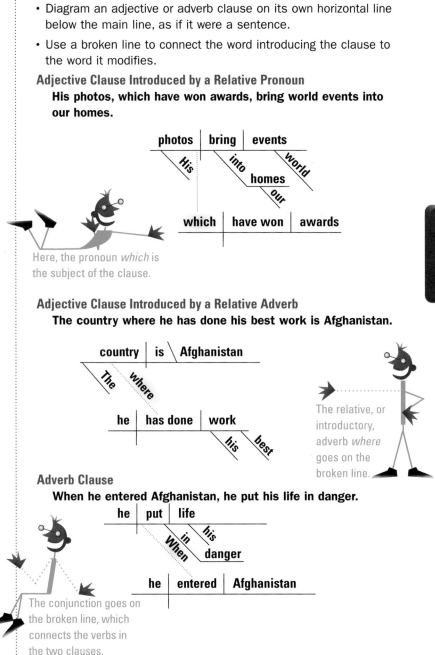

Here, the pronoun *which* is the subject of the clause.

Adjective Clause Introduced by a Relative Adverb

The country where he has done his best work is Afghanistan.

The relative, or introductory, adverb *where* goes on the broken line.

Adverb Clause

When he entered Afghanistan, he put his life in danger.

The conjunction goes on the broken line, which connects the verbs in the two clauses.

CLAUSES

B. CONCEPT CHECK: Adjective and Adverb Clauses

Use what you have learned to diagram these sentences.

War in Afghanistan
1. Afghan rebels who were fighting a civil war smuggled Steve into the country.
2. After he made his first trip in 1979, he was entranced by Afghanistan.
3. The villages where he was taken were bombed.

Noun Clauses

- Diagram the subordinate clause on a separate line that is attached to the main line with a forked line.

- Place the forked line in the diagram according to the role of the noun clause in the sentence.

- Diagram the word introducing the noun clause according to its function in the clause.

Noun Clause Used as a Subject
Whatever he has photographed has been very dramatic.

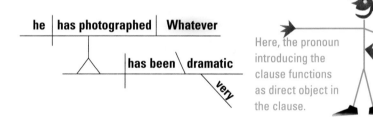

Here, the pronoun introducing the clause functions as direct object in the clause.

C. CONCEPT CHECK: Noun Clauses

Use what you have learned to diagram these sentences.

The Horrors of War
1. His portrait of an Afghan girl gives whoever sees it a haunting image of war.
2. What he photographed in Afghanistan was published in newsmagazines.
3. The editors liked what he had done.

Compound-Complex Sentences

- Diagram the independent clauses first.
- Attach each subordinate clause to the word it modifies.

McCurry takes precautions, but he knows that anything can happen.

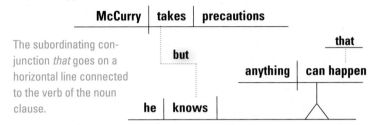

The subordinating conjunction *that* goes on a horizontal line connected to the verb of the noun clause.

D. CONCEPT CHECK: Compound-Complex Sentences

Use what you have learned to diagram these sentences.

The Life of a Photojournalist
1. He loved places where he had never been, and he enjoyed the different cultures.
2. He may shoot 500 rolls of film, but the editors choose a few that fit their needs.

E. MIXED REVIEW: Diagramming

Diagram the following sentences. Look for all types of clauses.

Trouble in India
1. Steve McCurry traveled to India.
2. He attended a festival for Ganesh, which is the elephant god.
3. Villagers carried the statue to the sea, where they submerged it.
4. McCurry stood in the water and took pictures.
5. People submerged the idol, and McCurry photographed them.
6. As McCurry took pictures, angry young men approached him.
7. Some hit him, while others grabbed his camera.
8. No one had said that he should not photograph the submersion.
9. What he did not know almost killed him.
10. The people who had given permission only watched at first, but they finally rescued him.

CLAUSES

Grammar in Literature

Adding Variety with Sentence Structure

Writers often use different sentence structures to

• vary the rhythm of the narrative

• incorporate descriptive detail

In the following excerpt, the varied sentence structure mimics the lulling rhythm of a train ride.

A R A B Y
by James Joyce

I held a florin tightly in my hand as I strode down Buckingham Street towards the station. The sight of the streets thronged with buyers and glaring with gas recalled to me the purpose of my journey. I took my seat in a third-class carriage of a deserted train. After an intolerable delay the train moved out of the station slowly. It crept onward among ruinous houses and over the twinkling river. At Westland Row Station a crowd of people pressed to the carriage doors; but the porters moved them back, saying that it was a special train for the bazaar. I remained alone in the bare carriage. In a few minutes the train drew up beside an improvised wooden platform. I passed out on to the road and saw by the lighted dial of a clock that it was ten minutes to ten. In front of me was a large building which displayed the magical name.

An adverb clause helps create a more complete image of the narrator.

A longer compound-complex sentence creates a long, rhythmic stretch.

A shorter, simple sentence creates a short beat.

A noun clause answers the question "What did he see?"

An adjective clause modifies *building*.

Good writers don't generally plan their sentence structures before they write them. But as they compose and revise, they use structures that create rhythm and emphasis well suited to a particular idea and place in the paragraph. Every sentence structure is based on one of three ways of arranging clauses:

Creating Variety in Sentence Structures	
Using a single independent clause	Focuses attention on a single idea. In a series, can create choppy rhythm.
Combining independent clauses	Connects ideas of equal importance. Can create a smooth and balanced flow.
Adding subordinate clauses	Adds another layer of ideas; can help create momentum and complexity.

PRACTICE AND APPLY: Sentence Combining

The following passage is made up of simple sentences. Follow the instructions below to vary the sentence structures.

> **(1)** We expected rain. **(2)** We did not expect a gale. **(3)** The wind was strong. **(4)** We could hardly move. **(5)** We tied and secured one sail. **(6)** Another would rip loose. **(7)** The wind would tear it to shreds. **(8)** The light ship rolled and pitched. **(9)** The waves batted it like a ball. **(10)** The waves grew taller and stronger. **(11)** We went below deck. **(12)** Everything was secured tightly. **(13)** It was four o'clock in the morning. **(14)** The storm began to weaken.

1. Combine sentences 1 and 2 to form a compound sentence.
2. Combine sentences 3 and 4 by changing one sentence into a subordinate clause.
3. Combine sentences 5, 6, and 7 to form a compound-complex sentence. (Hint: Start the clause with *As soon as.*)
4. Combine sentences 9 and 10 to form a complex sentence.
5. Combine sentences 13 and 14 to form a complex sentence.

After you have revised the paragraph, read both versions aloud with a partner. Are there other sentences that could be combined to improve the paragraph? How?

📁 **Working Portfolio:** Choose your most recent piece of writing and revise it by combining sentences and using a variety of sentence structures.

Mixed Review

A. Kinds of Clauses and Sentence Structure Read the passage. Then write the answers to the questions below it.

> **LITERARY MODEL**
>
> **(1)** He stepped forward, so that he could see all round and over the kit-bag. **(2)** Of course there was nothing there, nothing but the faded carpet and the bulging canvas sides. **(3)** He put out his hands and threw open the mouth of the sack where it had fallen over, being only three parts full, and then he saw for the first time that round the inside, some six inches from the top, there ran a broad smear of dull crimson. **(4)** It was an old and faded blood stain. **(5)** He uttered a scream, and drew back his hands as if they had been burnt. **(6)** At the same moment the kit-bag gave a faint, but unmistakable, lurch forward towards the door.
>
> —Algernon Blackwood, "The Kit-Bag"

1. What is the structure of sentence 1: compound, complex, or compound-complex?
2. What word or words introduce the second clause in sentence 1?
3. What kind of clause is in sentence 1: adjective, adverb, or noun clause?
4. Is sentence 2 a simple, compound, or complex sentence?
5. How many independent clauses are in sentence 3?
6. What kind of clause is *where it had fallen over* in sentence 3?
7. What is the use of the noun clause in sentence 3: subject, predicate nominative, or direct object?
8. Is sentence 4 a simple, compound, or complex sentence?
9. Is sentence 5 a compound, complex, or compound-complex sentence?
10. How many subordinate clauses are in sentence 6?

B. Identifying Sentence Fragments and Run-Ons Identify each set of underlined words as a phrase fragment, clause fragment, or run-on sentence. If there is nothing wrong with the underlined words, write "Correct."

   (1) <u>Dracula is big business, Romanians are delighted.</u> **(2)** <u>For the very first time in 1991.</u> Romanians could read Bram Stoker's novel. **(3)** <u>Even though it was first published in 1897.</u> Some critics theorize that Dracula was based on Vlad Tepes. **(4)** <u>Who was known as Vlad the Impaler.</u> **(5)** <u>It is his castle that tourists see on Dracula tours; however, they have to climb about 1,400 steps to get to it.</u>

Rewrite the paragraph in exercise B, correcting all fragments and run-on sentences.

Choose the letter of the term that correctly identifies each numbered part.

> When the UN celebrated the Decade of Women, Anita Desai was
> (1)
> invited to participate. Desai, whose works include eight novels, lived in
> (2)
> India at the time. Her assignment was to go to Norway, where she would
> (3)
> write about various women. Whoever had devised the program must have
> (4)
> been a diabolical genius, or so Desai thought. Her February trip began
> well but soon turned into a nightmare. After she put on the winter clothes
> (5)
> the Norwegians had given her, she boarded a steamer. The ship rose and
> (6)   (7)
> fell on gale-driven waves as it headed for the icy island of Frøya.
> The elements were against her, and Desai feared she would never see
> (8)
> land again. After the ship docked, she found her hostess. Who plunked her
> (9)
> in a car and drove into the stormy darkness. They arrived at the woman's
> (10)
> friend's house, the electricity was out, there was no heat.

1. A. independent clause
   B. subordinate clause
   C. simple sentence
   D. compound sentence

2. A. adverb clause
   B. noun clause
   C. essential adjective clause
   D. nonessential adjective clause

3. A. adjective clause
   B. adverb clause
   C. noun clause
   D. elliptical clause

4. A. noun clause acting as predicate
      nominative
   B. adjective clause modifying *genius*
   C. noun clause acting as appositive
   D. noun clause acting as subject

5. A. adverb clause modifying *boarded*
   B. adjective clause modifying *she*
   C. noun clause acting as object of
      preposition
   D. noun clause acting as subject

6. A. noun clause
   B. nonessential adjective clause
   C. essential adjective clause
   D. adverb clause

7. A. simple sentence
   B. compound sentence
   C. complex sentence
   D. compound-complex sentence

8. A. simple sentence
   B. compound sentence
   C. complex sentence
   D. compound-complex sentence

9. A. phrase fragment
   B. clause fragment
   C. run-on
   D. simple sentence

10. A. compound sentence
    B. compound-complex sentence
    C. run-on
    D. clause fragments

Student Help Desk

Using Clauses at a Glance

A clause contains a subject and a verb. An independent clause expresses a complete thought, but a subordinate clause doesn't.

| Since I bought a sidecar for my motorcycle, | I seem to have more friends. |

SUBORDINATE CLAUSE

- begins with a subordinating conjunction, relative pronoun, or relative adverb
- does not make sense on its own

INDEPENDENT CLAUSE

- makes sense on its own
- can be modified by the subordinate clause

Four Sentence Structures   A TRAVELER'S TALE

Simple Sentence

I dropped Alex's suitcase in the river.

Complex Sentence

I dropped it because the handles were so slippery.

Compound Sentence

I tried to fish it out, but then the crocodiles came along.

Compound-Complex Sentence

Alex threw a fit when she found out, and she has never forgiven me.

Fixing Fragments and Run-Ons

A Few Quick Fixes

What's the Problem?

Quick Fix

What's the Problem?	Quick Fix
Both the subject and the verb are missing; the fragment is a phrase. Into the water.	**Add a subject and verb.** The suitcase fell into the water.
The fragment is a subordinate clause. When Alex wasn't looking.	**Combine the fragment with an independent clause.** It happened when Alex wasn't looking.
The punctuation mark separating two complete thoughts is missing. The suitcase floated to the surface the crocodiles flocked to it.	**Add an end mark and start a new sentence, or use a semicolon.** The suitcase floated to the surface. The crocodiles flocked to it. The suitcase floated to the surface; the crocodiles flocked to it.
Two sentences are separated only by a comma. I threw in a bunch of bananas to distract them, the crocodiles ignored it. They obviously preferred Alex's toothpaste, they ate both tubes.	**Add a conjunction or change the comma to a semicolon.** I threw in a bunch of bananas to distract them, **but** the crocodiles ignored it. **Change one clause into a subordinate clause.** They obviously preferred Alex's toothpaste, **because** they ate both tubes.

CLAUSES

The Bottom Line

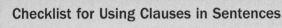

Checklist for Using Clauses in Sentences

Have I . . .

- ____ varied the structures of my sentences?
- ____ left fragments that should be part of a sentence?
- ____ separated complete ideas with the correct punctuation?
- ____ combined clauses to make ideas logical and clear?

Chapter 4

Using Verbs

Theme: Sleep
To Sleep, Perchance to Dream . . .

"If only I were up in the mountains! I would pick a spot in the sun, lie down, and take the nap of my life. I can just imagine it."

How many verbs can you identify in the preceding two lines? How many kinds of verbs have been used? Verbs come in many forms; used well, they can convey an infinite variety of actions and conditions in a compelling fashion. In this chapter, you'll learn how to use verbs correctly and captivate even your sleepiest reader.

Write Away: Sleep Stories
Write a short narrative that has something to do with sleep. For example, describe a time when you couldn't stay awake, when you couldn't fall asleep, or when you overslept. Save your narrative in your 🗂 **Working Portfolio.**

Write the letter that represents the best way to write each underlined section.

Some people can take naps anywhere, but few <u>have ever buyed</u> a nap.
                                                      (1)
Well, in Spain, people <u>are taken</u> naps in siesta shops. One adventuresome
                            (2)
soul recently tried it. He <u>will have reserved</u> a short massage and a half-
                                  (3)
hour nap and paid about ten dollars for them. He enjoyed the massage,

but he <u>does not fall</u> asleep. He disliked the New Age music that the
          (4)
shopkeeper <u>did play</u>. Naps are necessary for some people. <u>Highs and lows</u>
                (5)   (6)
<u>are had by us all</u> throughout the day. One writer wished <u>he was allowed</u>
to nap at his desk. Whenever he <u>sat</u> his head down, he was filled with
                                      (8)
guilt. He knew that his boss <u>will not approve</u>. However, a short nap <u>could</u>
                                    (9)   (10)
<u>of made</u> the writer feel refreshed and alert.

1. A. are ever buying
   B. will have ever buyed
   C. have ever bought
   D. Correct as is

2. A. have took
   B. take
   C. were taken
   D. Correct as is

3. A. had reserved
   B. will reserve
   C. reserves
   D. Correct as is

4. A. does not fallen
   B. did not fall
   C. did not fell
   D. Correct as is

5. A. will be playing
   B. has been playing
   C. played
   D. Correct as is

6. A. We are all having highs and
      lows
   B. We all like to have had highs
      and lows
   C. We all have highs and lows
   D. Correct as is

7. A. he were allowed
   B. he was allowing
   C. he is allowed
   D. Correct as is

8. A. had sat
   B. sets
   C. set
   D. Correct as is

9. A. will not be approving
   B. would not approve
   C. had not approved
   D. Correct as is

10. A. could have made
    B. would of made
    C. could have make
    D. Correct as is

Principal Parts of Verbs

❶ Here's the Idea

A verb is a word that shows action or a state of being. An **action verb** expresses mental or physical activity. A **linking verb** joins the subject of a sentence with a word or phrase that renames or describes the subject.

PROFESSIONAL MODEL

> Mr. Cho sleeps with the windows open because the fresh air helps him sleep better. When it rained last night, the windows were open, as usual, and his wife's favorite chair was all wet.

ACTION VERB

LINKING VERB

▶ **Every verb has four basic forms, called principal parts: the present, the present participle, the past, and the past participle.** These are used to make all of the verb's tenses and other forms.

The Four Principal Parts of a Verb			
Present	**Present Participle**	**Past**	**Past Participle**
drop	(is) dropping	dropped	(has) dropped
snore	(is) snoring	snored	(has) snored
break	(is) breaking	broke	(has) broken
lose	(is) losing	lost	(has) lost

Verbs can be regular or irregular. Most verbs are regular.

Regular Verbs

The past and past participle of a **regular verb** are formed by adding -ed or -d to the present part.

Regular Verbs			
Present	**Present Participle**	**Past**	**Past Participle**
call	(is) calling	called	(has) called
kick	(is) kicking	kicked	(has) kicked
clap	(is) clapping	clapped	(has) clapped

Note that some regular verbs require spelling changes, such as doubling the final consonant, to form the present participle and the past or past participle.

Irregular Verbs

The past and past participle of an **irregular verb,** like *ring,* are formed in several different ways. Because you can't make the tenses or other forms of a verb without knowing its principal parts, irregular verbs must be memorized.

Most irregular verbs fall into five basic groups. Learning these groups will help you remember the irregular verb parts.

Common Irregular Verbs				
	Present	**Present Participle**	**Past**	**Past Participle**
Group 1 The forms of the present, past, and past participle are the same.	**burst** cut put spread	(is) bursting (is) cutting (is) putting (is) spreading	**burst** cut put spread	(has) **burst** (has) cut (has) put (has) spread
Group 2 The forms of the past and past participle are the same.	**bring** fling lend say	(is) bringing (is) flinging (is) lending (is) saying	**brought** flung lent said	(has) **brought** (has) flung (has) lent (has) said
Group 3 The past participle is formed by adding *-n* or *-en* to the past.	**break** bear steal swear	(is) breaking (is) bearing (is) stealing (is) swearing	**broke** bore stole swore	(has) **broken** (has) borne (has) stolen (has) sworn
Group 4 The *i* in the present form changes to *a* in the past and to *u* in the past participle.	**begin** drink spring swim	(is) beginning (is) drinking (is) springing (is) swimming	**began** drank sprang *or* sprung swam	(has) **begun** (has) drunk (has) sprung (has) swum
Group 5 The past participle is formed from the present, in many cases by adding *-n, -en,* or *-ne.*	**blow** go eat shake	(is) blowing (is) going (is) eating (is) shaking	**blew** went ate shook	(has) **blown** (has) gone (has) eaten (has) shaken

For more irregular verbs, see the Student Help Desk, p. 126.

USING VERBS

❷ Why It Matters in Writing

The use of standard English is important for success in school and the work world. Teachers and employers may form an impression of you based on the way you use language. Errors in verb forms are especially noticeable. Notice the corrections in this model.

STUDENT MODEL

Zeke had never ~~did~~ *done* anything to get into trouble until he ~~fall~~ *fell* asleep in chemistry class. He knocked over the Bunsen burner and broke a vial of flammable liquid. That was the day the chem lab almost ~~blowed~~ *blew* up.

❸ Practice and Apply

REVISING: Correcting Errors in Principal Parts

Correct errors in the principal parts of verbs in the following passage. If a sentence does not have an error, write *Correct*.

An "A-pealing" Awakening

(1) Some people sprang into action at the first sound of their alarm clocks. **(2)** Others greet the day a little less eagerly. **(3)** Yet nearly all of us have stole a few minutes of extra sleep after we hit the snooze button of our alarm. **(4)** Thanks to alarm clocks, clock radios, and snooze buttons, the ways we wake up have change across the years. **(5)** Centuries ago, monasteries had a sexton, or custodian, who gotten up to ring the chapel bells during the night. **(6)** To help the sexton, a candle maker embedded miniature bells inside a wax candle. **(7)** With the help of this clever candle, the sexton waked up at regular intervals throughout the night. **(8)** Every hour, as the candle burned and the wax melted, a small bell fallen into a metal dish. **(9)** The clanging noise startle the sexton awake. **(10)** He then run to the chapel and rang the bells.

➡ **For a SELF-CHECK and more practice, see the EXERCISE BANK, p. 299.**

Verb Tenses

❶ Here's the Idea

▶ **A tense is a verb form that shows the time of an action or condition.**

The principal parts of a verb are used to form the three **simple tenses (present, past,** and **future)** and the three **perfect tenses (present perfect, past perfect,** and **future perfect).** These forms give us many ways to describe present, past, and future events. The verb's forms in all the tenses make up its **conjugation.**

Forming and Using Simple Tenses

Conjugation of Simple Tenses		
	Singular	**Plural**
Present		
First person	I rest	we rest
Second person	you rest	you rest
Third person	he, she, it rests	they rest
Past—present + -*d* or -*ed*		
First person	I rested	we rested
Second person	you rested	you rested
Third person	he, she, it rested	they rested
Future—*will* or *shall* + present		
First person	I will (shall) rest	we will (shall) rest
Second person	you will (shall) rest	you will (shall) rest
Third person	he, she, it will (shall) rest	they will (shall) rest

Using the Present Tense

The present tense shows that an action or condition

- is occurring in the present

    The technician hooks up the electrodes.

- occurs regularly

    The laboratory team conducts tests every day.

- is constantly or generally true at any given time

    Equipment monitors brain activity during sleep.

Many writers use the present tense to talk about historical events. This use of what is called the **historical present tense** gives readers a sense of being present at events.

In 1953 Kleitman and Aserinsky discover REM sleep.

Using the Past Tense
The past tense shows that an action or condition occurred in the past.

We decided last week to conduct the experiment.

Using the Future Tense
The future tense shows that an action or condition will occur at some time in the future. Note that some writers use *shall* with first-person subjects; however, *will* can be used correctly with all subjects.

Volunteers will sign up for the experiment next month.

Forming and Using Perfect Tenses

All perfect tenses are formed from the past participle of the verb.

Conjugation of Perfect Tenses		
	Singular	**Plural**
Present Perfect—*has* or *have* + past participle		
First person Second person Third person	I have rested you have rested he, she, it has rested	we have rested you have rested they have rested
Past Perfect—*had* + past participle		
First person Second person Third person	I had rested you had rested he, she, it had rested	we had rested you had rested they had rested
Future Perfect—*will have* or *shall have* + past participle		
First person Second person Third person	I will (shall) have rested you will (shall) have rested he, she, it will (shall) have rested	we will (shall) have rested you will (shall) have rested they will (shall) have rested

Using the Present Perfect Tense
The present perfect tense shows that an action or condition
- was completed at one or more indefinite times in the past

Sleep research has added to our understanding of the brain.

- started in the past and continues into the present

Since the 1950s, sleep research has aided physicians, psychologists, and parents.

CHAPTER 4

Using the Past Perfect Tense
The past perfect tense shows that a past action or condition preceded another past action or condition.

Aserinsky had observed **the eyes' moving during sleep and** decided **to explore these movements.**

When talking about two actions in the past, use the past perfect tense to express the action that happened first.

I had drunk **three glasses of water before I** went **to bed.**

Using the Future Perfect Tense
The future perfect tense shows that an action or condition in the future will precede another future action or condition.

The lab will have studied **5,000 sleepers when it** celebrates **its tenth anniversary next week.**

❷ Why It Matters in Writing

The correct use of verb tenses establishes the sequence of events for readers and can help them understand cause and effect. In this model, the use of the past perfect shows that Julia's condition had started before this midnight stroll.

PROFESSIONAL MODEL

Julia had always suffered from insomnia, so Angela was not surprised to hear her shuffling around in the middle of the night. Julia tiptoed downstairs for a slice of corn bread.

PAST PERFECT

PAST

❸ Practice and Apply

A. CONCEPT CHECK: Verb Tenses

Write the verb or verbs in each sentence and identify their tense.

The News on Narcolepsy

(1) In 1999, two separate groups of scientists discovered a possible genetic link to narcolepsy. **(2)** Both groups had performed research on animals. **(3)** But people, like animals, have long suffered from narcolepsy. **(4)** Those with the disorder fall asleep without warning. **(5)** They immediately enter the deepest kind of sleep. **(6)** Researchers have concluded that a damaged gene produces defective brain-cell receptors. **(7)** These receptors do not pick up signals from the protein hypocretin-2. **(8)** The research suggests that the protein plays an important role in sleep regulation. **(9)** One scientist predicts that these two studies will have redirected sleep research in no time. **(10)** Scientists will likely begin to look for medications that work on the brain's hypocretin system.

➡ **For a SELF-CHECK and more practice, see the EXERCISE BANK, p. 299.**

Change the tense of three verbs in the above paragraph, and rewrite the sentences with the new verbs.

B. REVISING: Using Verb Tenses

Revise the following paragraph, correcting errors in verb tense.

Sleep Test Report

DECEMBER 1

On November 20, Denzel arrived at the sleep laboratory for the test he has scheduled two weeks before. After getting settled, he take a battery of psychological tests. In the early evening, he ate dinner, went for a walk, watch TV, and read. Later in the evening, he will feel sleepy, so Peggy, the technician, attached the electrodes to his head. At 12:30 A.M., Denzel went to bed, will have sipped some water, and turned off the light. At 2:32 A.M., the electro-oculogram recorded rapid eye movement, and a few minutes later, Denzel had sat bolt upright in bed, reclined, rolled over, and fell asleep. All had proceeded quietly until 4:28 A.M., when he woke up, drank some water, rocked back and forth, reclined, and slept. At 6:30 A.M., he woke up and stretch. He has no memory of waking up during the night. On December 20, he will receive his test results.

Progressive and Emphatic Forms

❶ Here's the Idea

Progressive forms of verbs are used to describe ongoing occurrences: *writing, remembering, lifting.* Emphatic forms lend forcefulness to verbs. Both kinds of forms provide options for varied and detailed writing.

Using Progressive Forms

▶ **The progressive form of a verb expresses an event in progress.**

The six progressive forms are made by adding the simple and perfect tenses of *be* to the present participle of a verb.

Progressive Tenses		
	Shows an Event That . . .	**Example**
Present	**is** in progress	I **am pacing** the floor.
Past	**was** in progress	I **was pacing** the floor last night.
Future	**will be** in progress	I **will be pacing** the floor tomorrow night, too.
Present perfect	began in the past and is continuing in the present	I **have been pacing** every night.
Past perfect	was ongoing when it was interrupted by another past action	I **had been pacing** for hours when I decided to have a snack.
Future perfect	will have been ongoing by the time of a specified future action	By next Monday I **will have been pacing** the floor every night for two weeks.

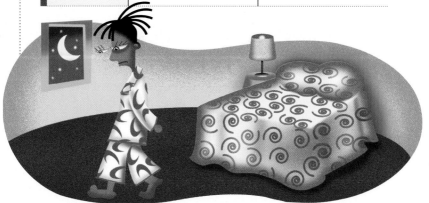

Using Emphatic Forms

▶ **The emphatic form gives special force to a verb.**

Emphatic forms are only used in the present and past tenses. They are made by adding *do* or *did* to the present tense of the verb.

Present Emphatic

Leon does have terrible trouble sleeping.

(*Does* emphasizes the verb *have*.)

Past Emphatic

Leon did make a doctor's appointment.

(*Did* emphasizes the verb *make*.)

The emphatic form is commonly used to correct or contradict.

I did turn off the lights last night.

❷ Why It Matters in Writing

The progressive and emphatic forms can demonstrate the relationship and importance of events in a text. Like any emphatic device, these forms lose their force if you overuse them.

PROFESSIONAL MODEL

Sleep researchers are beginning to understand sleep disorders much better than they did only 20 years ago. For years, many patients have been mistaking their own constant sleepiness for sheer laziness. Even today, not all physicians recognize the symptoms of sleep disorders such as sleep apnea, a temporary loss of breath during sleep.

Although sleep apnea is diagnosed most often in men, women do suffer from the condition and are underdiagnosed. This disorder leads to fatigue as well as high blood pressure, accidents, and even a shortened life span. Treatment does exist, so an accurate diagnosis can lead to real improvement in the life of someone suffering from this condition.

PRESENT PROGRESSIVE

shows that the action is continuing.

PRESENT PERFECT PROGRESSIVE

shows that this is a long-standing problem.

PRESENT EMPHATIC

shows contrast with the fact that it is men who are most often diagnosed.

PRESENT EMPHATIC

makes a strong point.

❸ Practice and Apply

A. CONCEPT CHECK: Progressive and Emphatic Forms

Identify the progressive and emphatic forms in the following sentences. Write the verb and identify its form and tense.

Sleepy in Seattle and Elsewhere

1. People are always calling themselves insomniacs, but a few restless nights do not qualify someone as a true insomniac.
2. Nonetheless, more than 60 million Americans do suffer from frequent or chronic insomnia.
3. Aaron has been experiencing insomnia since boyhood.
4. He had long been suffering from sleepless nights and groggy days when his parents consulted a doctor.
5. They were becoming increasingly worried about him.
6. The doctor prescribed changes in some of Aaron's habits because he had not been eating or exercising properly.
7. Aaron finally did change his lifestyle.
8. Among other things, he has been keeping a sleep diary.
9. By March, he will have been following this routine for a year.
10. Until then, the doctor will be checking Aaron's progress.

➜ **For a SELF-CHECK and more practice, see the EXERCISE BANK, p. 300.**

For a SELF-CHECK and more practice, see the EXERCISE BANK, p. 300.

B. REVISING: Using Progressive and Emphatic Verb Forms

Change the underlined verbs to progressive or emphatic forms.

Snore No More

For years Bob's wife and children <u>had begged</u> him to see a doctor about his snoring. One night they moved his favorite chair and a cot into the garage. Bob pretended not to notice, but he <u>got</u> the message and made an appointment.

The doctor said that although Bob was generally healthy, he <u>suffered</u> from obstructive apnea. In Bob's case, extra folds of tissue sagged and partially blocked his windpipe as he slept. This tissue <u>vibrated</u> every time he inhaled or exhaled, so Bob snored. Thanks to his family, Bob <u>will have</u> an operation that should give everyone a snoreless night's sleep.

C. WRITING: Adding Progressive and Emphatic Verb Forms

In your 🗀 **Working Portfolio,** find the narrative you wrote for the **Write Away** on page 102. Improve it where you can by replacing some of the verbs with progressive and emphatic forms.

Active and Passive Voice

❶ Here's the Idea

▶ **The voice of an action verb indicates whether the subject performs or receives the action.** Voice affects the meaning and tone of the sentence.

Active Voice

When the subject of a verb performs the action expressed by the verb, the verb is in the active voice.

> **The maid placed the fresh sheets on the bed.**

> **A chocolate rested on the pillow.**

Most of the sentences you write will be in the active voice. It is active verb forms that appear in the tables in this chapter.

Passive Voice

When the subject of a verb receives the action, the verb is in the passive voice.

> **The fresh sheets were placed on the bed by the maid.**

The passive voice is often used when the person or thing performing the action is indefinite or unknown.

> **Comfortable beds have been valued throughout the ages.**

Forming the Passive

To form the passive, use an appropriate tense of the verb *be* with the past participle of the main verb.

> **Metal beds were advertised as bug-proof in the late 1700s.**

> PAST ↗   ↖ PAST PARTICIPLE

❷ Why It Matters in Writing

The overuse of the passive voice creates dull or awkward sentences. When revising, look out for sentences in the passive voice that could be in the active.

Passive

> **Mattresses were stuffed with pine shavings by Americans in the 19th century.**

Active

> **Americans in the 19th century stuffed their mattresses with pine shavings.**

❸ Practice and Apply

A. CONCEPT CHECK: Active and Passive Voice

Write the main verb in each sentence and identify its voice.

Nights on the Go
1. The comfort of one's own bed cannot be overestimated.
2. Travelers have often embarked on adventures in sleeping.
3. Early travel accommodations resulted in great discomfort.
4. In the 1840s, Charles Dickens sailed to the United States.
5. His displeasure with his less-than-spacious stateroom aboard the ship was openly expressed.
6. Dickens compared the beds there with stacked coffins.
7. Arguably, the worst quarters were found on a canal boat.
8. At first, Dickens was surprised by the bookshelves in the room.
9. Then he spotted a "microscopic sheet and blanket."
10. People, not books, were shelved there for the night.

➜ For a SELF-CHECK and more exercises, see the EXERCISE BANK, p. 300.

Rewrite three of the above sentences, changing them from the passive to the active voice.

B. REVISING: Using Active and Passive Voice Effectively

Revise any sentences in the following paragraph that would be improved by a change from passive to active. You may have to add a subject.

Sleeping the Japanese Way
(1) In Japan, Western-style accommodations can be found. **(2)** However, for a taste of Japanese culture, the traditional Japanese inns are recommended by travel writers. **(3)** These inns, called *ryokan*, are known for their excellent personal service. **(4)** Tatami mats and an alcove for flowers and art are contained by most rooms. **(5)** Dinner is usually served in the room by a maid. **(6)** After dinner, the table is moved and futon bedding is placed on the floor. **(7)** A futon, a pad of tufted cotton, is used as a mattress. **(8)** In contrast to *ryokan,* a capsule hotel offers no-frills accommodations, in most cases to men only. **(9)** Each sleeping capsule is about the size of a coffin. **(10)** Inside, a television set and a futon mattress are provided by the hotel.

The Moods of Verbs

❶ Here's the Idea

▶ **The mood of a verb conveys the status of the action or condition it describes.** Some actions and conditions are factual; others exist only as ideas or possibilities.

Indicative Mood

The **indicative mood** is used to make statements and ask questions about factual actions and conditions. All the verb forms shown so far in this chapter are indicative.

Many writers have compared **life to a dream.**

Do **your dreams** have **sound and color?**

Imperative Mood

The **imperative mood** is used to give a command or make a request. In all sentences in the imperative mood, the understood subject is *you.*

Record **your dreams in a journal.**

Subjunctive Mood

The **subjunctive mood** is used primarily to express a wish or refer to actions and conditions that are contrary to fact. The subjunctive form is identical to the past form. The subjunctive of *be* is *were.*

Comparison of Indicative and Subjunctive Moods	
Indicative	**Subjunctive**
One dreamer wants to **be** a bird.	One dreamer wishes he **were** a bird.
If he **becomes** a bird, he **will** have wings and a beak.	If he **were** a bird, he **would have** wings and a beak.

HOT TIP

Another subjunctive form is used in formal communications when referring to a request or command.

The dream interpreter asks that you be **truthful.**

❷ Why It Matters in Writing

The subjunctive mood enables writers to point out that certain situations are contrary to fact.

If I knew **the right answer, I'd tell you.**

❸ Practice and Apply

A. CONCEPT CHECK: The Moods of Verbs

Identify the mood of the underlined verb in each sentence.

Interpreting Dreams

1. <u>Do</u> you <u>have</u> an interest in dream analysis?
2. Then <u>read</u> Dr. Gayle Delaney's book *In Your Dreams.*
3. Dr. Delaney <u>includes</u> suggestions for dream interpretation in the book.
4. She says that her methods of analysis <u>provide</u> insights into even the most outrageous and humorous dreams.
5. First, <u>wake</u> up without the help of an alarm clock after sleeping eight hours.
6. According to Dr. Delaney, this <u>will give</u> you a better chance of recalling your dreams.
7. After waking up, <u>write</u> all the details you can remember about the dream.
8. She recommends that dream elements <u>be sorted</u> into five categories: settings, characters, objects, feelings, and actions or behaviors.
9. Once the dream elements are recorded, <u>place</u> the major ones in their categories.
10. Then <u>identify</u> the most significant elements.

➜ **For a SELF-CHECK and more practice, see the EXERCISE BANK, p. 301.**

B. REVISING: Changing the Mood of Verbs

Rewrite each of the following sentences, changing the mood from indicative to subjunctive or imperative.

1. In a dream, one girl felt that her best friend was walking across her back.
2. A dream interpreter told the girl to consider how this dream made her feel.
3. The girl felt like a doormat.
4. "If you say something to your friend, what will you tell her?" the interpreter asked the girl.
5. "I want her to treat me with respect," the girl responded.

Problems with Verbs

❶ Here's the Idea

Verbs play an essential role in your writing; errors in verb use can detract from otherwise good writing. Common problems include misuse of tenses and confusion of similar verbs.

Improper Shifts in Tense

An **improper shift,** a common problem in writing, is the use of two different tenses to describe two or more actions that occur at the same time.

▶ **Use the same tense to describe two or more actions that occur at the same time.**

Improper Shift
> **Sleep scientists have been studying the sleeping brain, and psychologists study dreams.**

Correct
> **Sleep scientists** have been studying **the sleeping brain, and psychologists** have been studying **dreams.** (Both actions began at an indefinite time in the past and continue in the present.)

Improper Shift
> **Many people enjoy their nighttime dreams but considered their daydreams ordinary.**

Correct
> **Many people** enjoy **their night dreams but** consider **their daydreams ordinary.** (Both actions take place in the present.)

Although you want to avoid incorrect shifts in tense, sometimes a shift in tense is necessary to express a change in time or a sequence of events.

▶ **Use different verb tenses and forms to show how events are related in time or to emphasize them differently.**

> **Victor often** has dreamed **of becoming a concert pianist, but he still** refuses **to practice the piano every day.** (The verb tenses show that Victor's dreams occurred in the indefinite past, but his refusal to practice occurs in the present.)

Commonly Confused Verbs

Several pairs of verbs are often confused because they have similar spellings and meanings.

Commonly Confused Verbs			
	Meaning	**Principal Parts**	**Example**
lie	to rest in a flat position	lie, (is) lying, lay, (have) lain	Tell Tyler to **lie** down and take his nap.
lay	to place	lay, (is) laying, laid, (have) laid	I'll just **lay** the baby down and call you back.
rise	to go upward	rise, (is) rising, rose, (have) risen	Carmen lay in bed and waited for the sun to **rise**.
raise	to lift	raise, (is) raising, raised, (have) raised	She **raised** the blinds and let the sun pour in.
sit	to occupy a seat	sit, (is) sitting, sat, (have) sat	Will **sat** in the chair, exhausted.
set	to put or place	set, (is) setting, set, (have) set	I **set** the cake on the counter.
leave	to allow to remain	leave, (is) leaving, left, (have) left	Jerry's afraid to **leave** the cat and the dog alone.
let	to permit	let, (is) letting, let, (have) let	He never **lets** them sleep in the house.
bring	to carry toward	bring, (is) bringing, brought, (have) brought	Thanks for **bringing** all those pillows and blankets.
take	to carry away from	take, (is) taking, took, (have) taken	Yuri forgot to **take** her leftovers home with her.

One reason that *lie* and *lay* are often confused is that the past participle of *lie* is spelled *lay*.

She lies down for a nap every afternoon.

She lay down for a nap yesterday afternoon.

Incorrect Use of *Would Have*

Many people mistakenly use *would have* in *if* clauses to express a condition contrary to fact. In a case like the one below, use the past perfect tense.

Incorrect

If I would have used a warmer blanket, I would have slept better.

Correct

If I had used a warmer blanket, I would have slept better.

Misuse of *Would of, Should of, Could of,* or *Might of*

Because the words sound alike, many people mistakenly write *would of, should of, could of,* or *might of* in place of *would have, should have, could have,* or *might have.* Remember that *would have, should have, could have,* and *might have* are helping verbs.

Incorrect

Mirabel wished that she could of slept just ten minutes longer.

Correct

Mirabel wished that she could have slept just ten minutes longer.

❷ Why It Matters in Writing

Properly used tenses can help you express a complex sequence of events. Note the use of different tenses in the following model.

STUDENT MODEL

Miss Yolanda eventually boarded up her windows and bought locks for her doors. This was after she had stopped seeing her art students and just before she decided never to see anyone ever again. She had had enough.

PAST
Action occurs in the past.

PAST PERFECT
Action has been completed by the time the past actions occur.

❸ Practice and Apply

A. CONCEPT CHECK: Problems with Verbs

Correct the verb errors in the following sentences.

Surreal Images

1. Imagine that you are laying in bed and beginning to relax.
2. Just before you fall asleep, strange images and sounds flashed quickly through your mind.
3. A flower bursts open, sprouts wings, and raises in the air.
4. A famous actor enters your classroom and sets beside you.
5. Then you are outside the school, and no one leaves you enter.
6. In the next instant, an elephant asks you to take him some fresh straw.
7. If you would have been truly awake, this image might have stayed in your mind.
8. You might wish you could of held on to these flickering visions.
9. Such images occur during the state of drowsiness preceding sleep and were called hypnagogic hallucinations.
10. Unlike dreams, they have no structure or story line, nor had they been studied as thoroughly as dreams.
11. In some ways they resemble a five-second daydream that leaves you enter a fantasy world.
12. However, after one finished a daydream, he or she resumes the task at hand.
13. Dr. Eric Klinger discovered that daydreams will occupy up to 40 percent of our waking time.
14. Evidently, researchers should sit out plans to investigate the surreal presleep visions.
15. They should of started a long time ago.

➡ **For a SELF-CHECK and more exercises, see the EXERCISE BANK, p. 302.**

B. WRITING: Using Commonly Confused Verbs

Think of a bizarre image or situation that might be a hypnagogic hallucination. Write a short description or dialogue about the image, using one word from each of the following pairs.

bring / take   lie / lay   leave / let   sit / set

Create a cartoon, using one or more of the commonly confused verbs in the caption.

Grammar in Literature

Using Verb Tenses and Forms

Writers vary their use of verb tenses and forms to
- show the sequence of events
- show whether the subject is in control or is being acted upon
- make readers feel an immediate connection to events

Notice how the variety of verb tenses, forms, and voice in the paragraph below clearly establishes the sequence of events and draws readers into the action.

CIVIL PEACE
Chinua Achebe

He <u>was normally a heavy sleeper but that night he heard all the neighborhood noises die down one after another</u>. Even the night watchman who knocked the hour on some metal somewhere in the distance <u>had fallen</u> silent after knocking one o'clock. That must have been the last thought in Jonathan's mind before he <u>was finally carried</u> away himself. He couldn't have been gone for long, though, when he <u>was violently awakened</u> again.

"Who <u>is knocking</u>?" whispered his wife lying beside him on the floor.

"I don't know," he whispered back breathlessly.

The second time the knocking came it was so loud and imperious that the rickety old door could have fallen down.

"Who <u>is knocking</u>?" he asked then, his voice parched and trembling.

> **Past tense** establishes the time frame for the action.

> **Past perfect tense** indicates an action that had happened previously.

> **Passive voice** stresses the fact that Jonathan is not in control of what is happening to him.

> **Present progressive** form draws readers into the moment.

Effective Use of Verb Tenses and Forms

Tense	Use verb tenses carefully to let the reader know the order in which events occur.
Voice	In general, use the active voice for strong, graceful writing. Avoid the passive voice unless you want to shift the focus from the performer of an action to the action itself or unless the performer of the action is unknown.
Mood	The indicative mood is appropriate for most narratives. The imperative mood tends to engage the reader directly, and the subjunctive, in describing hypothetical situations, creates distance.

PRACTICE AND APPLY: Effective Use of Verb Tenses and Forms

Read the passage and respond to the items that follow.

> **(1)** Purun Bhagat <u>heaped</u> his fire high that night, for he was sure his brothers would need warmth; but never a beast came to the shrine, though he called and called till he <u>dropped</u> asleep, wondering what <u>had happened</u> in the woods. **(2)** It was in the black heart of the night, the rain drumming like a thousand drums, that he <u>was roused</u> by a plucking at his blanket, and, stretching out, felt the little hand of a *langur*. **(3)** "It <u>is</u> better here than in the trees," he <u>said</u> sleepily, loosening a fold of blanket; "<u>take</u> it and <u>be</u> warm." **(4)** The monkey caught his hand and pulled hard. **(5)** "Is it food, then?" said Purun Bhagat. **(6)** "Wait awhile, and I <u>will prepare</u> some." **(7)** As he kneeled to throw fuel on the fire the *langur* <u>ran</u> to the door of the shrine, crooned, and ran back again, plucking at the man's knee.
>
> —Rudyard Kipling, "The Miracle of Purun Bhagat"

1. Identify the tense of each underlined verb in the passage.
2. In sentence 1, which progressive form could you substitute for "called and called"?
3. Why do you think Kipling uses the passive voice in sentence 2?
4. Write all the verbs that are in the imperative mood.
5. Plot the events in the passage on a time line.

Working Portfolio: Return to the narrative you wrote for the **Write Away** on page 102. Revise it by varying verb tense, voice, and mood.

A. Principal Parts of Verbs, Verb Tenses, Progressive and Emphatic Forms
Correct the errors and problems in verb usage.

In Oz

1. One of the most popular dream-sequence movies of all time had been *The Wizard of Oz.*
2. Based on the book *The Wonderful Wizard of Oz* by L. Frank Baum, the movie premiere in 1939.
3. In it, Judy Garland plays Dorothy, the young Kansas girl whose dream took her to the enchanting land of Oz.
4. Her adventures in Oz begin after her house lands on a wicked witch, who afterwards lays dead beneath it.
5. The local citizens, the Munchkins, gather and treat Dorothy as though she was a good witch.
6. Charming characters like the Scarecrow, the Lion, and the Tin Man join Dorothy on her journey to the Emerald City, and they encountered many hazards along the way.
7. Dorothy was hoping that the wizard in the city will help her return home.
8. To her surprise, the wizard possess no magical powers.
9. Dorothy did return home, though, after she realizes that there's no place like it.
10. Today *The Wizard of Oz* remained a favorite of children and adults alike.

B. Voice, Mood, and Problems with Verbs Correct all the errors in verb usage and change passive voice to active voice when necessary.

> **STUDENT MODEL**
>
> **(1)** The premise of sleeping for hundreds of years is used by many filmmakers. **(2)** After all, life in the future has been wondered about by many of us. **(3)** In 1959, Walt Disney raised to the challenge of retelling the story of Sleeping Beauty. **(4)** If Sleeping Beauty would not have eaten a poisoned apple, she wouldn't of fallen asleep for the next 100 years. **(5)** She might of stayed asleep if a handsome prince hadn't kissed her. **(6)** Disney's animated movie was based on a fairy tale, but another movie approaches the idea from a comic standpoint. **(7)** *Sleeper*, made in 1973, establish the premise of sleep as suspended animation. **(8)** The sleeper was frozen in 1973 and will wake up in a drastically different world. **(9)** The comedy laid in his attempts at adjusting to the new world. **(10)** Movie critics have recommended that everyone sees both movies to appreciate how a single theme can be treated in very different ways.

Write the letter that represents the best way to write each underlined section.

Whenever Robert Louis Stevenson <u>sleep</u> as a child, he was terrified by
(1)
nightmares. His bad dreams <u>occured</u> regularly until he was in his
(2)
twenties. When he was six years old, he <u>has begun</u> to read tales in his
(3)
dreams. He <u>had been dreaming</u> such interesting stories that he lost
(4)
interest in printed tales. Consequently, Stevenson <u>did believe</u> that dreams
(5)
were the source of creativity. In fact, <u>parts of dreams were used by him</u> in
(6)
his work. Like his characters Jekyll and Hyde, Stevenson felt as though
he <u>be split</u> in two. The "Brownies," or little people in his head, created the
(7)
dream, and he <u>is</u> the spectator. As he <u>lied</u> in his bed, the Brownies <u>have</u>
(8)   (9)
<u>present</u> intricately plotted dramas.
(10)

1. A. was sleeping
   B. slept
   C. has slept
   D. Correct as is

2. A. occurs
   B. were occuring
   C. occurred
   D. Correct as is

3. A. began
   B. had begun
   C. begins
   D. Correct as is

4. A. is dreaming
   B. has been dreaming
   C. will be dreaming
   D. Correct as is

5. A. does believed
   B. believed
   C. done believe
   D. Correct as is

6. A. parts of dreams were using by
      him
   B. parts of dreams will be used by
      him
   C. he used parts of dreams
   D. Correct as is

7. A. was split
   B. were split
   C. is split
   D. Correct as is

8. A. is being
   B. has been
   C. was
   D. Correct as is

9. A. lay
   B. laid
   C. layed
   D. Correct as is

10. A. would of presented
    B. presented
    C. present
    D. Correct as is

Student Help Desk

Using Verbs at a Glance

Verbs are words that express action or a state of being. Verbs have **four principal parts** that form the basis for creating the verb tenses.

Present	Present Participle	Past	Past Participle
nod	**(is) nodding**	**nodded**	**(have) nodded**
	Add -*ing* to the present of regular and irregular verbs.	Add -*ed* to the present of regular verbs.	Consult a dictionary for spelling changes, such as a doubled consonant.

Common Irregular Verbs
If It's "Broke," Fix It!

	Present	Present Participle	Past	Past Participle
Group 1 The present, past, and past participle of these irregular verbs are the same.	**burst** cost hurt set	(is) bursting (is) costing (is) hurting (is) setting	**burst** cost hurt set	(have) **burst** (have) cost (have) hurt (have) set
Group 2 The past and past participle are the same.	**bring** get lead swing	(is) bringing (is) getting (is) leading (is) swinging	**brought** got led swung	(have) **brought** (have) got *or* gotten (have) led (have) swung
Group 3 The past participle of these verbs is formed by adding -*n* or -*en* to the past form.	**break** beat choose speak	(is) breaking (is) beating (is) choosing (is) speaking	**broke** beat chose spoke	(have) **broken** (have) beaten (have) chosen (have) spoken
Group 4 The *i* in the present form changes to *a* in the past and to *u* in the past participle.	**begin** ring shrink sink	(is) beginning (is) ringing (is) shrinking (is) sinking	**began** rang shrank sank	(have) **begun** (have) rung (have) shrunk (have) sunk
Group 5 The past participle in this group is formed from the present instead of the past.	**come** do give know	(is) coming (is) doing (is) giving (is) knowing	**came** did gave knew	(have) **come** (have) done (have) given (have) known

Using Verb Tenses

It's About Time

Talking About the Past

Past:
I slept well last night.

Present Perfect:
I have always slept well.

Past Progressive:
I was sleeping when the phone rang.

Past Perfect:
I had slept well the night before I took the test.

Past Perfect Progressive:
I had been sleeping soundly until the rooster crowed.

Talking About the Present

Present:
I sleep well as a rule.

Present Progressive:
I am sleeping like a log these days.

Present Perfect Progressive:
I have been sleeping soundly for many years now.

Talking About the Future

Future:
I will sleep better tomorrow.

Future Progressive:
I will be sleeping outdoors next week.

Future Perfect:
I will have slept eight hours when the alarm rings.

Future Perfect Progressive:
I will have been sleeping for an hour when you get home.

The Bottom Line

Checklist for Using Verbs

Have I . . .

_____ spelled regular and irregular verb forms correctly?

_____ used the most appropriate tense given the sequence of events?

_____ employed the passive voice effectively?

_____ used the subjunctive mood correctly?

_____ avoided improper shifts of tense?

_____ used the correct verb to express my meaning?

Chapter 5

Subject-Verb Agreement

Not everyone like to stay home and play Ping-Pong.

Theme: Sports and Exercise

Be a Sport

What's wrong with this poster? Besides the fact that these people are dangling in mid-air, the verb doesn't agree with the subject. The advertisers need a brush-up in subject-verb agreement.

Everyone likes to exercise differently. Some people seek out fantastic athletic adventures, while others prefer to work out close to home. It's a matter of matching the right activity to the right individual. Similarly, not every verb form agrees with every subject. It's up to you to match them up correctly.

Write Away: Sports Story
Write a paragraph describing your participation in some sport or other form of exercise. Save your paragraph in your 🗂 **Working Portfolio.**

Mark the letter that indicates the best way to rewrite each underlined section.

Tashi Wangchuk <u>Tenzing, a travel agent, were</u> a tired but happy man
$\quad\quad\quad\quad\quad\quad\quad\quad\quad\quad$ (1)
in May 1997, when he scaled Mount Everest. <u>Much of his family's history</u>
$\quad\quad\quad\quad\quad\quad\quad\quad\quad\quad\quad\quad\quad\quad\quad\quad\quad\quad\quad\quad\quad\quad\quad\quad\quad\quad\quad\quad\quad$ (2)
<u>involve</u> mountain climbing. In fact, one of his grandfathers, <u>Tenzing Norgay,</u>
$\quad\quad\quad\quad\quad\quad\quad\quad\quad\quad\quad\quad\quad\quad\quad\quad\quad\quad\quad\quad\quad\quad\quad\quad\quad\quad\quad\quad\quad$ (3)
<u>have</u> the honor of being among the first to climb Mount Everest. <u>Reaching</u>

<u>the summit makes</u> Tenzing the third generation of his family to climb the
$\quad$ (4)
mountain successfully. <u>Statistics for his climb is</u> in the record books. <u>Many</u>
$\quad\quad\quad\quad\quad\quad\quad\quad\quad\quad\quad\quad$ (5)
<u>people has cheered</u> Tenzing's successful climb. Yet, <u>there is a chance</u> that
$\quad$ (6) $\quad\quad\quad\quad\quad\quad\quad\quad\quad\quad\quad\quad\quad\quad\quad\quad\quad\quad\quad\quad$ (7)
his mountain-climbing days are over. He is not among those climbers <u>who</u>

<u>is planning</u> to repeat the climb. <u>Do this surprise you?</u> More than 700
$\quad$ (8) $\quad\quad\quad\quad\quad\quad\quad\quad\quad\quad\quad\quad$ (9)
people have scaled the mountain, and <u>90 percent of them tries</u> to scale the
$\quad\quad\quad\quad\quad\quad\quad\quad\quad\quad\quad\quad\quad\quad\quad\quad$ (10)
mountain again.

---

1. A. Tenzing, a travel agent, has been
   B. Tenzing, a travel agent, are
   C. Tenzing, a travel agent, was
   D. Correct as is

2. A. Much of his family's history were involved
   B. Much of his family's history have involved
   C. Much of his family's history involves
   D. Correct as is

3. A. Tenzing Norgay, has had
   B. Tenzing Norgay, was having
   C. Tenzing Norgay, has
   D. Correct as is

4. A. Reaching the summit make
   B. Reaching the summit have make
   C. Reaching the summit is making
   D. Correct as is

5. A. Statistics for his climb was
   B. Statistics for his climb has been
   C. Statistics for his climb are
   D. Correct as is

6. A. Many people is cheering
   B. Many people have cheered
   C. Many people was cheering
   D. Correct as is

7. A. there are a chance
   B. there have been a chance
   C. there were a chance
   D. Correct as is

8. A. who has been planning
   B. who are planning
   C. who was planning
   D. Correct as is

9. A. Have this surprised you?
   B. Does this surprise you?
   C. Are this a surprise?
   D. Correct as is

10. A. 90 percent of them has tried
    B. 90 percent of them have tried
    C. 90 percent of them is trying
    D. Correct as is

SUBJECT-VERB

Agreement in Person and Number

❶ Here's the Idea

▶ **A verb must agree with its subject in person and number.**

AGREE

Traditional karate dates back to the 17th century.

AGREE

Today, more than 1 million people practice traditional karate.

Agreement in Person and Number

▶ **Singular subjects take singular verbs; plural subjects take plural verbs.**

In the present tense of all verbs except *be,* the only verb form that changes is third-person singular. Add -s to create that form.

Forms of Verbs		
Person	**Singular**	**Plural**
First person	I matter	we matter
Second person	you matter	you matter
Third person	he/she/it matters	they matter

Every rule has exceptions. Remember: OY! To create the third-person-singular form of
• a verb ending in **o,** add -es (do → does)
• a verb ending in **y,** change the *y* to *i* and add -es (try → tries)

The forms of *be* are a special case.

Forms of *Be*				
PERSON	**PRESENT**		**PAST**	
	Singular	**Plural**	**Singular**	**Plural**
First person	I am	we are	I was	we were
Second person	you are	you are	you were	you were
Third person	he/she/it is	they are	he/she/it was	they were

Nouns that end in -s are usually plural.
Verbs that end in -s are usually singular.
For more information about singular and plural forms of nouns, see p. 6.

Words That Separate Subjects and Verbs

Don't be distracted by words that come between a subject and its verb. Mentally screen out these words to make sure that the verb agrees with the subject.

> Many teens of varying athletic ability practice karate.

Plural subject	Disregard words that come between a subject and its verb.	Plural verb

❷ Why It Matters in Writing

Words that separate the subject and the verb are a very common cause of errors in agreement, so watch for them carefully. Subject-verb agreement mistakes can confuse your readers.

STUDENT MODEL

A student, through training and practice, learn that the emotions control the physical body. The techniques of karate creates self-confidence, and the development of such confidence lead to stable emotions. This elimination of negative emotions benefit both the physical and the mental health of the karate student.

SUBJECT

VERB

SUBJECT-VERB

A. CONCEPT CHECK: Agreement in Person and Number

Identify the sentences with subjects and verbs that don't agree. In each case, write the correct verb. If a sentence is correct, write *Correct.*

The Fine Art of Karate

1. Today many people takes a martial art class for exercise, fun, and self-protection.
2. The martial arts, including karate, has their beginning in East Asia.
3. Karate, like the other martial arts, do not rely on weapons.
4. *Karate,* in fact, are a Japanese word meaning "empty hand."
5. Athletes use their hands and feet to direct blows at an opponent.
6. The techniques of karate includes stance and blocking and striking methods.
7. Technique, or the patterns of karate performance, has developed over the years.
8. A karate student, through specialized training programs, develop self-control and a disciplined approach to life.
9. Training programs focuses on breathing and physical exercises.
10. Based on performance, students of karate advances in rank.
11. The skill level of the students is symbolized by belt color.
12. White, for example, indicate the lowest rank in karate.
13. Black, in contrast, are the highest-ranking color.
14. The black belt, also known as the *dan,* has varying degrees of proficiency.
15. The tenth-degree black belt, achieved by only a few people, mark the highest level of proficiency.

➡ For a SELF-CHECK and more practice, see the EXERCISE BANK, p. 302.

B. REVISING: Errors in Subject-Verb Agreement

The following paragraph contains five errors in subject-verb agreement. Identify the errors and rewrite the sentences correctly.

Gi, a Karate Robe
Students in karate classes sometimes hears commands in a foreign language. Many instructors of karate uses Japanese commands. Terms for the sport of karate often comes from the Japanese language. The name for a karate training hall are *dōjō.* The simple white garment of students is a *gi.* The set of formal exercises, popular with instructors, are called *kata.*

Indefinite Pronouns as Subjects

❶ Here's the Idea

When used as subjects, some indefinite pronouns are always singular and some are always plural. Others can be either singular or plural, depending on how they're used.

Indefinite Pronouns

Always singular

another	either	neither	one
anybody	everybody	nobody	somebody
anyone	everyone	no one	someone
anything	everything	nothing	something
each	much		

Everyone in my family loves to go canoe sailing.

Always plural

both	few	many	several

Several of my friends enroll in the canoe sailing class each summer.

Singular or plural

all	more	none
any	most	some

AGREE

Some of the teenage crew are always surprised to learn that canoe sailing is not a new sport. (Plural)

Some refers to a number of individuals, so the verb, *are surprised,* is plural.

AGREE

Some of the instruction occurs on land. (Singular)

Some refers to an amount, so the verb, *is,* is singular.

For more information about indefinite pronouns, see pp. 160–161.

❷ Why It Matters in Writing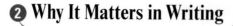

You'll often use indefinite pronouns to make general statements. Correct subject-verb agreement will help your readers understand whether the indefinite pronouns are singular or plural.

Most of the lake is **deep enough for sailing.**

> *Most* refers to one lake; verb is singular.

Most of the lakes are **deep enough for sailing.**

> *Most* refers to more than one lake; verb is plural.

❸ Practice and Apply

A. CONCEPT CHECK: Indefinite Pronouns as Subjects

Identify the sentences with subjects and verbs that don't agree. In each case, write the correct verb. If a sentence is correct, write *Correct.*

Sail, Paddle, or Both?

1. Anybody with an interest in canoeing have probably heard of John MacGregor.
2. Many considers him the founder of modern canoeing.
3. Someone as talented as MacGregor often excel in many areas.
4. One of MacGregor's accomplishments were the design and construction of the celebrated Rob Roy canoes.
5. Most of his books and lectures was promotions for the use and enjoyment of this double-paddle sailing canoe.
6. All of MacGregor's canoe designs features double paddles and masts with sails.
7. Both of these move a canoe swiftly through the water.
8. By the end of the 19th century, few of canoeing's fans were questioning the popularity of the sailing canoe.
9. Today, everything point to a renewed interest in this sporting vessel.
10. Many of the new and long-time enthusiasts competes in organized sail-canoe races.
11. Some of the race-sponsoring organizations includes the American Canoe Association, the Open Canoe Sailing Group, and the IC 10m Association.
12. Something now available to enthusiasts is competition in different classes of sailing canoes.

13. Some of the canoes performs better than others.
14. One are the 10-meter international canoe, the world's fastest single-pilot sailing vessel.
15. According to enthusiasts, nothing compare with the challenge and thrill of sail-canoe racing.

→ **For a SELF-CHECK and more practice, see the EXERCISE BANK, p. 303.**

B. PROOFREADING: Correcting Agreement Errors

The following paragraph contains five errors in subject-verb agreement. Identify the errors and rewrite the sentences correctly.

Sports Times Three

Anyone who loves biking, swimming, and running probably have dreams of competing in an Ironman Triathlon competition someday. Most of the amateur athletes who compete in the event participate in qualifying races. However, many of the race hopefuls enter the lottery that provides entrance to the race for 150 U.S. citizens and 75 international athletes. Each of the qualifying athletes have a chance in the triathlon. Something in addition to the arduous physical challenge draw the athletes. One of the competition's biggest attractions is its legendary $250,000 total in prizes. Each of the first finishers, male and female, receive $35,000. Everyone agree that the purse is a great incentive for an Ironman—or Ironwoman!

C. WRITING: Using Correct Subject-Verb Agreement

Write a short narrative about the photograph below, using at least three indefinite pronouns. Be sure to use correct subject-verb agreement.

Compound Subjects

LESSON 3

❶ Here's the Idea

A compound subject contains two or more subjects. Compound subjects may take either singular or plural verbs.

Parts Joined by *And*

▶ **A compound subject whose parts are joined by *and* usually requires a plural verb.**

A hoop and a ball are necessary for a pickup basketball game.

Some compounds function as a single unit and take singular verbs.

Track and field is my favorite sport.

Compound subjects preceded by *each, every,* or *many a* take a singular verb.

Every boy and girl on the team dreams of being discovered by a pro.

Parts Joined by *Or* or *Nor*

▶ **When the parts of a compound subject are joined by *or* or *nor*, the verb should agree with the part closest to it.**

Neither expensive hoops nor a fancy
AGREE
court is needed for a good game of

pickup basketball.

Neither a fancy court nor expensive
AGREE
hoops are needed for a good game

of pickup basketball.

❷ Why It Matters in Writing

When you are revising your writing, you may combine sentences by creating compound subjects. Remember to change the verbs in these combined sentences so they agree with their subjects.

DRAFT

The author of *Hoops Nation,* Chris Ballard, searches for the nation's best pickup basketball games. His friends help him in this quest.

REVISION

The author of *Hoops Nation,* Chris Ballard, and his friends search for the nation's best pickup basketball games.

SUBJECT

VERB

The revised compound subject requires a plural verb.

❸ Practice and Apply

CONCEPT CHECK: Agreement Between Compound Subjects and Verbs

Need a Pick-me-up?
Write the correct verb for every sentence in which subjects and verbs don't agree. If a sentence is correct, write *Correct.*

1. Players and spectators alike enjoys the thrill and excitement of a good basketball game.
2. Yet neither the pro arena nor college basketball courts is the only place for exciting games.
3. Many a school play lot and local gymnasium serve as a site for some great pickup basketball games.
4. A handful of players, a hoop, and a ball is the only requirements for a pickup game.
5. A pickup game's spontaneity and mix of players add to its excitement.
6. Both regulation basketball and pickup games has playing rules.
7. Governed by the honor system, either the offense or defense call the fouls in a pickup game.
8. Chris Ballard and his friends are avid fans of pickup games.
9. In 1996, Ballard and three of his basketball-loving friends was driving the nation's streets in search of pickup games.
10. Their 30,000-mile adventure and rating of pickup-playing sites is recorded in Ballard's book *Hoops Nation: A Guide to America's Best Pickup Basketball.*

➜ For a SELF-CHECK and more practice, see the EXERCISE BANK, p. 303.

SUBJECT-VERB

Other Confusing Subjects

❶ Here's the Idea

Collective Nouns

▶ **Collective nouns name groups of people or things. They can take either singular or plural verbs, depending on how they are used.**

Note that a collective noun can be singular or plural, depending on its use in a sentence. To decide whether the subject takes a singular or plural verb, ask yourself whether it refers to a number of individuals or to a single unit.

The team has won more medals than it deserves.

> *Team* refers to the group as a unit, so it takes a singular verb.

The team come from several different states.

> *Team* refers to a number of individuals, so it takes a plural verb.

Phrases and Clauses

▶ **Phrases or clauses used as subjects take singular verbs.**

⟐ INFINITIVE PHRASE

To win a competition is the goal of many young ice dancers.

⟐ GERUND PHRASE

Learning ice dancing requires a commitment to both dance and skating.

⟐ NOUN CLAUSE

What some people don't understand is the effort it takes to excel in both arenas.

Singular Nouns That End in -*s*

▶ **Some nouns that end in -s look plural but are actually singular. When used as subjects, these nouns take singular verbs.**

Examples include *news*, *measles*, and *economics*.

The news devotes a good deal of time to sports coverage.

Words that end in -*ics* (athletics, civics, economics, ethics, genetics, politics) may be singular or plural. They are singular when they refer to a school subject, a science, or activities. Otherwise they are plural. Often the plural form is preceded by a possessive noun or pronoun.

Some words referring to singular objects but ending in -*s*, like *glasses, scissors, pants,* and *shorts,* actually take plural verbs.

Warm-up pants help to prevent injury.

Numerical Amounts and Titles

▶ **Numerical amounts and titles often look like plurals. However, they usually refer to single units and take singular verbs.**

A hundred dollars is enough prize money for me.

***The Mighty Ducks* was a cute movie.**

A fractional number or percentage takes either a singular or plural verb, depending on its meaning in the sentence. When the number refers to a total amount, it takes a singular verb. When it refers to individual units, it takes a plural verb.

REFERS TO

One-tenth of the pair's final score is determined by the compulsory dance number.

REFERS TO

One-half of the final scores are given by local judges.

❷ Why It Matters in Writing

Using correct subject-verb agreement with phrases helps ensure that your readers focus on the important words.

STUDENT MODEL

People with ballet training have a head start in figure skating. Knowing how to perform arabesques provide^s ballet students with an advantage on the ice.

> Correct subject-verb agreement shifts the focus to the phrase as a whole, rather than to the word *arabesques*.

❸ Practice and Apply

A. CONCEPT CHECK: Other Confusing Subjects

Choose the correct verb form in parentheses to complete each of the following sentences.

Dancing on Ice
1. In ice dancing, athletics (combines, combine) with artistic interpretation for one beautiful performance.
2. Ice-skating and dancing at the same time (was, were) the idea of a ballet dancer, Jackson Haines, in the 1860s.
3. About 40 years later, the Olympics first (introduces, introduce) the world to figure skating competitions.
4. Then another 60 years (passes, pass) before ice dancing becomes an Olympic event in 1976.
5. An ice dancing team (has, have) many rules to follow.
6. The couple (is, are) required to skate together except for direction or position changes.
7. Performing lifts and spins (gives, give) ice dancers their only opportunity to have both skates off the ice.
8. Otherwise, keeping at least one skate on the ice (is, are) mandatory for each partner.
9. For the free dance, the pair (chooses, choose) its own music and tempo as well as dance steps.
10. To skate well in the free-dance events (is, are) important, since these events count as one-half of the score.

➡ **For a SELF-CHECK and more practice, see the EXERCISE BANK, p. 304.**

B. PROOFREADING: Correcting Errors in Agreement

The paragraph below contains errors in subject-verb agreement. Identify the errors and rewrite the sentences correctly.

With Precision
Enjoying skating and group dynamics may qualify you for a precision skating team. Such a team rely on the synchronized skating ability of its 16 to 24 members. To succeed in competition are a major goal of many teams. What is required of each competing team are performance in short and long programs. Viewing skaters from above enable the judges to better observe the team's footwork and line formations.

Special Agreement Problems

❶ Here's the Idea

The forms of some sentences can make identifying their subjects difficult.

Inverted Sentences and Questions

▶ **In inverted sentences and in many questions, subjects follow verbs.** When writing such a sentence, identify the subject and make the verb agree.

Near the top of the list of popular sports is **gymnastics.**

Why are **you so limber?**

In many questions, the subject will split the verb in two, falling after the helping verb and before the main verb.

Which athletic club will **she** join?

Here's How **Checking Verbs That Precede Subjects**

1. Identify the subject and the verb.

Instrumental to weightlifting is **the** barbell.

2. Rearrange the subject and verb, putting them in traditional order.

AGREE

The barbell is **instrumental to weightlifting.**

3. Check the agreement of the resulting sentence.

Imperatives and *Here* and *There* Sentences

▶ **The subject of an imperative sentence is almost always** *you,* **understood.**

[You] Improve **your physique and endurance by lifting weights.**

▶ **In sentences beginning with** *here* **and** *there,* **those words rarely function as subjects. The subjects usually follow the verbs.**

There is **no** substitute **for frequent repetitions.**

Here come **the reigning** champions!

Sentences with Predicate Nominatives

▶ **In a sentence containing a predicate nominative, the verb must agree with the subject, not the predicate nominative.**
Mentally screen out the predicate nominative to see the true subject.

Strong muscles are ~~one sign of a fit body.~~

One sign **of a fit body** is ~~strong muscles.~~

Relative Pronouns

▶ **When the relative pronoun *who*, *which*, or *that* is the subject of an adjective clause, its number is determined by its antecedent. Once you've determined the pronoun's number, you can determine the correct verb form.**

REFERS TO

Tom is the one who has **striped pants on.**

Who refers to the singular antecedent *one;* therefore, the clause has a singular verb: *has.*

REFERS TO

It is the striped pants **that** have **everyone's attention.**

That refers to the plural antecedent *pants;* therefore, the clause has a plural verb: *have.*

❷ Why It Matters in Writing

As you revise your writing, you often use inverted sentences and other sentence types to add variety and interest. Make sure you don't create problems in subject-verb agreement in the process.

STUDENT MODEL

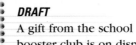

DRAFT	REVISION
A gift from the school booster club is on display next to the locker rooms. The club has donated a brand-new set of free weights for all students to use.	On display next to the locker rooms ~~are~~ *is* a gift from the school booster club. The club has donated a brand-new set of free weights for all students to use.

❸ Practice and Apply

Identify the sentences with subjects and verbs that don't agree. In each case, write the correct verb. If a sentence is correct, write *Correct*.

Iron-Pumping Kids

1. Imagine eight-year-olds pumping iron in weight-resistance programs.
2. Is such programs appropriate for children?
3. What does you think of children pumping iron next to adults in the gym?
4. Does they belong there?
5. There is certainly disagreement among experts about the answers to these questions.
6. Among supporters of resistance-training programs for children are the American Academy of Pediatrics.
7. According to a 1999 study, weight-resistance programs is a good approach to exercise for children.
8. This is the kind of exercise that increase upper-body strength and muscular endurance in children.
9. However, children who lifts weights should use lighter weights and do frequent repetitions.
10. Isn't the recommendations for adults just the opposite?
11. Adults who participates in resistance programs benefit most from lifting heavier weights.
12. Robert Malina provides a voice for the experts who disagrees with the study's conclusions.
13. He says there is better physical developmental programs available for children.
14. Among these is a program that develop movement skills.
15. There are also many traditional sports programs for children, such as basketball and soccer.

➜ **For a SELF-CHECK and more practice, see the EXERCISE BANK, p. 304.**

B. REVISING

Find your **Write Away** from page 128 in your 📁 **Working Portfolio.** Add variety to your work by using structures such as inverted sentences, questions, imperatives, or *here* and *there* sentences. Proofread for subject-verb agreement.

Real World Grammar

Yearbook Captions

Yearbook writers and editors are always writing about school clubs, teams, and their individual members. It can be hard to know whether these subjects are singular or plural, and writing about them can easily lead to errors in subject-verb agreement. Take a look at these page proofs from the Winnemac High School yearbook, where a proofreader has caught a few errors.

TRACK

At the Bradley Spring Invitational, Mara Hoff and Katrina Richardson, along with the rest of the team, proves that a semester of backbreaking practice pays off.

The verb *prove* must agree with the compound subject, *Mara Hoff* and *Katrina Richardson,* and not the intervening prepositional phrase.

❶ Each of the runners know that this is her last chance to bring home a trophy.

The indefinite pronoun *each* takes a singular verb.

❷ Neither Mark Wills nor Kevin Smith cave in to pressure as he approaches the finish line. The stunning result are victories for both! The crowd goes wild.

In compound subjects joined by *nor,* the verb agrees with the closest subject.

Result takes a singular verb.

Crowd refers to a singular unit and takes a singular verb.

❸ Katrina Richardson is an athlete who never get discouraged. Here she is, pulling up from the rear.

The relative pronoun *who* has a singular antecedent, *athlete,* and takes a singular verb.

Grammar in Yearbook Writing

Errors	How to Fix Them
Subjects separated from verbs	A yearbook writer will often add intervening phrases to help identify or modify the subject. Mentally screen out these words to make the verb agree with the subject.
Collective nouns	Yearbooks are all about school clubs, groups, and teams. Pay close attention to whether collective nouns refer to a single unit, taking a singular verb, or to a number of individuals, taking a plural verb.
Titles and numerical amounts	Titles, as well as numerical amounts, such as sports scores, times, and monetary amounts, can cause confusion in subject-verb agreement. Remember that they usually take singular verbs.

Check the following yearbook page before it goes to press. Revise the text below, correcting errors in subject-verb agreement.

FRISBEE TEAM

"The Little Macks" are the name of Winnemac High's Ultimate Frisbee team. They know how to toss that disk!

❶ One of the most experienced players are senior Betty Velez, who started the team as a freshman.

❷ Here comes the team's arch-rivals, the San Marino Floppy Disks.

❸ Captain Desiree Talbot, queen of the end zones, go for the winning catch.

A. Subject-Verb Agreement Identify the sentences with subjects and verbs that don't agree. In each case, write the correct verb. If a sentence is correct, write *Correct.*

1. Adults with an interest in fitness and biking makes up the more than 33 million adult cyclists in the United States.
2. No one doubt that many people cycle only for entertainment, not for competition.
3. Seeking economical, environmentally sound methods of transportation have been the motivation for other cyclists.
4. The movie *Breaking Away*, released in 1979, focus on Indiana high school students in Bloomington's Little 500 international bicycle relay.
5. Increasing interest in bicycling were one result of this Academy Award–winning film.
6. Why are the popularity of competitive biking events rising?
7. Among the reasons is probably recent American successes in the Tour de France.
8. Greg LeMond's victory by just eight seconds were a dramatic climax for the 1989 Tour de France.
9. Almost everyone was cheering for American Lance Armstrong in the 1999 Tour de France.
10. He is the cyclist who was able to win the tour after a courageous battle with and defeat of cancer.

B. Subject-Verb Agreement Edit and proofread the following paragraph, correcting all errors in subject-verb agreement.

STUDENT MODEL

Imagine that you and your friends has planned a Saturday morning bike ride through the local forest preserve. Neither you nor your pals expects any problems down the road, right? However, since it is best to be prepared, take along a bike-repair tool kit. What should be in a basic tool kit? Bikers who has experience agree that a kit should include at least a spare inner tube, a patch, tire levers, a pressure gauge, a pump, and some wrenches. If you are planning a very long road trip, considers the value of an extended tool kit. Included in the extended kit is chain links, nuts, bolts, washers, extra spokes, specialized wrenches, and cables. Being prepared for any biking emergency give you the confidence and peace of mind to truly enjoy your trip!

Mark the letter that indicates the best revision for each underlined section.

Many of today's teens plays soccer. According to the United States
(1)
Youth Soccer Association, participation in the sport have boomed since the
(2)
late 1960s. Everyone agree that the 1999 Women's World Cup
(3)
Championship helped spark more interest in soccer. Adults and children
(4)
was glued to the television. The United States women's team were playing
(5)
great soccer. At the end of the final game, neither the Americans nor the
(6)
Chinese team were leading. The Americans, who was able to score more
(7)
penalty kicks, finally won the cup in overtime. The news of their victory
(8)
have made the players celebrities. What is soccer's attraction for young
(9)
people? Just visits a soccer field, and you will see them enjoying fast-
(10)
paced plays and juggling drills. (Yes, you can use your head to juggle.)

1. A. Many of today's teens has
      played
   B. Many of today's teens was
      playing
   C. Many of today's teens play
   D. Correct as is

2. A. has boomed
   B. were booming
   C. are booming
   D. Correct as is

3. A. Everyone have agreed
   B. Everyone agrees
   C. Everyone are agreeing
   D. Correct as is

4. A. Adults and children have glued
   B. Adults and children is glued
   C. Adults and children were glued
   D. Correct as is

5. A. team are playing
   B. team was playing
   C. team have been playing
   D. Correct as is

6. A. neither the Americans nor the
      Chinese team was leading

B. neither the Americans nor the
   Chinese team have led
C. neither the Americans nor the
   Chinese team have been leading
D. Correct as is

7. A. who is able
   B. who were able
   C. who has been able
   D. Correct as is

8. A. The news of their victory were
      making
   B. The news of their victory has
      made
   C. The news of their victory have
      been making
   D. Correct as is

9. A. What are soccer's attraction
   B. What was soccer's attraction
   C. What were soccer's attraction
   D. Correct as is

10. A. Just have visit
    B. Just has visit
    C. Just visit
    D. Correct as is

Student Help Desk

Subject-Verb Agreement at a Glance

Verbs must agree with their subjects in person and number.

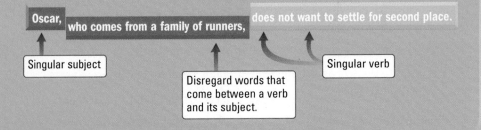

Oscar, | who comes from a family of runners, | does not want to settle for second place.

Singular subject

Disregard words that come between a verb and its subject.

Singular verb

CHAPTER 5

Agreement Problems   Sneaky Subjects

Here are some subjects that may try to throw you a fastball.

Type of Subject	Number of Verb	Examples
Phrase or clause	singular	**Working as a team** produces a winning season.
Singular noun ending in -s	singular	**Athletics** provides a fantastic pastime.
Numerical amount	singular	**A thousand light years** away from the game is where the pitcher's mind was.
Title	singular	*Hoop Dreams* is my favorite movie.
Compound subjects joined by *and*	plural	The **coaches and their assistants** discuss the plays for the game.
Compound subject joined by *or* or *nor*	number of closer part of subject	Neither the batter nor the **coach** wants to admit defeat.
		Neither the batter nor the **coaches** want to admit defeat.
Indefinite pronouns	singular or plural	**Everyone** wants to play.
		Few like warming the bench.
Collective noun	singular or plural	The **team** holler at one other.
		The **team** practices.

148 Grammar, Usage, and Mechanics

Agreement Problems   They'll FOUL You Up!

Type of Sentence	Problem	Example
Inverted	Subject follows verb.	Out on the field stands the most respected umpire.
Question	Subject often follows verb or helping verb.	Did you record the statistics of the play?
Imperative	Subject (you) may not be stated.	Next time, (you) go to the outfield and watch for the ball.
Beginning with here or there	Subject follows verb.	Here is the protective equipment that the umpire wears.
With predicate nominative	Predicate nominative does not affect number of verb.	Our umpires are the best example of professionalism in the league.

The Bottom Line

Checklist for Subject-Verb Agreement
Have I . . .

____ mentally screened out words between the subject and verb?

____ determined the number of each indefinite pronoun used as a subject?

____ used the correct verb forms with compound subjects?

____ mentally put inverted sentences and questions in their normal order to check agreement?

____ used correct verb forms in imperative sentences?

____ found the true subject in sentences beginning with *here* or *there*?

____ mentally screened out predicate nominatives in order to check agreement?

Chapter 6

Using Pronouns

> **I** will never understand why **they** cook on TV. **I** can't smell **it.** Can't taste **it.** At the end of the show **they** hold **it** up to the camera, "Well, here **it** is. **You** can't have any. Thanks for watching. Goodbye."

Theme: Humor and Humorists

What's So Funny?

Every comedian knows the importance of words. In fact, most believe that pronouns are particularly important. Need proof? Just try to tell a joke without using such words as *I, he, she, who,* or *me.* You probably won't get very far.

Pronouns are critical in everyday conversation and writing, as well. In fact, mistakes in pronoun usage can cause problems that are annoying but funny. In this chapter, you'll learn to avoid such errors.

Write Away: Who's Who?
Write a short comic monologue in which you describe something funny that has happened to you. Don't be afraid to exaggerate. Share your monologue; then save it in your 📁 **Working Portfolio.**

Choose the letter of the best revision for each underlined section.

No one knows <u>whom</u> told the first joke or even when people first started to
(1)
laugh. Caves don't have cartoons with punch lines on <u>they</u> walls—at least,
(2)
none that <u>we</u> know of. However, laughing does seem to be a distinctly human
(3)
activity—and one that <u>us</u> humans have always enjoyed. Quite probably even
(4)
Neanderthals chuckled when one of <u>they</u> slipped on a discarded banana peel
(5)
on <u>their</u> way to a hunt. Of course, their sense of humor was probably very
(6)
different from <u>us</u>. For example, Neanderthals probably were not known for
(7)
<u>them</u> clever word play. Of course, <u>between you and I</u>, that's okay, since puns
(8)   (9)
are not my favorite kind of humor. Anyway, <u>your friends and yourself</u> might
(10)
enjoy contemplating what that first joke might have been as you think about
the lives of early humans.

1. A. whomever
   B. whoever
   C. who
   D. Correct as is

2. A. its
   B. their
   C. they're
   D. Correct as is

3. A. us
   B. our
   C. they
   D. Correct as is

4. A. them
   B. we
   C. our
   D. Correct as is

5. A. them
   B. him or her
   C. theirs
   D. Correct as is

6. A. his
   B. her
   C. his or her
   D. Correct as is

7. A. ours
   B. our
   C. we
   D. Correct as is

8. A. they
   B. him
   C. their
   D. Correct as is

9. A. between you and he
   B. between you and they
   C. between you and me
   D. Correct as is

10. A. yourself and your friends
    B. your friends and you
    C. yourselves
    D. Correct as is

LESSON 1

Nominative and Objective Cases

❶ Here's the Idea

▶ **Personal pronouns take on different forms depending on how they are used in sentences. The form of the pronoun is called its case.**

There are three pronoun cases: nominative, objective, and possessive. The chart below shows all of the personal pronouns sorted by case, number (singular or plural), and person.

Personal Pronouns	Nominative	Objective	Possessive
Singular			
First Person	I	me	my, mine
Second Person	you	you	your, yours
Third Person	he, she, it	him, her, it	his, her, hers, its
Plural			
First Person	we	us	our, ours
Second Person	you	you	your, yours
Third Person	they	them	their, theirs

People often confuse the nominative and objective cases of pronouns. To figure out which case is correct, look at how the pronoun functions in the sentence.

The Nominative Case

▶ **The nominative form of a personal pronoun is used when the pronoun functions as a subject.** That's true whether the pronoun functions alone or as part of a compound subject.

We saw Billy Crystal on TV last night. **He** was hilarious.
⤴SUBJECT   ⤴SUBJECT

He and Whoopi are Mom's favorite comedians.
⤴ COMPOUND SUBJECT

A word or group of words that comes after a linking verb and renames or identifies the subject is a **predicate nominative.**

▶ **When a pronoun serves as a predicate nominative, it is called a predicate pronoun and takes the nominative case.**

IDENTIFIES

The winner of the comedy contest was **she.**
PREDICATE PRONOUN ⤴

The Objective Case

▶ **The objective form of a personal pronoun is used when the pronoun functions as a direct object, an indirect object, or an object of a preposition.**

When the Second City comedians were in town, I saw them.
DIRECT OBJECT

Since Nanako likes comedy, I bought her a ticket too.
INDIRECT OBJECT

After the show, Nanako got autographs for us.
OBJECT OF A PREPOSITION

Also use the objective case of the pronoun when it is part of a compound object.

I was really excited when one actor wrote Nanako and me funny messages.   COMPOUND INDIRECT OBJECT

To make sure you're using the correct case of the pronoun in a compound construction, look at each part separately.

Here's How Choosing Correct Case

Dad took pictures of Nanako and (I/me).

Nanako and (I/me) posed for Dad.

1. Try each pronoun from the compound construction alone in the sentence.

   Dad took pictures of I. Dad took pictures of me. (Objective case correct)
   I posed for Dad. Me posed for Dad. (Nominative case correct)

2. Choose the correct case for the sentence.

   Dad took pictures of Nanako and me.
   Nanako and I posed for Dad.

Also use the objective form of the pronoun when it's used with an infinitive. An **infinitive** is the base form of a verb preceded by the word *to—to applaud, to laugh, to joke.*

Cora and I went to see Roseanne. We got to meet her backstage.   OBJECT OF THE INFINITIVE

I didn't expect the only fans backstage to be us.
OBJECT OF THE INFINITIVE

② Why It Matters in Writing

People are so frequently reminded to say "and I" in compound constructions that they often wind up using it incorrectly, especially when they are trying to sound formal. For example, notice the misuses of the pronoun in these lines from a speech.

> The principal has chosen Ms. Gould and ~~I~~ *me* to head up the new anti-violence initiative at the school. This program is of critical importance, so you will see total commitment from both my partner and ~~I~~ *me*.

③ Practice and Apply

CONCEPT CHECK: Nominative and Objective Cases

Write the correct pronoun from those in parentheses. Then identify the pronoun as nominative (N) or objective (O).

A Little Comic Relief

1. When Bob Zmuda got the idea to do a comedy fundraiser for the homeless, people said that (he/him) was crazy.
2. However, when Chris Albrecht told (he/him) that his cable network would sponsor it, the fundraiser became possible.
3. Soon Whoopi Goldberg, Billy Crystal, and Robin Williams said that (they/them) would host the Comic Relief show.
4. With (they/them) aboard, other comics also signed on.
5. Each of (they/them) had different reasons for helping out.
6. Comic Paul Rodriguez said that his family and (he/him) moved a lot because his parents were migrant workers.
7. "I've known hardships," (he/him) explained.
8. "But for a stroke of luck, it could be any of (us/we)," said comic Louis Anderson the following year.
9. When the hosts introduced the Comic Relief show on March 29, 1986, none of (they/them) knew if anyone would watch.
10. Yet, "By evening's end, (we/us) had raised $2.5 million," notes Zmuda.

➡ For a SELF-CHECK and more practice, see the EXERCISE BANK, p. 305.

Possessive Case

LESSON 2

❶ Here's the Idea

▶ **Personal pronouns that show ownership or relationship are in the possessive case.**

The possessive pronouns *mine, ours, yours, his, hers, its,* and *theirs* can function as the subject, predicate nominative, or object of a sentence.

> **Those Dave Barry books are hers. His is my favorite column.**
>   PREDICATE NOMINATIVE ↗   ↖ SUBJECT

> **If you'd like to read one of Barry's books, I'll lend you mine.**
>   DIRECT OBJECT ↗

The possessive pronouns *my, your, his, her, its,* and *their* can be used to modify nouns or gerunds, which function as nouns. The pronoun comes before the noun or gerund it modifies.

> **I have all of his books. His writing always cracks me up.**
>   NOUN ↗   ↖ GERUND

Don't use the possessive case for pronouns that precede participles. Gerunds and present participles both end in *-ing,* but only the gerund acts as a noun.

> ↙POSSESSIVE   OBJECTIVE ↘
> **His reading makes me laugh. I've heard him reading on tape.**
>   GERUND ↗   PRESENT PARTICIPLE ↗

 Don't confuse these possessives and contractions: *its* and *it's, your* and *you're, their* and *they're,* or *theirs* and *there's.*

❷ Why It Matters in Writing

By using a possessive pronoun with a gerund or gerund phrase, you can focus your reader's attention on an activity or action.

Emphasizes Activity or Action:
   Imagine his using that silly expression!

Shift focus to the actor with an objective pronoun and a participle.

Emphasizes Actor:
   Imagine him using that silly expression!

❸ Practice and Apply

A. CONCEPT CHECK: Possessive Case

Write the correct pronoun from those in parentheses.

Class Clown Becomes Comic

1. The late Art Buchwald, a well-known humorist, posed a theory about where humor writers get (they're/their) ideas.

2. (His/He) thinking was that most humorists have unhappy childhoods.

3. The budding comic makes people laugh to win (their/them) attention.

4. Of course, this theory isn't only (him/his).

5. Apparently, though, playing the clown helped Buchwald get through (him/his) childhood.

➔ **For a SELF-CHECK and more practice, see the EXERCISE BANK, p. 305.**

B. REVISING: Emphasizing Actions and Actors

Write the pronoun from those in parentheses that will best emphasize whatever is indicated following the sentence, the actor(s) or the action.

Example: I watched (his/him) directing the cast. (actor)
Answer: I watched him directing the cast.

Comic Genius Mocks Movies

1. Mel Brooks's fans rave about (his/him) mocking so many kinds of movies. (action)

2. They love (his/him) poking fun at westerns in *Blazing Saddles.* (action)

3. They watch Gene Wilder and Madeline Kahn in *Young Frankenstein* to see (them/their) joking about horror movies. (actors)

4. They marvel at (his/him) parodying the theater by coming up with a plot about producers who want to create a flop. (actor)

5. You'll also hear (them/their) raving about *High Anxiety* as a great parody of Alfred Hitchcock thrillers. (action)

Write a sentence about a man running to the theater that emphasizes the action "running to the theater." Be sure to use the appropriate pronoun before this phrase.

LESSON 3 — *Who* and *Whom*

❶ Here's the Idea

▶ **The case of the pronoun *who* is determined by the pronoun's function in a sentence.**

Forms of *Who* and *Whoever*	
Nominative	who, whoever
Objective	whom, whomever
Possessive	whose, whosever

Who and *whom* can be used to ask questions and to introduce subordinate clauses. *Whose* and *whosever* can be used to show ownership or relationships.

> **It's the Marx brothers whose comic genius I love.**

Don't use *who's* for *whose*. *Who's* is the contraction of "who is."

Who and *Whom* in Questions

Who is the nominative form. In a question, *who* is used as a subject or as a predicate pronoun.

> **Who made the film *Duck Soup*? The filmmaker was who?**
> ▲ SUBJECT   PREDICATE PRONOUN ▲

Whom is the objective form. In a question, *whom* is used as a direct or indirect object of a verb or as the object of a preposition.

> **Whom could we ask? To whom might we write?**
> ▲ DIRECT OBJECT   ▲ OBJECT OF PREPOSITION

Here's How Choosing *Who* or *Whom* in a Question

(Who/Whom) shall I send it to?

1. Rewrite the question as a statement.
   I shall send it to (who/whom).

2. Figure out whether the pronoun is used as a subject, an object, a predicate pronoun, or an object of a preposition and choose the correct form. The pronoun in the sentence above is the object of a preposition. The correct form is *whom*.
   I shall send it to whom.

3. Use the correct form in the question.
   Whom shall I send it to?

Who and *Whom* in Subordinate Clauses

Who and *whom* can also be used to introduce subordinate clauses. To figure out whether to use *who* or *whom* in a subordinate clause, look at how the pronoun functions in the clause. Use *who* when the pronoun functions as the subject of the subordinate clause.

Groucho is the Marx brother who is the best known.

SUBJECT → SUBORDINATE CLAUSE

Use *whom* when the pronoun functions as an object in the subordinate clause.

The brother whom we all know best is Groucho.

DIRECT OBJECT → SUBORDINATE CLAUSE

Here's How Choosing *Who* or *Whom* in a Clause

Groucho is a comic (who/whom) others impersonate.

1. Identify the subordinate clause in the sentence.

   (who/whom) others impersonate

2. Figure out whether the clause needs a nominative or an objective pronoun. You may have to rearrange the clause to figure this out.

   Others impersonate (who/whom). (The clause needs an objective pronoun.)

3. Use the correct form in the sentence.

   Groucho is a comic whom others impersonate.

---

❷ Why It Matters in Writing

Many people mistakenly assume that *whom* is the more formal version of *who*. They therefore use *whom* incorrectly in formal writing such as letters of inquiry, complaint, and application.

STUDENT MODEL

To Whom It May Concern:

            Whoever
~~Whomever~~ ran the sound system at the Comedy Café last night
                                   who
needs a hearing test. Of course, anyone ~~whom~~ regularly listens at
that volume would have to have hearing problems. However, I'd
                                        who
recommend your sound person be someone ~~whom~~ is sensitive
enough to hear sound at something less than a deafening level.

❸ Practice and Apply

Write the correct pronoun from those in parentheses.

A Comedy Duo

1. Stan Laurel and Oliver Hardy were a comedy team (who's/whose) antics in silent films and early "talkies" still make people laugh.
2. Laurel and Hardy, (who/whom) were masters of slapstick, could turn even a simple task into a series of accidents.
3. (Whoever/Whomever) watched these comedians regularly delighted in anticipating the mishaps the two would always get into.
4. Laurel was the one on (who/whom) Hardy usually blamed the situation, saying, "Here's another fine mess you've gotten us into."
5. The mess they get into in *The Music Box* involves a piano chasing the duo, (who/whom) are trying to move it up a steep hill at the time.

➡ **For a SELF-CHECK and more practice, see the EXERCISE BANK, p. 306.**

Rewrite the following opening paragraph to a letter of application to theater school, correcting the case of *who* and *whoever*.

A Solo Act

To Whom It May Concern:

    I am a comedic actor interested in attending your theater school. Whoever you contact among my references will tell you that I am the funniest person at my high school. I am the one whom is cast in the lead comedy roles at school. I'm the one on whom people count to cheer them up with jokes and slapstick. I'm also probably the first person who people think of when they hear the term *class clown*. I'm a person whose talent lies in making whomever is around me laugh. In other words, I'm someone whom could be an asset to your school— if you'll give me the chance to attend.

LESSON 4 Pronoun-Antecedent Agreement

① Here's the Idea

▶ **A pronoun must agree with its antecedent in number, gender, and person.** An **antecedent** is the word—a noun or another pronoun—that a pronoun replaces or refers to.

Agreement in Number

A singular antecedent requires a singular pronoun.

REFERS TO

Colonel Blake **leaned back in his chair and fell over.**

A plural antecedent requires a plural pronoun.

REFERS TO

The doctors **brought their complaints to Blake.**

A plural pronoun is used to refer to nouns or pronouns joined by *and.* A pronoun that refers to nouns or pronouns joined by *or* or *nor* should agree with the noun or pronoun nearest to it.

REFERS TO

The stars and creator of *M*A*S*H* were excited that their show was nominated for several Emmys.

REFERS TO

Neither the creator nor the actors realized how well their work would be received. PLURAL PRONOUN

REFERS TO

Neither the actors nor the creator realized how well his work would be received. SINGULAR PRONOUN

Number and Indefinite Pronouns

Making a personal pronoun agree in number with an indefinite pronoun can be difficult because the number of an indefinite pronoun is not always obvious. For help determining the number of an indefinite pronoun, refer to the chart at the top of the next page.

Indefinite Pronouns

Always Singular			Always Plural	Singular or Plural
another	everybody	one	both	all
anybody	everyone	somebody	few	any
anyone	everything	someone	many	most
anything	neither	nothing	several	none
each	no one	something		some
either	nobody			

Use a singular personal pronoun to refer to a singular indefinite pronoun and a plural personal pronoun to refer to a plural indefinite pronoun.

REFERS TO

Each of the old sitcoms still has its fans.

SINGULAR INDEFINITE PRONOUN   SINGULAR PERSONAL PRONOUN

REFERS TO

Many of today's producers base their movies on old sitcoms.

PLURAL INDEFINITE PRONOUN   PLURAL PERSONAL PRONOUN

If the indefinite pronoun antecedent can be singular or plural, use the meaning of the sentence to determine the number of the personal pronoun.

Some of the old humor has lost its appeal.

However, some of the shows still have their zip.

Number and Collective Nouns

A **collective noun,** such as *audience* or *cast,* may be referred to by a singular or a plural pronoun.

Refer to a collective noun by a singular pronoun if the noun is a group acting together as one unit.

The surgical team demonstrated its skill on every M*A*S*H episode. (The unit acted as a single whole.)

Refer to a collective noun by a plural pronoun if the group's members or parts are acting independently or individually.

The surgical team played their childish pranks, too.
(Each member played his or her prank independently.)

Agreement in Gender and Person

The gender of a pronoun must be the same as the gender of its antecedent.

Hawkeye refused to wear his officer's uniform.

When the antecedent of a singular pronoun could be either feminine or masculine, use the phrase *his or her* rather than saying *his*.

Any officer out of his or her uniform was breaking rules.

The person of a pronoun must agree with the person of its antecedent. The pronouns *one, everyone,* and *everybody* are in the third person. They are referred to by *he, his, him, she, her,* and *hers*.

his or her
Everyone must bring ~~your~~ script to the rehearsal.

❷ Why It Matters in Writing

The pronoun you use to refer to a collective noun can help you signal whether you're referring to the group acting as a whole unit or as individual members.

> **STUDENT MODEL**
>
> The Class Clowns Comedy Troupe has just returned   **NOUN**
> from its first national tour. Although the troupe were   **PRONOUN**
> excited to see their families again, they do admit to
> feeling a little disappointed that the tour is over.

Here the troupe improvises a new sketch for its upcoming show.

A. CONCEPT CHECK: Pronoun-Antecedent Agreement

Rewrite each sentence so that the pronoun agrees with its antecedent. Write *Correct* if the pronoun already agrees with its antecedent.

A Comedy About War?
1. The show *M*A*S*H* was about a U.S. Army medical unit during the Korean War and their comic and tragic moments.
2. Hardly anyone wanted to risk their neck on a dark comedy.
3. The directors often shot their scenes in the operating room.
4. Neither the producer nor the actors wanted his work interrupted by a laugh track.
5. Some former MASH doctors told its stories to the writers.
6. Everyone at one MASH unit dyed their hair and clothes red.
7. Each of the show's characters had their own particular focus.
8. Hawkeye and Trapper John, army surgeons, took every chance to express their irreverent attitudes toward the army.
9. Margaret Houlihan and Major Burns spent his or her time noting violations of army rules.
10. Many on *M*A*S*H* considered the show their best work.

➡ **For a SELF-CHECK and more practice, see the EXERCISE BANK, p. 306.**

B. PROOFREADING AND REVISING: Making Pronouns and Antecedents Agree

Write the pronoun from those in parentheses that agrees with its antecedent.

A Show About Nothing?
1. In interviews, the *Seinfeld* ensemble were fond of joking that (its/their) show was about nothing.
2. The group was able to get (its/their) humor from everyday interactions that occur in ordinary settings.
3. The crew shot "The Parking Garage" on a set in Studio City to avoid having to haul (its/their) cameras anywhere.
4. The writing staff often wove three or four subplots into (its/their) half-hour *Seinfeld* scripts.
5. The cast had other roles to (its/their) credit before coming on this show.

In your 🗀 **Working Portfolio,** find your **Write Away** paragraph from page 150 and check it for pronoun-antecedent agreement errors.

Other Pronoun Problems

❶ Here's the Idea

Pronouns and Appositives

▶ **A pronoun may be used *with* an appositive, *in* an appositive, or in a comparison.** An **appositive** is a noun or pronoun that identifies or renames another noun or pronoun.

***We* and *Us* with Appositives** The pronoun *we* or *us* is sometimes followed by an appositive. To decide whether to use the nominative case, *we,* or the objective case, *us,* before the appositive, follow the instructions below.

> **Here's How** Using *We* and *Us* with Appositives
>
> **The female comic performed for (we/us) girls.**
>
> 1. Drop the appositive from the sentence. Try each pronoun separately in the sentence.
>
>   **The female comic performed for we.** (INCORRECT)
>
>   **The female comic performed for us.** (CORRECT)
>
> 2. Determine whether the pronoun is a subject or an object. In this sentence, the pronoun is the object of the preposition *for.*
>
> 3. Write the sentence using the correct case.
>
>   **The female comic performed for us girls.**

Pronouns as Appositives Pronouns used as appositives are in the same case as the noun or pronoun to which they refer. To figure out the correct form of the pronoun to use as an appositive, follow the instructions below.

> **Here's How** Using Pronouns in Appositives
>
> **The audience applauded for the comics, Elaine and (she/her).**
>
> 1. Try each pronoun separately in the sentence.
>
>   **The audience applauded for she.** (INCORRECT)
>
>   **The audience applauded for her.** (CORRECT)
>
> 2. Determine whether the pronoun is a subject or an object. In this sentence, the pronoun is the object of the preposition *for.*
>
> 3. Write the sentence, using the correct case.
>
>   **The audience applauded for the comics, Elaine and her.**

Pronouns in Comparisons

You can make comparisons by beginning a clause with *than* or *as*.

Judy knows more jokes than he knows.

If you omit the final words of such a clause, the clause is said to be **elliptical**.

Judy knows more jokes than he.

To determine which pronoun to use in an elliptical clause, fill in the unstated words and try out each option.

Steve tells as many jokes as (her/she).

Steve tells as many jokes as her [does]. (INCORRECT)

Steve tells as many jokes as she [does]. (CORRECT)

Reflexive and Intensive Pronouns

You can use a pronoun ending in *-self* or *-selves* **reflexively**—that is, to refer to a preceding noun or pronoun—or **intensively**—that is, for emphasis.

I laughed myself silly at their show. (REFLEXIVE)

I myself prefer Judy's jokes. (INTENSIVE)

It is incorrect to use reflexive or intensive pronouns without an antecedent.

Steve joined Judy and myself after the show.
(INCORRECT SINCE THERE IS NO ANTECEDENT FOR *MYSELF*)

Hisself and *theirselves* are never correct. Do not use them.

❷ Why It Matters in Writing

In elliptical clauses, the meaning of a sentence can determine the case of the pronoun.

I applauded the actress longer than he. (Meaning: "I applauded the actress longer than he applauded her.")

I applauded the actress longer than him. (Meaning: "I applauded the actress longer than I applauded him.")

❸ Practice and Apply

A. CONCEPT CHECK: Other Pronoun Problems

Write the correct pronoun from those in parentheses.

Inside the Open-Mike Comedy Circuit

1. (We/Us) comedy lovers enjoy open-mike comedy nights.
2. There, people who dream of becoming stand-up comics try to generate as much laughter as (them/they) can.
3. Of course, some just perform to enjoy (themselves/them).
4. Professional comics may be more reliably funny, but many of the amateurs are just as good as (they/them).
5. In fact, some of these talented performers will (them/themselves) become stars one day.
6. Noting that long-time comic Tim Allen also haunted Detroit open mikes for years, one rising star hopes to do at least as well as (he/him).
7. Another wonders why she puts (her/herself) through this.
8. Then she admits, "(We/Us) comics need a lot of attention."
9. By trying out material on (we/us) audience members, these amateurs see what works and develop a stage personality.
10. Meanwhile, we—my friends and (I/me)—have a good time.

→ **For a SELF-CHECK and more practice, see the EXERCISE BANK, p. 307.**

B. REVISING: Correcting Agreement Problems

Write the pronoun from those in parentheses that will best complete each sentence.

Stand-Up to Sitcom

When you consider how many stand-up comedians get their own sitcoms, you begin to wonder whether any other group of entertainers is more sought after by television networks than **(1)** (they/them). Of course, basing sitcoms on stand-up acts makes sense. A sitcom based on a comedian's stage personality and material should be at least as successful with TV audiences as **(2)** (he or she/him or her) is with club audiences—and quite often it is.

However, **(3)** (we/us) viewers don't always go for shows starring our favorite stand-up performers. For example, although Margaret Cho **(4)** (her/herself) is talented, her sitcom, *An All-American Girl,* didn't last long. Likewise, Jeff Foxworthy didn't fare much better than **(5)** (she/her) with his sitcom. Nevertheless, of all the people network executives could get to star on sitcoms, stand-up comics still appear to be at the top of their list.

Pronoun Reference Problems

❶ Here's the Idea

A pronoun should always refer clearly to a specific, stated antecedent.

General Reference

If a pronoun refers to a general idea rather than a specific noun, readers may be confused. To fix this problem, rewrite the sentence or sentences to make the antecedent clear. Doing so may involve replacing the pronoun with a noun or gerund.

General:

> **Meredyth meditates before going onstage. This improves her performance.** (*This* generally relates to the verb *meditates*, but a verb cannot be the antecedent for a pronoun.)

Revised:

> **Meredyth meditates before going onstage. Meditating improves her performance.** (The gerund *meditating* replaces the general reference *this*.)

WATCH OUT *It, they, this, which,* and *that* are words for which writers often mistakenly fail to provide clear antecedents.

Indefinite Reference

When a pronoun lacks an antecedent entirely, the result is an indefinite reference. Writers most often make this mistake with *it, they,* and *you.*

Indefinite:
> **In this review it says that the political jokes are devastating.** (Who or what is *it?*)

Revised:
> **This reviewer says that the political jokes are devastating.**

Indefinite:
> **In political comedy shows, you continually have to update the material.** (Whom does *you* refer to? Not the reader!)

Revised:
> **In political comedy shows, the comedians continually have to update the material.**

Ambiguous Reference

Ambiguous means "having two or more possible meanings." An ambiguous reference occurs when there is more than one possible antecedent to choose from. Writers inadvertently make references ambiguous when they put a noun or pronoun between the pronoun and its intended antecedent.

Ambiguous:

> **Tony waved to Jack while he told Nancy a joke.** (Who told Nancy a joke, Tony or Jack?)

Revised:

> OPTION 1: **While he waved to Jack, Tony told Nancy a joke.**

> OPTION 2: **While Tony waved to him, Jack told Nancy a joke.**

Gender-Biased Reference

Using the pronoun *his* to refer to an antecedent that could be masculine or feminine results in a gender-biased reference. You can avoid this problem by saying *his or her*—or *he or she*—depending on the pronoun case required. Here are some other ways to avoid making gender-biased references.

Here's How **Making Gender-Free References**

A political comic knows that his material will earn the hostility of politicians.

Strategies	Example
Revise the sentence to make the antecedent and pronoun reference plural.	**Political comics know their material will earn the hostility of politicians.**
Eliminate the possessive pronoun.	**The writer of political comedy knows that such material will earn the hostility of politicians.**
Rewrite the sentence to include the key information as an adjective clause beginning with *who*.	**A comic who chooses political material knowingly earns the hostility of politicians.**

❷ Why It Matters in Writing

Using clear pronoun references is especially important when you need to provide precise directions.

Unclear:

Before you place the ad in the magazine, find out how much it costs. (Find out how much what costs, the ad or the magazine?)

Revised:

OPTION 1: **Find out how much the ad costs before you place it in the magazine.**

OPTION 2: **Find out how much the magazine costs before you place the ad in it.**

❸ Practice and Apply

PRONOUNS

CONCEPT CHECK: Pronoun Reference Problems

Rewrite the sentences to correct the problems. For each ambiguous reference, there is more than one correct answer.

Live from New York . . .

1. George Carlin wanted to wear jeans on the first broadcast of *Saturday Night Live,* but this was a problem for the network.
2. It says in the book *Saturday Night Live: The First Twenty Years* that Carlin wore a suit with a T-shirt instead.
3. If you like to watch vintage *Saturday Night Live* on cable TV, read this book about it.
4. They say that Dan Aykroyd was in "The Coneheads" skits.
5. A guest host must stay on his toes.
6. In the skit "The Nerds," you had a guy named Todd DiLaMuca.
7. Bill Murray played Todd, and he was on the show for four seasons.
8. On "Weekend Update" they satirize current events.
9. If you work on comedy writing as well as performing, this might get you on the program someday.
10. After you choose a piece of dialogue from a *Saturday Night Live* skit, memorize it with a partner.

➡ **For a SELF-CHECK and more practice, see the EXERCISE BANK, p. 308.**

Real World Grammar

Humorous Anecdotes

"He said. . . . Then she said. . . ." When you're relating an anecdote, even a humorous one, you need to make clear who said and did what. In other words, you need to know how to use pronouns properly.

Here's an anecdote a student wrote to begin a speech she planned to make at a neighbor's 75th birthday celebration. The comments are from her English teacher.

Rough Draft of Speech

Mrs. Muldoon and myself like to think we were meant to be friends. It happened when I was twelve. I had declared that I would find my own way to my new piano teacher's house. Clutching the directions, I had gotten to 4542 Elm. Then, as it instructed, I walked right in.

"Hello?" I called, but it remained quiet. Not wanting to pry into private rooms, I myself sat ? down at the piano and started playing. I figured the music would attract my teacher's attention.

"How lovely!" said Mrs. Muldoon, clapping when I had finished. "Now who might you be?"

I introduced myself, she made us lemonade, and ourselves spent the afternoon playing. Then I tried to pay for my lesson, and it revealed my mistake. In my nervousness, I had confused 4542 for 4245!

The pronoun myself needs an antecedent. Watch out for this problem throughout!

What happened when you were twelve? This it and others I've circled are missing clear antecedents.

You yourself played as opposed to someone else?

What revealed your mistake? You've got a general reference problem here.

Using Pronouns Correctly in Writing

Avoid general and indefinite references	To avoid creating empty or unclear sentences, be sure each pronoun refers to a specific, stated antecedent.
Intensive and reflexive pronouns	When you want to emphasize a noun or pronoun, use an intensive pronoun. Use a reflexive pronoun only to refer to a noun or pronoun that precedes it in the sentence.

Revised Speech

Mrs. Muldoon and I like to think we were meant to be friends. Our friendship began when I was twelve. I had declared that I would find my own way to my new piano teacher's house. Clutching the directions, I had gotten myself to 4542 Elm. Then, as the directions instructed, I walked right in.

"Hello?" I called, but the house remained quiet. Not wanting to pry into private rooms, I sat myself down at the piano and started playing. I figured the music would attract my teacher's attention.

"How lovely!" said Mrs. Muldoon, clapping when I had finished. "Now who might you be?"

I introduced myself, she made us lemonade, and we spent the afternoon playing. Then I tried to pay for my lesson, and my handing her the money led us to discover my mistake. In my nervousness, I had confused 4542 for 4245!

PRACTICE AND APPLY: Revising

A friend has asked you to check over an anecdote he's written to present at his sister's wedding reception. Check it for pronoun errors. Then revise it to correct those errors.

STUDENT MODEL

A few years ago, our parents took my sister and myself on a trip to France. Liz and myself had taken Spanish but not French. Our mom and dad knew even less French than we. After an excellent meal, the waiter asked, "How was your food?"

"Bolo!" said Liz. Well, they don't say "bolo" in French. Nobody could have been more embarrassed than myself.

However, the waiter just smiled at Liz and said, "I think you mean *bon*, mademoiselle." Then he gave her a free dessert!

That sort of experience is typical for Liz. She's so friendly and tries so hard that they always respond positively to her. In fact, with her great enthusiasm, she's bound to make as wonderful a life companion as she has been a traveling companion and sister.

A. Using Pronouns Write the correct pronoun from those given in parentheses.

Critics often note that actor and comedian Jim Carrey can transform himself into **(1)** (whoever/whomever) he chooses to play. **(2)** (He/Him) plays slapstick comedy parts and serious dramatic roles equally well. However, few point out that he has also worked a transformation in **(3)** (him/himself) and his life.

Yes, as a child he was the goofy one **(4)** (who/whom) entertained **(5)** (his/their) friends with **(6)** (his/him) clowning. By 16, though, when he and his siblings were going from **(7)** (his/their) school to night shifts at a local factory, he had become an angry young man. His anger didn't let up until the family quit **(8)** (its/their) jobs and began living out of a camper. Then, according to Carrey, **(9)** (they/them) finally began to be happy and like **(10)** (them/themselves) again. Meanwhile, Carrey also began performing stand-up comedy, and by the time he was 19, his success at that began to change all their lives even more dramatically.

B. Pronoun Reference Problems The ten underlined pronouns in the following passage have reference problems. Rewrite the paragraph to eliminate those problems.

They say that actor Jim Carrey has contributed to the "dumbing" of America. This probably comes from his roles in *Ace Ventura: Pet Detective, The Mask,* and *Dumb and Dumber.* However, in an article by Jack Kroll that appeared in *Newsweek,* it praises him for bringing comedy "back to its dumb roots." Kroll describes his energy as lawless and innocent. For his part, he says, "It's not up to me to educate America." Carrey goes on to explain that he's trying to give them relief.

Carrey seems to have enjoyed bringing people "relief" since he was old enough to sit in a high chair. Innocently, he made faces while he was eating. This caused his family to laugh, which inspired him to make more faces around them. Then, when Carrey was eight, he discovered that if you made funny faces for a classmate, he'd laugh. So Carrey began entertaining classmates in the schoolyard and the classroom—although at least one teacher didn't think this was the appropriate place. When she caught him clowning around in class, she had him show what he was doing at the front of the room. However, when the students laughed at his goofy antics, the teacher let him perform at the end of class so that they wouldn't be disrupted. These performances, and the laughter he got later that year at the school's holiday play, clinched his love for acting goofy.

Mastery Test: What Did You Learn?

Choose the letter of the best revision for each underlined section.

Just about everyone has <u>their</u> own favorite Dave Barry book. <u>Us</u> history
(1)   (2)
buffs enjoy Barry's book on U.S. history, *Dave Barry Slept Here*. <u>It was him</u>
(3)
who made up the historical anecdotes in the book, however. In other words,
the collection of essays is not exactly known for <u>it's</u> historical accuracy.
(4)
These essays are better known for <u>their</u> omissions of the "dull parts" of
(5)
history. Of course, Barry's humor makes <u>him</u> writing anything but dull.
(6)
<u>In one essay it says</u> that Abraham Lincoln invented the telephone. In
(7)
another, Barry reports that Orville and Wilbur Wright canceled <u>their</u> first
(8)
flight because of "equipment problems at O'Hare." <u>Anyone whom</u> knows
(9)
history will also love the way Barry spoofs historical texts with absurd
footnotes such as "1. It doesn't matter." Whether or not the book becomes
your favorite, though, after reading it you'll probably agree that few if any
humorists are funnier than <u>him</u>.
(10)

1. A. his
   B. they're
   C. his or her
   D. Correct as is

2. A. We
   B. Our
   C. My
   D. Correct as is

3. A. He was the one
   B. Him was the one
   C. He is
   D. Correct as is

4. A. their
   B. his
   C. its
   D. Correct as is

5. A. his or her
   B. they
   C. its
   D. Correct as is

6. A. his
   B. its
   C. their
   D. Correct as is

7. A. In one essay he says
   B. In one essay they say
   C. It says in one essay
   D. Correct as is

8. A. his
   B. his or her
   C. they
   D. Correct as is

9. A. Everyone whom
   B. Anyone who
   C. Whomever
   D. Correct as is

10. A. it
    B. his
    C. he
    D. Correct as is

Student Help Desk

Using Pronouns at a Glance

Nominative Case

I	we
you	you
he	they
she	
it	
who	

Use this case when

- the pronoun is a **subject**
- the pronoun is a **predicate nominative**

Objective Case

me	us
you	you
him	them
her	
it	
whom	

Use this case when

- the pronoun is the **direct object of a verb**
- the pronoun is the **indirect object of a verb**
- the pronoun is the **object of a preposition**

Possessive Case

my/mine	our/ours
your/yours	your/yours
his	their/theirs
her/hers	
its	
whose	

Use this case for

- pronouns that show ownership or relationship

Indefinite Pronouns   Some Special
Team Players

When you're referring to an indefinite pronoun with a personal pronoun, make sure the two agree in number.

Singular	another, anybody, anyone, anything, each, either, everybody, everyone, everything, neither, nobody, no one, one, somebody, someone, nothing, something
Plural	both, few, many, several
Singular or Plural	all, some, any, most, none

Possessive Pronoun Errors
Catch These Yourself (Your spell checker won't!)

Correct	Incorrect
its	it's
their	they're
your	you're
whose	who's

Pronoun Problems — Coaching Tips

PROBLEM The pronoun is part of an elliptical clause.

Example: We like that old-time comedy better than (he/him). [likes it]

Tips: • Restate the sentence, putting the missing words back into the clause. (Here, you would add "likes it.")
• Choose the pronoun case that's correct in the new sentence.

PROBLEM The pronoun is used with an appositive.

Example: (We/Us) fans of old-time comedy routines ought to start a club.

Tips: • Restate the sentence without the appositive. (Here, you would drop "fans of old-time comedy routines.")
• Choose the pronoun case that's correct in the new sentence.

PROBLEM The pronoun is used as an appositive.

Example: The members— you, Koren, and (I/me)—could share all our albums.

Tips: • Restate the sentence without the noun identified by the appositive. (Here, you would drop "The members.")
• Choose the pronoun case that's correct in the new sentence.

The Bottom Line

Checklist for Using Pronouns

Have I . . .

____ used the nominative case for pronouns functioning as subjects or predicate nominatives?

____ used the objective case for pronouns functioning as objects?

____ used the possessive case for pronouns that show ownership?

____ used *who* and *whom* correctly?

____ made all pronouns agree with their antecedents in number, gender, and person?

____ used the correct cases of pronouns in compound structures, comparisons, and appositives?

____ eliminated any general, indefinite, ambiguous, or gender-biased references?

Chapter 7

Using Modifiers

1996

*W*ho are you reading curiously
  this poem of mine
a hundred years from now?
*S*hall I be able to send to you
  —steeped in the love of my heart—
the faintest touch of this spring
  morning's joy,
  the scent of a flower,
    a bird-song's note,
  a spark of today's blaze of color
    a hundred years from now?

February 1896
      Rabindranath Tagore

Theme: Memory

Turning Experiences into Words

This is the first stanza of a poem written more than one hundred years ago. The poet is trying to communicate his experiences and re-create his memories through words. You, too, have had many interesting experiences with your classmates, friends, and family members that you can share in writing. Each time you write a diary entry, a personal note, or a poem, you re-create your memories. The use of modifiers such as adjectives and adverbs helps make your written memories vivid and unique.

Write Away: Describe Today
Imagine that one hundred years from today someone will read your writing. Create a descriptive paragraph about yourself or something you are experiencing on this particular day. Place your writing in your 🗀 **Working Portfolio.**

Mark the letter that indicates the best way to write each underlined section.

How <u>good</u> is your memory? Are you able to recall names, dates, and
(1)
places <u>effortlessly</u>? If you can, you probably have a memory <u>that is more</u>
(2)   (3)
<u>sharp than average</u>. However, <u>it is difficulter</u> to recall entire pages of text.
                                                              (4)
A British writer and adventurer, T. E. Lawrence, accomplished one of the

<u>most incrediblest feats</u> in literature. It's difficult to imagine a writer
(5)
toiling <u>more laboriously than he</u> over his manuscript for *Seven Pillars of*
                    (6)
Wisdom, his account of his Arabian adventures. He took the manuscript to

his advisor, whom he trusted <u>more than anyone</u>. <u>After these discussion,</u>
                                                    (7)   (8)
Lawrence put the manuscript in an empty briefcase and left for home.

While changing trains, <u>the briefcase was lost</u>. Lawrence <u>hardly had no</u>
                                    (9)   (10)
<u>choice</u> but to rewrite the manuscript from memory!

1. A. better
   B. best
   C. most good
   D. Correct as is

2. A. more effortless
   B. most effortless
   C. effortless
   D. Correct as is

3. A. that is more sharper than
      average
   B. that is sharpest than average
   C. that is sharper than average
   D. Correct as is

4. A. it is more difficulter
   B. it is most difficultest
   C. it is more difficult
   D. Correct as is

5. A. most incredible feats
   B. more incredibler feats
   C. most incredibler feats
   D. Correct as is

6. A. more laborious than he
   B. most laboriously than he
   C. laboriously than he
   D. Correct as is

7. A. more than anyone did.
   B. more than anyone else.
   C. most than anyone.
   D. Correct as is

8. A. After those discussion
   B. After this discussion
   C. After this discussions
   D. Correct as is

9. A. he lost the briefcase.
   B. the briefcase was lost by him.
   C. by him the briefcase was lost.
   D. Correct as is

10. A. hardly didn't have a choice
    B. hardly had none choice
    C. had no choice
    D. Correct as is

Using Adjectives and Adverbs

1 Here's the Idea

Modifiers are words that describe other words or give more specific information about (modify) their meanings. Modifiers function as either adjectives or adverbs.

For a review of adjectives and adverbs see p. 16.

Using Adjectives

▶ **Adjectives modify nouns or pronouns.** Adjectives answer the questions *which one, what kind, how many,* and *how much.*

Which one? **this** recollection, **that** reminder, **those** memories

What kind? **wonderful** memory, **fond** letter, **poignant** memoir

How many? **ten** scrapbooks, **many** entries, **few** mementos

How much? **some** facts, **enough** experience, **plentiful** life

Other words—nouns, pronouns, and participles—can also function as adjectives.

Other Words Used as Adjectives	
Nouns	*psychology class, brain waves*
Possessive nouns and pronouns	*my memory, your ancestors, our past, Lawrence's manuscript*
Indefinite pronouns	*any doctor, few people, many seniors*
Demonstrative pronouns	*that fact, those pictures*
Participles	*locked diary, missing image*
Numbers	*five books, two museums*

Using Adverbs

▶ **Adverbs modify verbs, adjectives, or other adverbs.** Adverbs answer the questions *where, when, how,* and *to what extent?*

Salespeople daily depend on their memory of names.   **WHEN**

Some remember names easily. Others remember   **HOW**

best the ones they study carefully.   **TO WHAT EXTENT**

❷ Why It Matters in Writing

Modifiers add detail and convey a fuller image of your subject. Notice how the modifiers in the excerpt below give a detailed picture of the woman.

> **LITERARY MODEL**
>
> She was **young, brilliant, extremely modern, exquisitely well dressed, amazingly well read** in the **newest** of the **new** books, and her parties were the **most delicious** mixture of the **really important** people and . . . artists—**quaint** creatures, discoveries of hers, some of them **too terrifying** for words, but others **quite presentable** and **amusing.**
>
> —Katherine Mansfield, "A Cup of Tea"

❸ Practice and Apply

CONCEPT CHECK: Using Adjectives and Adverbs

Identify the words that function as modifiers in the following sentences. Do not include articles. What word does each modify?

In Search of Memory
1. Your memory system involves different areas of your brain.
2. Sensors transmit messages readily to your amazing memory.
3. Researchers speculate that different portions of the brain perform varying memory functions.
4. Short-term memory holds limited information.
5. Investigations strongly suggest that long-term memory makes the biggest demands on brain power.
6. People with Alzheimer's disease lose their short-term memory first.
7. As the disease progresses, their brains almost completely shut down, resulting in loss of body control.
8. Senile people, on the other hand, experience memory loss but less severe brain deterioration.
9. Old people sometimes lose many memories.
10. Many old people can learn as quickly as youngsters.

➡ **For a SELF-CHECK and more exercises, see the EXERCISE BANK, p. 308.**

LESSON 2 Using Comparisons

1 Here's the Idea

You can use modifiers to compare two or more things. There are three forms, or degrees, of comparison.

Making Comparisons	
The **basic form** of an adjective or adverb modifies one person, thing, or action.	Our vacation was **expensive.**
The **comparative** form compares two.	Our hotel bills were **costlier** than our transportation bills.
The **superlative** form compares three or more.	Of all our expenses, food was the **most exorbitant.**

Regular Comparisons

Most modifiers change in regular ways to show comparisons.

Regular Forms of Comparison			
Rule	Base Form	Comparative	Superlative
For one-syllable words, and most two-syllable words, add -er or -est.	rich	richer	richest
Some two-syllable words use more or most.	secret	more secret	most secret
For most three-syllable words and adverbs ending in -ly, use more and most.	populous rapidly	more populous more rapidly	most populous most rapidly

LITERARY MODEL

At the square's most populous corner should be—and was—the short taxi rank.

THREE-SYLLABLE WORD

—Elizabeth Bowen, "The Demon Lover"

When comparing one person or thing to all others, use the comparative form.

He is better at remembering dates than any other student in the class.

To show a negative comparison, you can use the word *less* or *least* with most modifiers.

I'm less likely to get homesick than my sister. I'm the least likely person to get homesick of anyone I know.

Less refers only to amounts or quantity. To describe numbers of things that can be counted, use *fewer*.

My grandparents had fewer opportunities in the 1950s because they had less education.

Irregular Comparisons

Some modifiers form comparatives and superlatives in unique ways.

Common Irregular Comparisons		
Base Form	**Comparative**	**Superlative**
good	better	best
bad	worse	worst
well	better	best
many	more	most
much	more	most

❷ Why It Matters in Writing

Often, the strongest and clearest way a writer can communicate ideas to readers is by comparing one subject to another, whether the writing is about a thing or a feeling.

> **PROFESSIONAL MODEL**
>
> Never will I forget being eye-level with the crust of the **largest, juiciest, most delectable** piece of blueberry pie I've ever seen. The pie rose like a purple mountain only a foot from my face, and it completely obliterated all other thoughts I had. As I recall, its appearance was far **better** than its taste; yet it still gleams **brighter** in my memory than all of the lovely lakes we saw on our trip.

❸ Practice and Apply

A. CONCEPT CHECK: Modifiers in Comparisons

For each sentence below, rewrite the incorrect modifier correctly.

Example: The brilliant, tormented Marcel Proust was one of the eccentricest writers who ever lived.

Answer: most eccentric

Memory of Things Past

1. Even the mundanest experience can trigger memory.
2. The most deep memories can be jogged just by hearing a song.
3. No one knew best how to use memory than the famous writer Marcel Proust.
4. To avoid even the minorest distractions, Proust often wrote in his cork-lined room.
5. A perfectionist, Proust demanded that his coffee be prepared in the painstakingest manner.
6. Proust showed this same attention to detail in his writing, and he kept to the demandingest writing schedules.
7. He felt no regret about calling friends in the middle of the night for the minisculest piece of information for his novels.
8. Proust once hired musicians to perform their bestest music for him at daybreak.
9. Yet Proust, admired for his ability to recall memories, often claimed that his memory was among the worse.
10. He believed memory could be triggered by the simpler things.
11. The writer claimed ordinary sights, sounds, and tastes could change the present into the meaningfuller past.
12. In his last volume, *Time Regained,* Proust writes in the memorabliest way about two stones that remind him of Venice.
13. When he hears the chime of a spoon, he recalls the more harsh sound of a hammer on a train wheel.
14. The roughness of a napkin brings back the memory of the even roughest towel he used on a boyhood trip.
15. Think how many of the wonderfulest memories would surface if you found a favorite toy or souvenir in your attic!

→ **For a SELF-CHECK and more exercises, see the EXERCISE BANK, p. 309.**

B. WRITING: Making Comparisons

Think about three photographs of yourself that were taken years apart. Use comparative forms as you write a description of your photos.

Problems with Comparisons

❶ Here's the Idea

As a writer, you want your readers to fully understand your ideas. The explanations that follow will help you to avoid three of the most troublesome constructions dealing with comparisons—double comparisons, illogical comparisons, and incomplete comparisons.

Double Comparisons

▶ **Do not use both -er and more at the same time to form the comparative.**

▶ **Do not use both -est and most at the same time to form the superlative.**

Nonstandard: **Names can be more harder to recall than places.**

Revised: **Names can be harder to recall than places.**

Nonstandard: **Angie has the most comfortablest house of any of my friends.**

Revised: **Angie has the most comfortable house of any of my friends.**

Illogical and Incomplete Comparisons

Illogical and incomplete comparisons often occur when writers accidentally leave out small but important words from the comparison. The following examples can help you avoid these problems in your writing:

▶ **Use the word other or else to compare an individual member with the rest of the group.** In the following sentence, the writer's wording is confusing. Does the writer mean that rock 'n' roll isn't music?

Illogical: **Rock 'n' roll was more popular on the radio than any music.**

Because rock 'n' roll is a type of music, the writer should have written the sentence this way:

Revised: **Rock 'n' roll was more popular on the radio than any other music.**

> **When you are making a compound comparison, use *than* or *as* after the first modifier to avoid an incomplete comparison.** In the following sentence, the reader may wonder, better than what?

> *Incomplete:* **Young people seem to like color films better.**

> *Revised:* **Young people seem to like color films better than black-and-white films.**

Don't omit the verb in the second part of the comparison if it's needed to complete or clarify the meaning.

> *Confusing:* **She likes old movies better than her dad.** (SHE LIKES OLD MOVIES BETTER THAN SHE LIKES HER DAD?)

> *Revised:* **She likes old movies better than her dad does.**

❷ Why It Matters in Writing

Using modifiers correctly results in clearer writing. In the anecdote below, the writer could improve his sentences by correcting double and incomplete comparisons.

STUDENT MODEL

Grandpa loved fishing ~~more~~ better than Grandma. *did* I can't imagine anyone *else* besides Grandma being as patient about her husband's ~~most~~ strongest desire, which was to be on the lake when the fish were biting. One morning—I remember this incident better than any *other* one—Grandpa crept down to his boat while it was still dark. He figured his chances of not getting caught were better *than if he waited until dawn.* Anyway, by the time he had rowed out to the middle of the lake, it was light. Looking down, he saw a note from Grandma in the bottom of the boat that said, "You're the big one that got away."

❸ Practice and Apply

A. CONCEPT CHECK: Problems with Comparisons

Directions: Identify and correct double and illogical comparisons in the sentences that follow.

Example: Eudora Welty is as talented as any Southern writer of her generation.

Answer: as talented as any other

One Writer's Beginnings
1. Few writers could paint a word portrait as vividly as Eudora Welty.
2. Welty explored the most deepest human bonds and emotions in her novels.
3. Growing up in the American South, Welty was as aware of the sounds and sights around her as any writer.
4. She had the most happiest childhood, which she described in her memoir, *One Writer's Beginnings.*
5. Welty recalled the most vividest memories.
6. *One Writer's Beginnings* remained on the *New York Times* bestseller list for forty-six weeks and provided the most personalest glimpse of this Southern writer's life.
7. Eudora's mother loved reading as much as her daughter.
8. She encouraged Eudora's most creativest daydreams.
9. Mrs. Welty recited poetry to her daughter as tenderly and beautifully as any mother.
10. Eudora loved a good story more than other children.
11. She conjured up the most fondest stories from childhood.
12. Her sensitive, detailed fiction relied on the most intensest powerful words.
13. The editors of Webster's Dictionary believe that there are few writers more powerfuler than Welty, and they quote her 33 times.
14. Welty had a better ear for dialogue and accents than most writers.
15. Eudora's power of memory, which grew even more stronger with age, spanned almost a century.

➡ **For a SELF-CHECK and more exercises, see the EXERCISE BANK, p. 309**

B. REVISING: Making Writing Clearer

In your 🗂 **Working Portfolio,** find the paragraph you wrote for the **Write Away** on page 176. Make your writing clearer by finding and revising any modifier and comparison errors.

Other Modifier Problems

LESSON 4

❶ Here's the Idea

Common modifier problems include the misuse of *this, that, these,* and *those,* misplaced modifiers, dangling modifiers, and double negatives.

This/That, These/Those, and *Them*

This, that, these, and *those* are demonstrative pronouns that can be used as adjectives. Three rules will help you avoid mistakes in using them.

Kind, sort, and type Use singular demonstrative pronouns with the words *kind, sort,* and *type.*

> **This kind of hobby, collecting movie posters, is educational.**
> (SINGULAR)

> **These types of posters from World War II are old!** (PLURAL)

Here/There Never use *here* or *there* with demonstrative adjectives. The adjective already points out which one: it doesn't need any help.

> **This here poster of James Dean is from 1955.**

Them/These/Those Never use the pronoun *them* as an adjective in place of *these* or *those.*

> ***Nonstandard:* Them legends of Hollywood are amazing.**

> ***Standard:* Those legends of Hollywood are amazing.**

Adverb or Adjective?

Many words have both adjective and adverb forms. It you're not sure which form of a word to use, look at the word that it modifies. If the modified word is a noun or pronoun, use the adjective form. If it's a verb, adjective, or adverb, use the adverb form.

> **Real posters can be really hard to identify.**

> **The expert collector identifies fakes expertly.**

Two pairs of words—*good* and *well, bad* and *badly*—cause writers special problems.

Good = Adjective————— MODIFIES ———————

Adjective: Jhana is a **good** photo researcher.

                    MODIFIES
Predicate
Adjective: She feels **good** when she finds a rare photo.

Well = Adjective or Adverb

Predicate
Adjective: Jhana missed an exhibit of Civil War scenes

                    MODIFIES

         because she didn't feel **well**.

                    MODIFIES
Adverb: She handled her disappointment **well**.

Bad = Adjective————— MODIFIES ———————

Adjective: Once she made a **bad** purchase of forged photos.

                    MODIFIES
Predicate
Adjective: I felt **bad** for her.

Badly = Adverb————— MODIFIES ———————

Adverb: That time she was cheated **badly**.

Never write "I feel badly" when referring to a state of mind or health. You are literally saying that you feel (touch things) poorly.

Misplaced and Dangling Modifiers

▶ **A misplaced modifier is a word or phrase that is placed so far away from the word it modifies that the meaning of the sentence is unclear or incorrect.**

Draft: I sent a poster to Mom rolled in a tube. (THIS SOUNDS AS IF MOM WERE ROLLED IN A TUBE.)

                    MODIFIES

Revision: I sent a poster **rolled in a tube** to Mom.

Draft: I found my autograph collection **looking through old files.** (WAS THE COLLECTION LOOKING THROUGH OLD FILES?)

                    MODIFIES

Revision: **Looking through old files,** I found my autograph collection.

MODIFIERS

> A dangling modifier is a word or phrase that does not clearly modify any noun or pronoun in a sentence.

> *Draft:* **Encouraged by Mark Twain, the memoirs were published.** (CAN MEMOIRS FEEL ENCOURAGED?)

> *Revision:* **Encouraged by Mark Twain, former President Grant published his memoirs.**

For more about misplaced and dangling modifiers, see p. 271.

Double Negatives

> A double negative is the use of two or more negative words to express one negative. The words *hardly, barely, scarcely,* and *never* function as negatives, so they should not be used with other negative words.

> *Draft:* **Congresswoman Pat Schroeder reminisces that voters in Colorado wouldn't hardly consider her a political candidate.**

> *Revision:* **Congresswoman Pat Schroeder reminisces that voters in Colorado wouldn't consider her a political candidate.**

Although people often use the phrases *can't help but* and *haven't but* in speech, they are incorrect because they create double negatives.

Drabble by Kevin Fagan

❷ Why It Matters in Writing

Misplaced and dangling modifiers can alter the meaning of a sentence, as well as confuse the reader.

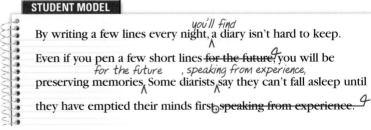

STUDENT MODEL

By writing a few lines every night, a diary isn't hard to keep. ~~you'll find~~

Even if you pen a few short lines ~~for the future,~~ you will be preserving memories. Some diarists say they can't fall asleep until *for the future* , *speaking from experience,*

they have emptied their minds first. ~~speaking from experience.~~

CHAPTER 7

③ Practice and Apply

A. CONCEPT CHECK: Other Modifier Problems

Correct the modifier being used incorrectly in the sentences below. Watch for dangling modifiers, misplaced modifiers, and double negatives.

Goodbye to All That

1. Poet Robert Graves barely didn't survive World War I.
2. Graves was affected by them years as a soldier.
3. Recovering from the trauma of War World I, the reminiscences of Graves were recorded in his book *Goodbye to All That*.
4. In the first section of the book, Graves says he couldn't never forget his boarding-school days.
5. Feeling badly from loneliness, Graves tried hard to make friends at school.
6. Graves spends the second half of his autobiography fighting in World War I.
7. As a keen observer of war in the trenches, the confusion of the young infantrymen is described good by Graves.
8. Seriously wounded in battle, the government reported Graves dead.
9. Writing humorously, his supposed death interfered with check cashing.
10. The final portion of Graves's autobiography deals with his belief that he wasn't scarcely the same man after the war.

➜ For a SELF-CHECK and more exercises, see the EXERCISE BANK, p. 310.

B. REVISING: Correcting Modifier Problems

On a separate sheet of paper, revise the model below by correcting the modifier problems.

STUDENT MODEL

> Occurring at the old Riverview amusement park, one of my worse childhood memories involves a ride called the "Wild Mouse." No more better example of how I am the less likely to enjoy these kind of roller-coaster rides can be found. The "Wild Mouse" made me feel badly just looking at it! I held my ticket for the ride crumpled in my hand. As the line dwindled, and less people stood between me and the dreaded ride, I couldn't hardly breathe.

Grammar in Literature

Modifiers and Communicating Ideas

World War I exhausted Great Britain's emotional and physical resources. Recalling what it was like to serve as a nurse during the war, Vera Brittain tells her story in *Testament of Youth*.

In the passage below, Brittain uses modifiers to communicate her strong feelings about the need to treat the future of humanity as more important than the aims of a war.

from TESTAMENT of Youth

Vera Brittain

In spite of the War, which destroyed so much hope, so much beauty, so much promise, life is still here to be lived; so long as I am in the world, how can I ignore the obligation to be part of it, cope with its problems, suffer claims and interruptions? The surge and swell of its movements, its changes, its tendencies, still mold me and the surviving remnant of my generation whether we wish it or not, and no one now living will ever understand so clearly as ourselves, whose lives have been darkened by the universal breakdown of reason in 1914, how completely the future of civilized humanity depends upon the success of our present halting endeavors to control

our political and social passions, and to substitute for our destructive impulses the vitalizing authority of constructive thought. To rescue mankind from that domination by the irrational which leads to war could surely be a more exultant fight than war itself, a fight capable of enlarging the souls of men and women with the same heightened conscious-ness of living, and uniting them in one dedicated community whose common purpose transcends the individual. Only the purpose itself would be different, for its achievement would mean, not death, but life.

Brittain repeats *so much* to stress the extensive loss caused by the war.

Brittain chooses precise modifiers such as *universal* to convey how complete the breakdown of reason was.

The adjectives *destructive* and *constructive* sharply contrast the conflicting influences on people during the war.

The positive connotations associated with the modifiers *heightened, dedicated,* and *common* strengthen Brittain's call for change.

How Brittain Uses Modifiers

Kind	Example
Adjectives	It is more effective to use a few carefully chosen adjectives than a long string of overused adjectives. (*universal breakdown, halting endeavors, vitalizing authority*)
Adverbs	The adverbs *very* and *so* can be used to intensify what you are saying. However, be careful that you don't overuse them. For example, instead of saying *very fast,* choose a more precise modifier, such as *rapidly.*
Comparisons	Comparisons allow you to talk about the differences between people, actions, or things. You can help readers visualize your ideas when you tell them that a building is the tallest building in the world.

PRACTICE AND APPLY: Using Modifiers Correctly

In the following paragraph, modifiers can be added to improve the sentences. On a separate sheet of paper, write an appropriate modifier for each numbered blank.

    Many young people look to Colin L. Powell, a man revered by millions around the world, as a(n) **(1)**_____ model. Powell was raised in the South Bronx, a poor neighborhood. He recalls that his parents had little to offer him except two **(2)**_____ traits: a strong work ethic and belief in the importance of education. After he enrolled in the ROTC program at the City College of New York, his true calling was **(3)**_____ found. ROTC provided him with a(n) **(4)**_____ springboard into military life. His **(5)**_____ military career included service in Vietnam and work as a presidential assistant for national security affairs. But **(6)**_____ Americans got to know General Powell during his Gulf War television appearances. He **(7)**_____ appeared on the news. In 1995, he published *My American Journey,* a memoir that became a bestseller. Many people **(8)**_____ urged Powell to run for political office. As a **(9)**_____ general, he might have succeeded. Instead, under George W. Bush, he became Secretary of State, a position that made him a(n) **(10)**_____ adviser to the president.

A. Modifiers used for description and comparison. Read the following passage. Then write the answers to the questions below it.

(1) People remember Florence Nightingale as a benevolent nurse who tended to the victims of war. **(2)** Florence's path to her chosen career was unexpectedly original. **(3)** The daughter of wealthy parents, who had toured Europe more extensively than most people, Florence was named after her birthplace in Italy. **(4)** As a privileged child, she had more genteeler options than nursing. **(5)** In 1851, Florence began the nursing training that no one loved more. **(6)** As a nurse with as much talent as any medical professional, Florence became superintendent of a hospital in London. **(7)** These kinds of attributes helped Florence make a contribution to the world of nursing. **(8)** Nightingale became famous after she nursed the sick at the battlefront so heroically of the Crimean War. **(9)** Working tirelessly, the mortality rate among the soldiers dropped dramatically. **(10)** Without the vision of Florence Nightingale, the respect accorded to nursing as a medical profession wouldn't hardly exist today.

1. What is the adjective in sentence 1?
2. Name the adverb in sentence 2 and identify what it modifies.
3. What is the comparative adverb in sentence 3?
4. What is the error in sentence 4? How should you correct it?
5. What words need to be added to sentence 5 to complete the comparison?
6. What word needs to be added to sentence 6 to clarify the comparison?
7. Why use *these* instead of *this* in Sentence 7?
8. How should you rewrite sentence 8 so that the modifier is next to the word(s) it modifies?
9. How should you rewrite sentence 9 correctly?
10. How should you rewrite sentence 10 correctly?

B. Fixing problems with modifiers Rewrite the following paragraph, correcting any comparison errors.

The Basis of Computer Memory

A computer speaks a language of only two numerals: 0 and 1. This simplest two-numeral form of communication is called machine language. The numerals combine to form more large binary numbers. Machine language is more better for writing instructions for the chips and microprocessing devices that drive computing machines, such as computers, printers, hard disk drives, and so on. This language, basicer than any human language, is the mostest efficient means of creating a computer's memory.

Write the letter that represents the best way to write each underlined section.

Aikido is <u>a more modern martial art</u> that originated in Japan. This form
(1)
of self-defense focuses on handling <u>an opponent effective</u> without causing
(2)
injury or death. After experiencing a vision in 1925, Morihei Ueshiba began

to perfect this martial art, <u>which is gentler</u> in nature than judo or jujitsu.
(3)
Morihei wanted to break away from military arts such as jujitsu and develop

the <u>better peaceable</u> martial art of all. The development of aikido and the life
(4)
of its fascinating founder is one of the <u>most interestingest</u> stories. Morihei
(5)
was rejected by the army because soldiers had to be <u>taller than him</u>.
(6)
Undaunted by <u>these sort of requirement</u>, Morihei increased his height with
(7)
weights attached to his legs. When he was finally accepted into the military,

his career <u>was extraordinary</u>. He was <u>fast</u> on marches than mounted officers.
(8)   (9)
His tenacity <u>didn't hardly end</u> with his military career; as a master of aikido,
(10)
he was known for legendary physical feats and spiritual depth.

1. A. a more moderner martial art
   B. a most modernest martial art
   C. a modern martial art
   D. Correct as is

2. A. an opponent effectively
   B. effective an opponent
   C. an effectively opponent
   D. Correct as is

3. A. which is gentle
   B. which is more gentler
   C. which is most gentlest
   D. Correct as is

4. A. most peaceable
   B. more better peaceable
   C. more peacefulest
   D. Correct as is

5. A. most interesting
   B. more interestinger
   C. interestingest
   D. Correct as is

6. A. taller than he was taller.
   B. taller than he was.
   C. tallest than he was.
   D. Correct as is

7. A. those sort of requirement
   B. that sorts of requirements
   C. this sort of requirement
   D. Correct as is

8. A. was extraordinarier.
   B. was much extraordinary.
   C. was the extraordinariest.
   D. Correct as is

9. A. fastest
   B. faster
   C. fasterer
   D. Correct as is

10. A. didn't scarcely end
    B. didn't barely end
    C. didn't end
    D. Correct as is

Student Help Desk

Modifiers at a Glance

I have such a **poor** memory that I **finally** went to see a **respected** doctor about it. He said, "How **long** have you had this **unfortunate** problem?" I said **innocently**, "What problem?"

> **Adjectives** describe *which one*, *what kind*, *how many*, or *how much*.

> **Adverbs** describe *how*, *where*, *when*, or *to what degree*.

Degrees of Comparison

Make ~~Less~~ *Fewer* Mistakes

Modifier	Example	Use to show
-er	My grandpa is **older** than anyone in our family.	comparative degree for most one- and two-syllable modifiers
-est	He is the **oldest** person in town.	superlative degree for most one- and two-syllable modifiers
more	The old man is **more stubborn** than anyone I know.	comparative degree for some two-syllable and all three-syllable modifiers and with adverbs that end in *-ly*
most	He becomes **most argumentative** about dates and places.	superlative degree for some two-syllable and all three-syllable modifiers and with adverbs that end in *-ly*
less	Sometimes, I wish he were a little **less concerned** about baseball batting averages from fifty years ago.	comparative degree for a smaller quantity of something
fewer	On the other hand, we have **fewer** disagreements about baseball than before.	comparative degree for a smaller number of individual things
least	He's the **least likely** person to surf the Internet for facts, but now he's learned how!	used to show negative superlative degree

Misplaced Modifiers — You Must Remember This

Problem	Strategy	Revision
Henry Ford said, "History is bunk" dismissively.	Keep modifiers close to the words they modify.	Henry Ford said **dismissively,** "History is bunk."
Flipping through the scrapbook, an unidentified photograph startled her.	Eliminate dangling modifiers.	Flipping through the scrapbook, **she** was startled by an unidentified photograph.

Avoid Double Negatives — Aye, aye? No, no!

Incorrect	Correct
On Veterans Day, I **can't not help** admiring the brave men and women in the armed forces.	On Veterans Day, I **can't help** admiring the brave men and women in the armed forces.
When I remember their distinguished service, I **haven't hardly** anything but respect for them.	When I remember their distinguished service, I **haven't anything** but respect for them.
Many brave veterans **didn't scarcely** have a chance to enjoy their youths before they were called to serve their country.	Many veterans **scarcely had** a chance to enjoy their own youth before they were called to serve.

The Bottom Line

Checklist for Using Modifiers

If you can answer yes to all the questions below, chances are that your writing will live on in your readers' memories!

Have I . . .

____ used adjectives and adverbs correctly?

____ used the correct form of comparatives?

____ used the correct form of superlatives?

____ avoided double or illogical comparisons?

____ used no more than one negative word such as *not* to express one negative?

____ used irregular forms correctly?

____ formed complete comparisons by including words such as *than, or,* and *other?*

Chapter 8

Capitalization

Dustin polish promoted

Dustin polish, who worked at the bureau and sat on both the bench and the president's cabinet, is expected to shine in the new foreign office, according to the high-ranking officials who promoted polish for this post.

ion 1   13

Theme: Powerful People—from Politicians to Poets

Capital Confusion

Could you tell from this article that Mr. Dustin Polish worked at the Federal Bureau of Investigation, served as a judge on the Bench, and was an advisor in the president's Cabinet? Probably not. In fact, without proper capitalization, it reads more like an ad for furniture polish than an announcement about a politician.

To better ensure that you convey what you truly intend to communicate, you need to use capitals correctly. This chapter can help you learn to do that.

Write Away: Capital Power

Take a few minutes to write a paragraph about someone you consider to be a powerful person. Then place your writing in your 🗀 **Working Portfolio.**

Diagnostic Test: What Do You Know?

For each underlined group of words, choose the letter of the correct revision.

As the <u>twentieth century</u> drew to a close, newscasters and journalists
(1)
began creating lists of the century's most powerful people. *Time* <u>Magazine</u>
(2)
put out special issues on the topic. Peter Jennings, <u>News Anchor for the</u>
(3)
<u>American Broadcasting Company (ABC)</u>, collaborated on a book <u>entitled *the*</u>
(4)
Century. It identifies Nelson Mandela, first <u>black President of South Africa,</u>
(5)
as a powerful figure for having put an end to <u>south Africa's Apartheid</u>
(6)
<u>system</u>, which had long denied blacks the right to vote. Although "<u>no Prince</u>
(7)
in his social attitudes and his politics," according to Lee Iacocca, Henry Ford
made most lists for instituting industrial mass production; building a car
<u>Working Class People</u> could afford, <u>the model t</u>; and campaigning to pave
(8)   (9)
the way for his vehicles with an <u>interstate-highway system</u>.
(10)

1. A. Twentieth Century
   B. Twentieth century
   C. twentieth Century
   D. Correct as is

2. A. *time* magazine
   B. *TIME* Magazine
   C. *Time* magazine
   D. Correct as is

3. A. News Anchor for the American
      Broadcasting company (ABC)
   B. news anchor for the American
      Broadcasting Company (ABC)
   C. news anchor for the American
      broadcasting company (Abc)
   D. Correct as is

4. A. Entitled *the century*
   B. entitled *The century*
   C. entitled *The Century*
   D. Correct as is

5. A. black president of South Africa
   B. black president of south Africa
   C. Black President of South Africa
   D. Correct as is

6. A. south Africa's apartheid system
   B. South Africa's Apartheid
      System
   C. South Africa's apartheid system
   D. Correct as is

7. A. No prince
   B. no prince
   C. No Prince
   D. Correct as is

8. A. Working Class people
   B. working class people
   C. working Class people
   D. Correct as is

9. A. The Model T
   B. The Model t
   C. the Model T
   D. Correct as is

10. A. Interstate-highway system
    B. Interstate-Highway system
    C. Interstate-Highway System
    D. Correct as is

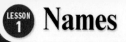

Names

❶ Here's the Idea

Proper Nouns and Adjectives

▶ **Capitalize proper nouns and proper adjectives.**

A **common noun,** which is not capitalized, names a general class or a type of person, place, or thing. A **proper noun,** which is capitalized, names a specific person, place, or thing. A **proper adjective** is formed from a proper noun and is also capitalized. Compare these three types of items in the following chart.

Nouns and Adjectives		
Common Nouns	**Proper Nouns**	**Proper Adjectives**
philosopher	Confucius	Confucian saying
country	China	Chinese philosopher
planet	Mars	Martian soil

When proper nouns and adjectives occur in compound words, always capitalize the first element of a hyphenated compound. Capitalize the second element if it is a proper noun.

    Japanese-made automobiles   Anglo-Saxon kingdom

Prefixes such as *pre-, anti-, sub-,* and *non-* are not capitalized when joined with proper nouns and adjectives.

    pre-Nixon   anti-Communist   non-European

Names of Individuals

▶ **Capitalize people's names and initials.**

    Elizabeth Dole   John F. Kennedy   A. E. Housman

Many names contain parts such as *de, du, mac, O',* and *van.* Capitalization of these parts varies. Always verify the capitalization of a name with the person or check the name in a reliable reference source. Here are some examples.

    Danny De Vito   Charles de Gaulle

    W. E. B. DuBois   Daphne du Maurier

    John D. MacArthur   Charles Macintosh

    Martin Van Buren   Vincent van Gogh

> **The abbreviations *Jr.* and *Sr.*, which fall after a person's name, are part of the name and should always be capitalized.**

The abbreviations are always preceded by a comma. Within a sentence, they are also followed by a comma.

> Former IBM president Thomas Watson, Jr., once burst into tears at the thought of going to work for IBM, then still his father's company.

Thomas Watson, Sr., poses with his son, Thomas Watson, Jr.

Titles of Individuals

> **Titles and abbreviations of titles are capitalized in certain situations.**

• **When used in direct address:**

> "How do you feel about your award, Professor?"

• **When used before personal names:**

General Omar Bradley	Mother Teresa
Dr. Joan Borysenko	Hon. Thomas Maselli

In general, don't capitalize a title when it follows a person's name or is used alone.

> Adela Suarez, professor of sociology, received an award.
>
> The president of the university may actually present it.

However, do capitalize abbreviations of titles when they follow names.

> Kim Hwang, **D.D.S.**   Deborah Tannen, **Ph.D.**

Don't capitalize the prefix *ex-*, the suffix *-elect,* or the words *former* or *late* when used with a title.

> Mayor-elect Williams   the late Justice Thurgood Marshall

In formal writing, use the word *former* rather than the prefix *ex-:* former President Bush, rather than ex-President Bush.

Family Relationships

▶ **Capitalize words indicating family relationships only when they are used as parts of names or in direct address.** Don't capitalize family names preceded by articles or possessive words.

In our family, Aunt Esther wields great power.

My uncle and cousins exercise power behind the scenes.

❷ Practice and Apply

A. CONCEPT CHECK: Names

Rewrite the words that are incorrectly capitalized in these sentences.

Thoughts on Power and the Powerful
1. In *Powerful People,* journalist roy rowan talks about people who have held powerful positions.
2. He points out that the truly powerful, such as general Douglas MacArthur, often have a confident, calm presence.
3. He says that energy and persistence are key as well, noting that ross perot, a former candidate for President of the united states, bounced back from failures by staying in motion.
4. To obtain power, rowan says that people need a sense of purpose, a clear goal, and a plan for obtaining their goal.
5. He notes, however, that Fathers often can't pass on power to their offspring.

➡ For a SELF-CHECK and more practice, see the EXERCISE BANK, p. 311.

B. PROOFREADING: Correcting Errors in Capitalization

Rewrite the words that are incorrectly capitalized in this passage.

Different Kinds of Power

Parents, teachers, and Politicians have different kinds of power. Mr. and mrs. o'Malley can decide what's best for their Sons and shape their characters in subtle ways. In the classroom, professor Jorge del río, ph.d., can have an impact on how students think, and calculus Teacher Jaime Escalante can even inspire students to perform better on tests. Some politicians, on the other hand, such as former ruler of china chairman mao zedong, simply wield power over people, making laws and decisions that profoundly affect their lives.

Other Names and Places

❶ Here's the Idea

Capitalize the names of nationalities and languages, and capitalize religious terms. Also capitalize certain geographical names, regions, and historical and calendar items.

Ethnic Groups, Languages, and Nationalities

▶ **Capitalize the names of ethnic groups, races, languages, and nationalities, along with adjectives formed from these names.**

Navajo	Portuguese	Israeli
Hispanic	Caucasian	French

Religious Terms

▶ **Capitalize the names of religions and their followers, religious denominations, sacred days, sacred writings, and deities.**

In the following passage, Etty Hillesum, a Dutch Jew who died in Auschwitz in 1943, writes about her experiences in the transit camp of Westerbork.

> **LITERARY MODEL**
>
> My God, are the doors really being shut now?   **DEITY**
> Yes, they are. Shut on the herded, densely packed
> mass of people inside....The train gives a   **RELIGIOUS FOLLOWERS**
> piercing whistle. And 1,020 Jews leave Holland....
>   Opening the Bible at random I find this: **SACRED WRITING**
> "The Lord is my high tower." I am sitting on my
> rucksack in the middle of a full freight car.
>
> —Etty Hillesum, *Letters from Westerbork*

The words *god* and *goddess* are not capitalized when they refer to the deities of ancient mythology.

Hermes, the god of commerce, invention, cunning, and theft, was also the messenger of ancient Greek gods.

Geographical Names

▶ **In geographical names and names of regions, capitalize each word except articles and prepositions.**

Geographical Names and Regions		
Cities, states	London Paris	West Virginia Oregon State
Regions	West Coast East	Highlands Pacific Northwest
Countries	Congo Thailand	Uruguay New Zealand
Parts of the world	South America Europe	Northern Hemisphere North Pole
Land features	Ural Mountains Death Valley	Sahara Desert Grand Canyon
Bodies of water	Adriatic Sea English Channel	Lake Huron Amazon River
Streets, highways	No. 10 Downing Street Lake Shore Drive	Route 66 Park Avenue

Do not capitalize words that indicate general directions or locations.

Many prospectors made a fortune out West. (SPECIFIC REGION)

They headed west to search for gold. (GENERAL DIRECTION)

The Wilkie family settled on the west side of the city. (GENERAL LOCATION)

Historical and Calendar Items

▶ **Capitalize the names of historical events, historical periods, and calendar items, including days, months, and holidays.**

Historical and Calendar Items		
Historical events	Seven Years' War Russian Revolution	V-J Day Battle of Waterloo
Historical periods	Bronze Age Han Dynasty	Edwardian Era Industrial Revolution
Calendar items	Tuesday March	Arbor Day New Year's Eve

Don't capitalize the names of seasons: spring, summer, winter, fall.

❷ Practice and Apply

A. CONCEPT CHECK: Other Names and Places

Rewrite the words that contain capitalization errors, using correct capitalization.

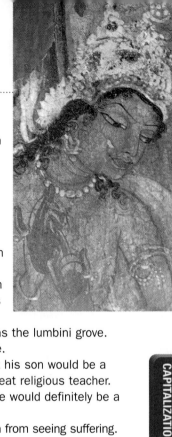

Gautama Buddha's Beginnings

1. Most buddhists believe that other enlightened ones existed before Siddhartha Gautama.
2. However, buddhism as a religion began with Siddhartha.
3. He was born about 2,500 years ago in kosala, which was north of the ganges river near what is now nepal.
4. Buddhist texts identify his birthplace as the lumbini grove.
5. Gautama was actually an indian prince.
6. A Holy man told Gautama's father that his son would be a great ruler, or, if he saw suffering, a great religious teacher.
7. A man from the himalayas predicted he would definitely be a great religious teacher.
8. So, the indian king tried to keep his son from seeing suffering.
9. When Gautama eventually saw the sick, elderly, dead, and holy, he was moved to do as indians had done for centuries.
10. He went off to the Forest alone to seek truth in Silence.

➜ For a SELF-CHECK and more exercises, see the EXERCISE BANK, p. 311.

B. PROOFREADING: Capitalizing Names and Places

Rewrite the words that are incorrectly capitalized in this passage.

Gautama's Journey

After Siddhartha left the Palace, he met two holy men who taught him to meditate and invited him to teach, too. Thinking he should be more spiritually advanced to teach, he left them to learn from the Temple priests. When the Priests' animal sacrifices offended him, however, he left them as well.

Next, in magadha, he met five ascetics and, copying them to gain insight, nearly starved to death. When he got too weak to get out of the nairanjana river after bathing, though, he gave up self-denial. The ascetics then left him.

Finally, while meditating under a tree at bodh gaya, he had the realization that the source of all suffering is desire. On his way to the city of varanasi to share this and other insights, he came upon the ascetics in deer park. They became his first followers.

CAPITALIZATION

A. Capitalizing Names and Places For each sentence, rewrite the words that should be capitalized. Do not include words that are already capitalized correctly.

1. Publishing tycoon william randolph hearst was once one of the most avid and yet least particular collectors in the world.
2. He filled warehouses with english furniture, moorish pottery, egyptian statues, but also worthless knickknacks.
3. He bought a welsh castle and a farm once owned by president lincoln.
4. When he wanted to move a spanish monastery he'd purchased, he built a railroad to move it stone by stone.
5. He did not need these places, since his father had a ranch in san simeon, california, overlooking the pacific ocean.
6. Still, when he inherited this estate from his father, senator George Hearst, he added a spanish-style castle to it.
7. He gave his mansion the spanish name La Cuesta Encantada, which in english means "The Enchanted Hill."
8. Then he filled this home with such treasures as the bed once owned by cardinal richelieu.
9. Only when Hearst's health began to fail after world war II did he leave this mountain retreat.
10. He spent his last days in a beverly hills mansion, where he died on august 14, 1951, at the age of 88.

B. Proofreading for Errors in Capitalization Rewrite the words that are incorrectly capitalized in this passage.

Many of the most successful creative geniuses—architects, actors, film directors, physicists—are also some of the most arrogant. For example, Frank lloyd Wright, undoubtedly an architectural genius, openly declared himself arrogant. Ironically, however, Wright was the son of a unitarian minister who failed at almost everything he tried—from running a music conservatory in madison, wisconsin, to serving as a minister. Of course, these very failures could have been what caused Wright's Mother to devote herself to Frank, her eldest Son, which no doubt increased his sense of self-importance.

Similarly, the brilliant midwest-born actor and director Orson Welles was said to have had a rather grand self-image. In an english school magazine, reviewer Kenneth Tynan wrote that Welles was a major prophet and a self-made man who loved his maker.

Then there's british physicist Ernest Rutherford. He discovered the atom's nucleus but was also arrogant enough to boast that he could do research at the north pole.

CHAPTER 8

Organizations and Other Subjects

❶ Here's the Idea

Capitalize the names of organizations and institutions, certain astronomical terms, vehicles, and monuments. Some school subjects and terms and the names of awards, special events, and brand names should also be capitalized.

Organizations and Institutions

▶ **Capitalize all important words in the names of organizations, including teams and businesses. Capitalize all important words in the names of institutions, including schools, hospitals, and government and political bodies.**

Organizations and Institutions	
Organizations	American Cancer Society Association for Women in Science
Businesses	Ford Motor Company Blockbuster Incorporated
Institutions	New York University Los Angeles Public Library
Government bodies	Senate Department of Education
Political parties	Republican Party Democratic Party

Don't capitalize words such as *democratic, republican, socialist* and *communist* when they refer to principles or forms of government. Capitalize them when they refer to specific political parties.

The United States has a democratic government.

The Democratic Party will be meeting soon.

HEARING ROOM
INTERIOR AND INSULAR AFFAIRS
EXECUTIVE SESSION

If this sign were not in all capital letters, only one word would begin with a lower case letter. Do you know which one?

Capitalization **205**

Astronomical Terms

▶ **Capitalize the names of stars, planets, galaxies, constellations, and other specific objects in the universe.**

Do not capitalize *sun* and *moon*. Capitalize *earth* only when it is used with other capitalized astronomical terms. Never capitalize *earth* when it is preceded by the article *the* or when it refers to land or soil.

> Scientists know that Venus and Earth are similar in size.

> Most people only see the moon or the sun rise over the earth.

Vehicles and Landmarks

▶ **Capitalize the names of specific ships, trains, airplanes, and spacecraft. Also capitalize the names of buildings, bridges, monuments, memorials, and other landmarks.**

Queen Elizabeth II	*U.S.S. Constellation*
Broadway Limited	Homestead National Monument
Spruce Goose	Korean War Veterans' Memorial

Notice that the names of ships, trains, airplanes, and spacecraft are italicized.

School Subjects and Terms

▶ **Capitalize the names of school subjects only when they refer to specific courses. Also capitalize any proper nouns and adjectives that are part of these names.**

▶ **Capitalize the words *freshman, sophomore, junior,* and *senior* only when they are part of a proper noun.**

STUDENT MODEL

The power struggle between Jessica and Tom to be chairperson of the Senior Prom Committee turned ugly today. The social studies teacher used their conflict to examine democratic elections, which was interesting. By Intermediate French, though, the two were arguing so loudly that Mrs. Picard made them argue in French. Thank heavens the committee votes tomorrow after Calculus 100.

PART OF A PROPER NOUN

NAMES A GENERAL SCHOOL SUBJECT

NAMES A SPECIFIC COURSE

Awards, Special Events, and Brand Names

▶ **Capitalize brand names and the names of awards and special events.**

Awards, Events, and Brand Names	
Awards	Grammy Award, Victoria Cross, Pulitzer Prize
Special events	Ingham County Fair, Farm Aid Concert, World Series
Brand names	Healthy Crunch, Pocketpal, Studymate

A common noun following a brand name is not capitalized.

    Healthy Crunch cereal   Pocketpal phone

❷ Practice and Apply

CONCEPT CHECK: Organizations and Other Subjects

Rewrite the words that contain capitalization errors, using correct capitalization. If a sentence is correct, write *Correct*.

Champions of Women's Rights

1. Perhaps you learned about the seneca falls convention of 1848, also called the Women's Rights Convention.
2. It was the first Convention for women's rights in History.
3. In my Junior year, I learned that Elizabeth Cady Stanton, Sarah and Angelina Grimké, and Lucretia Mott organized it.
4. Susan B. Anthony, later a champion of women's rights, was still devoted to the woman's state temperance society.
5. By 1852 Anthony, Stanton's junior in age, had begun working for women's rights with Stanton.
6. After about ten years of campaigning, they won their first victory in New York State.
7. They also started the national woman suffrage association.
8. To many women, this organization must have been like the north star beckoning to lost travelers in the wilderness.
9. Hoping to free women as well as the slaves, they worked with the abolitionists to pass the Thirteenth Amendment.
10. Shortly before her death, Anthony was recognized for her work at a Special Dinner in Her Honor.

➜ **For a SELF-CHECK and more practice, see the EXERCISE BANK, p. 312.**

In your 🗂 **Working Portfolio,** find your **Write Away** paragraph from page 196 and correct any errors in capitalization you find.

CAPITALIZATION

First Words and Titles

❶ Here's the Idea

First Words

▶ **Capitalize the first word of every sentence and line of traditional poetry.**

> **LITERARY MODEL**
>
> Do not go gentle into that good night,
>
> Old age should burn and rave at close of day;
>
> Rage, rage against the dying of the light.
>
> —Dylan Thomas, "Do Not Go Gentle into That Good Night"

Contemporary poetry often does not follow this convention. If you choose to omit capital letters in your own poems, make sure your meaning is still clear.

▶ **Capitalize the first word of a direct quotation only when the quotation is a complete sentence and is not connected grammatically to the sentence in which it appears.**

"Have you seen the holiday classic *Scrooge?*" Ed asked.

Ed is fond of calling his favorite old movies "classics."

▶ **In a divided quotation, do not capitalize the first word of the second part unless it starts a new sentence.**

"We watch old movies," said Ed, "especially during the holidays."

"*Scrooge* is my favorite," he said. "Which one do you like best?"

▶ **When quoting fewer than four lines of poetry, use slash marks between the lines and mimic the capitalization in the poem.**

The grand old Duke of York / He had ten thousand men

▶ **Capitalize the first word of each item in an outline and the letters that introduce major subsections.**

I. Life of Dylan Thomas
    A. Early years
        1. Family
        2. Education
    B. Adult years

▶ **In a letter, capitalize the first word of the greeting, the word *Sir* or *Madam*, and the first word of the closing.**

My dear Karyn,   Dear Sir,   Your friend,

Pronoun *I*

▶ **Always capitalize the pronoun *I*.**

Well, I hope I'll live a long and happy life.

Titles

▶ **Capitalize the first, last, and all other important words in a title, including verbs.** Do not capitalize conjunctions, articles, or prepositions of fewer than five letters unless they begin the title.

Book Title	*Paradise Lost*
Short Story Title	"A Sunrise on the Veld"
Movie Title	*Shakespeare in Love*
Play Title	*The Tragedy of Macbeth*

❷ Practice and Apply

CONCEPT CHECK: First Words and Titles

Rewrite the words that are incorrectly capitalized in this passage.

Can Sniffles Snuff Out Lives?

Some great people have died from seemingly minor ailments. suffragist Susan B. Anthony died from a cold. Oscar Wilde, the author of *the Importance Of Being Earnest,* died from an ear infection. Even Influenza—now called "The flu"—has been "The great equalizer" of many.

However, nothing can do away with some people's sense of humor. Wilde's sense of humor appears to have been intact to the end, and many of his witty remarks are still repeated today. His last words are said to have been, "my wallpaper and i are fighting a duel to the death. one or the other of us has to go." Then, too, there's a tombstone that says, "I told you i was sick!"

➡ **For a SELF-CHECK and more practice, see the EXERCISE BANK, p. 312.**

Abbreviations

① Here's the Idea

Capitalize abbreviations of place names, abbreviations related to time, and abbreviations of organizations and government agencies.

Place Names

▶ **Capitalize the abbreviations of cities, states, countries, and other places.**

N.Y.C.	**U.S.A.**	Vancouver, **B.C.**
CA	**U.K.**	**M**ex.

Use a state abbreviation only in an address or reference—not in formal writing.

Time

▶ **Capitalize the abbreviations B.C., A.D., A.M., and P.M. and the abbreviations for time zones.**

The Han dynasty ruled China from approximately 206 B.C. to A.D. 220.

The documentary on the governor's trip to Beijing airs at 7:00 P.M. EST.

Archaeologists believe that these life-size clay figures represent the troops meant to guard China's first sovereign emperor, Qin Shihuangdi, after his death in about 210 B.C.

Organization Names

▶ **Capitalize abbreviations of the names of organizations and agencies formed by using the initial letters of the complete name.**

Notice that these abbreviations usually do not take periods.

AAUW (American Association of University Women)

CIA (Central Intelligence Agency)

SEATO (Southeast Asia Treaty Organization)

UNESCO (United Nations Educational, Scientific, and Cultural Organization)

❷ Practice and Apply

....

A. CONCEPT CHECK: Abbreviations

Rewrite the words that contain capitalization errors, using correct capitalization. If a sentence is correct as is, write *Correct.*

> **Power Behind the Sports Scene**
> **1.** The athletes in the nfl, nba, wcw, and other professional leagues get a lot of attention in the media.
> **2.** Turn on any major network—cbs, abc, nbc—and within minutes you're likely to see something about an athlete.
> **3.** Espn broadcasts sports almost continuously, a.m. and p.m.
> **4.** However, executives in corporations such as gm become behind-the-scenes players when the corporation sponsors a broadcast or uses an athlete to promote a product.
> **5.** What's more, in the wrestling industry, the "players" with the greatest influence actually include the wcw commissioner, the wcw president, and the booking agents.

➡ For a SELF-CHECK and more practice, see the EXERCISE BANK, p. 313.

B. PROOFREADING: Capitalizing Abbreviations Correctly

Rewrite the words that are incorrectly capitalized in this passage.

> **The Power Behind the President**
>   Although Eleanor Roosevelt was known as a shy girl growing up in Ny, she overcame her shyness as the wife of President Franklin D. Roosevelt. To aid her ailing husband, Eleanor attended meetings of such agencies as the Works Progress Administration (wpa) and the National Youth Administration (Nya).
>   When Franklin D. Roosevelt died on April 12, 1945, at 3:30 p.m., however, many thought Eleanor would retire from public life. Instead, though, she accepted President Truman's appointment as a national delegate to the un. By the end of her long political career, she was admired by the world for her advocacy of human rights and world peace.

CAPITALIZATION

Real World Grammar

Press Release

A press release is a great way to announce a performance or other newsworthy item. Before sending one out, however, you need to check it for errors—including those in capitalization. Capitalization errors can confuse readers and make a sloppy, unprofessional impression that leaves readers wondering if the event you're announcing will be equally sloppy—not an impression you want to convey when you're hoping to get people to pay to see a show!

The following press release was well written, but the choir director still found errors in it. Would you have spotted these?

Press Release

Who: Saxton High School Senior Choir, directed by mr. leon Daniels

Capitalize people's names and titles used before them—even when abbreviated.

What: *Broadway alive!* a salute to Broadway musicals

This is an important word in a title—cap it!

Why: To raise funds to send the choir to Alaska this summer

Where: SHS Auditorium

When: friday, January 12, 7:00 P.M.

The day of the week should be capitalized.

Tickets: $5 per ticket in advance, $7.50 at the door. Tickets can be purchased at the school office between 9 A.M. and 3:30 P.M.

Additional Facts About the Concert

This salute to Broadway shows will include selections from *Grease!*, *a Chorus Line*, *the Lion King*, *the King and I*, and other popular musicals.

Capitalize first words in titles.

All money raised will help pay for the choir's tour of Alaska, where they have been invited to perform at summer festivals in Juneau, Fairbanks, and Nome. "I heard the choir sing last Spring," said Mr. Edward Klasky, ex-President of the Nome Chamber of Commerce, "And they gave an electrifying performance. I simply had to invite them to our state."

Seasons shouldn't be capitalized!

In general, lowercase titles that follow names.

Lowercase the first word of a divided quotation.

In addition to these major cities, the choir's itinerary will include a visit to denali national park.

Capitalize names of specific places.

Using Grammar in Writing

Titles of Works and Individuals	Verify the spelling and the wording of all names of people, titles, and abbreviations of titles, and capitalize them correctly so as to avoid confusing and/or offending people.
First Words in Quotations	Check your quotations for accuracy and be sure to capitalize divided quotations correctly.
Places and Dates	To avoid sending people to the wrong place at the wrong time, capitalize the names of specific places, days of the week, and months. However, do not capitalize the names of seasons.

PRACTICE AND APPLY: Writing

Correct all errors in capitalization in this rough draft of a press release the students wrote to announce their Thank-You Concert.

Press Release

Who: SHS Choir, directed by mr. Leon Daniels

What: <u>Broadway alive!</u> a salute to Broadway musicals

Why: To thank the community for helping us get to alaska this past Summer

Where: sorello band shell in Huston park

When: saturday, august 10, 8:00 PM

Tickets: Free!

Additional Facts About the Concert

"The trip wouldn't have been possible," said mrs. Arletta Mae Jones, Chairperson of the Association of friends of the Choir (AFC), "Without the generous support of the community."

Dwayne Robinson, who will be a freshman at Grand Valley College in the Fall, said, "We all want to show our gratitude to our families and friends for the trip of a lifetime."

The audiences throughout alaska were so receptive that the choir heard "Encore!" after every performance.

A. Using Capitalization Correctly Rewrite the words that contain capitalization errors, using correct capitalization.

1. England may have its Kings and Queens, but the united states has its own kind of "Royalty."
2. "Royal" americans include the exceptionally glamorous, talented, rich, and powerful—typically actors, comedians, Rock stars, Athletes, Senators, and Ceos, to name a few.
3. In fact, the status of an olympic runner can be just as high as that of a President or a Prime Minister.
4. The academy awards show, broadcast on tv each Spring, presents oscars to movie industry people. winning an oscar can give a person the clout to make additional films.
5. Ronald Reagan, Former President of the United States, used his movie star power to help him become a Governor and then the u.s. president.
6. Sports heroes sometimes use their status to earn money by endorsing breakfast cereals or trips to places such as disneyland.
7. The superbowl, the nba championships, and the world series can make an athlete the king of a particular sport.
8. Retired chicago bulls star Michael Jordan was treated so much like royalty that he was nicknamed "His Airness."
9. In a speech at Harvard university, James Russell Lowell said, "wealth may be an excellent thing, for it means power, it means leisure, it means Liberty."
10. Of course, some of the wealthiest people on earth not only have power, they also have a place on *forbes's* list of the 400 richest americans.

B. Identifying Errors in Capitalization Rewrite the words that are incorrectly capitalized in this passage.

STUDENT MODEL

Two especially powerful people, both in physical ability as well as in the capacity to inspire others, are major league baseball stars mark mcgwire and sammy sosa. As the 1990s drew to a close, these two men, respectively playing for the st. louis cardinals and the chicago cubs, belted out home run after home run in an attempt to set the all-time record. mcgwire, with his record-setting 70 home runs in the 1998 season, tied or set more than 30 major league, national league, and team records. sosa, who won the national league's mvp award in 1998, thrilled wrigley field fans by being the first major leaguer ever to hit 66 homers in a season. Both men continued to compete for a place in the *guinness book of records* in 1999.

For each underlined group of words, choose the letter of the correct revision.

Folk singer and songwriter Woodrow Wilson "woody" Guthrie believed
(1)   (2)
music had the power to change society. During the 1930s and 1940s, his

music spoke to the american people about the issues they cared about. At
(3)
15, Guthrie traveled East and West, visiting migrant camps. He then went
(4)
to live with his Father in Pampa, Texas, before getting involved in the
(5)
growing Folk Song Movement. Guthrie recorded songs for RCA Victor and
(6)
Folkways Records, now owned by the Smithsonian institution. His impact
(7)
was felt on into the 1960s with his song "This land is your land" and his
(8)
influence on folk-rockers such as Bob Dylan. Honored in the Rock and Roll

Hall of Fame in Cleveland, oh, Guthrie and his songs have become "a
(9)
national possession, like Yellowstone and Yosemite," according to critic
(10)
Clifton Fadiman.

1. A. Folk Singer and Songwriter
   B. Folk singer and Songwriter
   C. folk singer and songwriter
   D. Correct as is

2. A. wilson "woody" Guthrie
   B. Wilson "Woody" Guthrie
   C. wilson "woody" guthrie
   D. Correct as is

3. A. American people
   B. American People
   C. american People
   D. Correct as is

4. A. East and west
   B. east and West
   C. east and west
   D. Correct as is

5. A. father in pampa, texas
   B. father in Pampa, Texas
   C. Father in pampa, Texas
   D. Correct as is

6. A. growing Folk Song movement
   B. growing folk song movement
   C. growing folk Song Movement
   D. Correct as is

7. A. Folkways Records, now owned
      by the smithsonian institution
   B. Folkways records, now owned
      by the Smithsonian Institution
   C. Folkways Records, now owned
      by the Smithsonian Institution
   D. Correct as is

8. A. This Land Is Your Land
   B. This Land is your Land
   C. This land is Your land
   D. Correct as is

9. A. Cleveland, OH
   B. Cleveland, Oh
   C. Cleveland, oH
   D. Correct as is

10. A. like yellowstone and yosemite
    B. Like Yellowstone and Yosemite
    C. like yellowstone and Yosemite
    D. Correct as is

Student Help Desk

Capitalization at a Glance

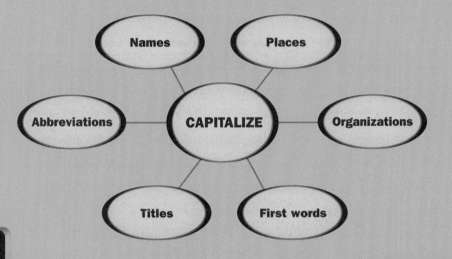

```
        Names              Places

Abbreviations    CAPITALIZE      Organizations

        Titles            First words
```

Correct Capitalization

When to "Pump It Up"

It's proper to capitalize proper nouns and proper adjectives.	Keep common nouns and adjectives all lowercase.
Mayor Daley	the mayor
Aunt Julia	my aunt
Neptune, Rigel, Milky Way	planet, comet, the earth
Northeast, North Shore	drive northeast, sit on the shore
August, Flag Day	summer months, fall days, winter, flag
Aphrodite, Apollo, Zeus	goddess, gods
Socialist Party	socialist government
Economics 101	economics book

Acronyms and Abbreviations — A Capital Education

Matters of Degree

B.A. Bachelor of Arts

B.S. Bachelor of Science

C.P.A. Certified Public Accountant

L.P.N. Licensed Practical Nurse

M.B.A. Master of Business Administration

Tests of Knowledge

ACT American College Testing

CEEB College Entrance Examination Board

GED general equivalency diploma

GRE Graduate Record Examination

SAT Scholastic Assessment Test

Classified Information

EOE Equal Opportunity Employer

FT, PT full-time, part-time

HR Human Resources

SASE self-addressed stamped envelope

Capitals Online — Making Capital Connections

L-Net

Back | Forward | Reload | Home | Images | Print | Security | Stop

Location:

Internet Etiquette

NEVER USE ALL CAPITALS FOR AN ENTIRE MESSAGE. Doing so is called "shouting" and is considered rude.

You can use all caps for Internet "slang" to respond more quickly in chat rooms and instant messages. For example, try these:

- **IMHO:** in my humble opinion
- **BTW:** by the way
- **LOL:** laughing out loud

Addresses and Searches

Be sure to use the appropriate cases in e-mail addresses and Internet searches. Doing this will help ensure you make the connection or find the information you desire.

NEVER USE ALL CAPITALS IN A MESSAGE

Theme: Human Behavior
Signs and Signals

These pedestrians have several ways of knowing whether it's safe to cross the street: the messages displayed on the crosswalk signals, the colors of the signals, and the warnings of their friends. The friends are both speaking the same words, but are they saying the same thing? Notice how a single exclamation point changed the meaning of these words. End marks and commas are powerful. Be sure to use them correctly.

Write Away: Perception Reflection
Can you think of a time when you and a friend or relative saw the same incident or interpreted the same information in very different ways? Why? Write about it, and then save your writing in your 🗀 **Writing Portfolio.**

For each underlined group of words, choose the correct revision.

> Do you prefer a sporty car or a four-wheel-drive sports utility <u>vehicle</u>
> (1)
> Your answers to that and other questions may be just what researchers
> want to <u>know.</u> Identifying people's attitudes and behaviors is <u>interesting</u>
> (2)   (3)
> <u>and fun!</u> but it's also serious business. Conducting opinion <u>polls. Surveyors</u>
>   (4)
> help presidential candidates identify how voters feel about current <u>issues</u>
>   (5)
> <u>and matters</u> of public concern. Researchers can help business owners gauge
> customer response to new products, <u>services packaging,</u> and advertising.
>   (6)
> Despite the many <u>differences among us</u> we all have things in common.
>   (7)
> The fact that we are often <u>the same, not different,</u> simplifies things for
>   (8)
> researchers. <u>Suppose for example</u> that a researcher is studying color
>   (9)
> preferences. Fortunately, the researcher doesn't have to contact every
> seventeen year old from <u>Cairo Illinois</u> to Cairo, Egypt. Instead, he or she
>   (10)
> can poll a representative sample of seventeen year olds and form a
> generalization based on their answers.

1. A. vehicle.
   B. vehicle?
   C. vehicle!
   D. Correct as is

2. A. know,
   B. know!
   C. know?
   D. Correct as is

3. A. interesting, and fun,
   B. interesting, and fun
   C. interesting and fun,
   D. Correct as is

4. A. polls? Surveyors
   B. polls, surveyors
   C. polls surveyors
   D. Correct as is

5. A. issues and matters,
   B. issues. And matters
   C. issues, and matters
   D. Correct as is

6. A. services, packaging,
   B. services, packaging
   C. services packaging
   D. Correct as is

7. A. differences, among us,
   B. differences among us,
   C. differences, among us
   D. Correct as is

8. A. the same not different
   B. the same, not different
   C. the same not different,
   D. Correct as is

9. A. Suppose, for example
   B. Suppose, for example,
   C. Suppose for, example
   D. Correct as is

10. A. Cairo, Illinois,
    B. Cairo, Illinois
    C. Cairo Illinois,
    D. Correct as is

Periods and Other End Marks

❶ Here's the Idea

Periods, question marks, and exclamation points are **end marks.**
An end mark can change the entire meaning of a sentence.

End Marks

Essential Endings		
End Mark	**Use after . . .**	**Example**
Period	• a declarative sentence	Researchers study colors and consumer behavior.
	• an imperative sentence	Choose your favorite color.
	• an indirect question	He asked me if I liked the color red.
Exclamation Point	• an exclamatory sentence	I never knew the color red stimulates the appetite!
	• a strong interjection	Wow!
	• words that express a sound	Wham!
Question Mark	• an interrogative sentence	Is that why many cafés have red tablecloths?
	• a declarative sentence that asks a question	Mom painted the kitchen walls red?

For more about using end marks with direct quotations and parentheses, see p. 248 and p. 252.

Other Uses of Periods

Periods are also used in abbreviations and outlines.

Putting Periods to Work		
Usage	**Rule**	**Example**
Outline	Use a period after each number or letter in an outline or list.	A. Preference for blue 　1. Dark blue 　2. Light blue B. Preference for yellow
Abbreviation	Use a period with an abbreviation or an initial.	Dr. M. Grant, Jr. *i.e.,* orange, yellow, etc. Tues., 3:40 P.M.

Some abbreviations do not require a period: metric abbreviations (km, ml), acronyms and abbreviations pronounced letter by letter (NASA, FBI), two-letter abbreviations for states' names (AL, WY), and positions on the compass (NNE, SW).

❷ Practice and Apply

A. CONCEPT CHECK: Periods and Other End Marks

Write each word that should be followed by an end mark, adding periods, question marks, and exclamation points as needed.

> **Color Is Just Color, Right? Wrong!**
> 1. Color experts have been asked why color preferences change
> 2. Such shifts reflect changes in consumers' lifestyles
> 3. Yuck That's how people used to react to green food packaging
> 4. Why They might have associated green with mold
> 5. Now consumers equate green with health and nature
> 6. Research suggests that green makes objects seem less heavy
> 7. At one company, employees complained that their red toolboxes weighed too much
> 8. The company secretly painted the toolboxes green
> 9. What do you think happened
> 10. Employees were thrilled that their "new" toolboxes were so light and easy to carry

➜ **For a SELF-CHECK and more practice, see the EXERCISE BANK, p. 313.**

B. PROOFREADING: Using End Marks Correctly

Proofread the passage below. Write the words before and after an end-mark mistake, inserting the correct end mark between them.

> **Henry Ford Would Be Amazed!**
>   In the early 1900s, Henry Ford said that people could buy a car from Ford Motor Co in any color "so long as it's black." Wow What a difference a century makes. Now cars come in an array of colors. You might ask how color experts help manufacturers choose colors? Did you know that color preferences change depending on the type of car. Buyers want brightly colored sports cars. Color preferences reflect social values! In the environmentally conscious 1990s, cars featured colors from nature H Ford's preference continues to attract many buyers? For them, black means "luxury."

COMMAS

Commas in Sentence Parts

❶ Here's the Idea

Although comma usage may vary for stylistic purposes, the following rules help writers communicate clearly to their readers in the absence of the kinds of nonverbal cues (such as pauses and body language) that we use in oral communication.

Commas with Introductory Elements

▶ **Use a comma after mild interjections or introductory words such as *oh, yes, no,* and *well.***

Yes, experts use tests to determine personality traits.

▶ **Use a comma after an introductory prepositional phrase that contains additional prepositional phrases.**

From introvert to extrovert, every personality type has been classified.

▶ **Use a comma after an introductory adverb or adverbial clause.**

Often, these assessments can help you match your career to your personality.

Although you may think you can't be classified, your personality-test results can reveal plenty about you.

▶ **Use a comma after an introductory participial or infinitive phrase.**

PARTICIPIAL PHRASE
Testing extensively, the experts have gathered data to back up their personality assessments.

INFINITIVE PHRASE
To help people find the right job, counselors often administer one or more of these tests.

For more on clauses, see p. 74, and for more on phrases, see p. 48.

Commas with Interrupters

▶ **Use commas to set off nouns of direct address,** nouns that name or speak directly to the reader.

Jeff, you should take the Myers-Briggs Type Indicator.

Use commas to set off a parenthetical expression, a word or phrase inserted into a sentence as commentary or to relate ideas within the sentence. *However, therefore, for example, by the way,* and *after all* are examples of parenthetical expressions.

PARENTHETICAL

The Myers-Briggs Type Indicator, **by the way,** is probably the most widely used personality test in the country.

NOT PARENTHETICAL

Can you judge the accuracy of the test **by the way** you feel about the results?

Be sure to use a comma to separate a question tagged onto the end of a sentence from the rest of the sentence.

It's fun to take these kinds of tests, **don't you think?**

Commas with Nonessential Clauses and Phrases

Use commas to set off nonessential clauses and nonessential participial phrases.

NONESSENTIAL CLAUSE

The Myers-Briggs Type Indicator, **which was developed by Katharine Briggs and Isabel Briggs Myers,** designates 16 distinct personality types.

NONESSENTIAL PARTICIPIAL PHRASE

A test interpreter, **judging responses to a number of questions,** can suggest career paths that match the test subject's personality type.

Use commas to set off a nonessential appositive. Commas aren't necessary with essential appositives.

NONESSENTIAL APPOSITIVE

The Myers-Briggs Type Indicator, **the MBTI®,** is used by many career counselors.

ESSENTIAL APPOSITIVE

The book *Do What You Are* is based on the MBTI®.

Sometimes only the use of commas indicates whether a clause or phrase is essential or nonessential.

NONESSENTIAL CLAUSE

The test subject**,** **who took the test on Tuesday,** scored higher in the thinking category. (THIS PARTICULAR TEST SUBJECT TOOK THE TEST ON TUESDAY AND SCORED HIGHER IN THE THINKING CATEGORY.)

ESSENTIAL CLAUSE

The test subject **who takes the test on Tuesday** scores higher in the thinking category. (ANY TEST SUBJECT WHO TAKES THE TEST ON TUESDAY SCORES HIGHER IN THE THINKING CATEGORY.)

For more on clauses, see p. 74, and for more on phrases, see p. 48.

Commas with Compound Sentences

▶ **Use a comma before the conjunction that joins the two independent clauses of a compound sentence.**

independent clause, **and** **independent clause**

Those who score high in the judgment category of the MBTI® prefer to lead highly structured lives**,** **but** those who score high in the perception category prefer a more flexible lifestyle.

 Make sure you're punctuating a compound sentence, not a simple sentence with a compound predicate.

COMPOUND PREDICATE (NO COMMA NEEDED)

Twelve subjects **took** the test and **showed** a higher preference for extroversion than introversion.

For more about compound sentences, see p. 86.

Commas with Series or Lists

▶ **Use a comma after every item in a series except the last one.**

A Myers-Briggs score high in **introversion,** **intuition,** **thinking,** **and judging** is typical of scientists.

▶ **Use a comma between two or more adjectives of equal rank that modify the same noun.**

Personality assessment is a **vital,** **interesting** profession.

Do not use a comma if one adjective in a series modifies another.

The test subjects filed into the **pale green** examination room.

 To tell if a series of adjectives requires a comma, place the word *and* between the adjectives. If the sentence still makes sense, replace *and* with a comma.

❷ Practice and Apply

A. CONCEPT CHECK: Commas in Sentence Parts

Eighteen commas are missing from the paragraph below. Write the words before and after the missing comma, adding the comma in between them.

Does This Interest You?

(1) Are you looking for a popular well-respected self-assessment tool? **(2)** One such tool is the Strong Interest Inventory also known as the SII. **(3)** Living up to its name this "test" helps identify your interests. **(4)** Please note students that the SII results are reported as various scales and they can be used to compare your scores with those of others. **(5)** One such scale is the Occupational Scale which compares your scores with those of workers in selected fields. **(6)** By comparing scores the test can identify occupations where workers have similar interests. **(7)** Yes research shows that people with similar interests are likely to find satisfaction in similar careers. **(8)** Dr. John Holland a psychologist developed the theory on which another scale of the SII is based. **(9)** Holland's theory states that all people and all job environments can be sorted into six "vocational types": realistic investigative artistic social enterprising and conventional. **(10)** Consider your test results as guides not dictates for investigating career options.

➜ For a SELF-CHECK and more practice, see the EXERCISE BANK, p. 314.

B. WRITING: Summarize

The following statistics present the eight MBTI® categories and how they are distributed through a representative U.S. sample of adults ages 18 to 94. Analyze the data below and write a paragraph summarizing your findings. Be sure to use commas correctly.

Extrovert 46%
Introvert 54%

Intuitive 32%
Sensor 68%

Feeling 48%
Thinking 52%

Judging 58%
Perceiving 42%

Fixing Comma Problems

❶ Here's the Idea

Many good writers use commas stylistically, especially to clarify words or phrases used as modifiers. When you use too few or too many commas, however, your message can become muddled. Avoid common comma errors and you'll enhance your writing style.

Adding Commas for Clarity

▶ **Use a comma to separate words that might be misread.**

> **Unclear:** Both women and men claim researchers may share the same opinions, but they communicate them differently.

> **Clearer:** Both women and men, claim researchers, may share the same opinions, but they communicate them differently.

▶ **Use a comma to replace an omitted word or words.**

> Studies show that women are more inclined to try to build rapport; **men, to give direct orders.** (Men are more inclined to give direct orders.)

▶ **When establishing contrast, use a comma to set off antithetical phrases that begin with words such as *not* and *unlike*.**

> American women, **unlike American men,** tend to pepper their conversations with courtesy words and questions.

Reading each sentence aloud can help you recognize confusing punctuation. Then you can assess whether you need to add or delete a comma or simply rework the text.

Eliminating Comma Splices

▶ **Never use a comma alone to separate two independent clauses.** This error is a type of run-on sentence called a **comma splice.** A comma splice can confuse readers and is considered a serious usage error. Always add a coordinating conjunction *(and, but, or)* or use a period or semicolon to separate the clauses.

> A man and woman might share the same opinion, ^*but* differing communication styles may lead them to think they disagree.

For more about run-on sentences, see p. 90.

For more about run-on sentences, see p. 90.

② Practice and Apply

A. CONCEPT CHECK: Fixing Comma Problems

Rewrite the sentences below, correcting any errors in comma usage. In some cases, there may be more than one way to correct the error. If a sentence needs no corrections, write *Correct.*

Body Language

1. Research confirms, that different groups of people communicate differently.
2. Often body language not spoken language causes problems among people from different cultures.
3. For example the gesture that means "okay" in the United States can mean "worthless," in France.
4. In Taiwan the correct way to beckon someone is, to wave the hand with the palm down.
5. Startled by such a gesture American visitors in Taiwan may think they are being told to go away.
6. Many Americans consider a pat on the head an affectionate gesture; most Asians just the opposite.
7. For some eye contact is a source of misunderstanding.
8. Many Europeans prefer direct eye contact, while many Latin Americans avoid eye contact, to show respect.
9. While simply standing around people from different cultures can make each other uncomfortable.
10. Generally, southern Europeans and Middle Easterners prefer less than 18 inches of personal space; Asians and Africans more than 36 inches.

➡️ **For a SELF-CHECK and more practice, see the EXERCISE BANK, p. 314.**

B. REVISING: Improving Your Usage of Commas

Open your 📁 **Writing Portfolio** and take out the writing you did for the **Write Away** on page 218. Revise the piece, fixing any comma problems that you find. In some cases, you may discover that reworking an entire sentence (rather than adding, removing, or moving commas) is the best way to eliminate confusion and improve your writing.

COMMAS

Other Comma Rules

LESSON 4

❶ Here's the Idea

Other Uses for Commas

Use a Comma	Example
To set off a personal title or a business abbreviation	Joe Pollster, CEO of Pigeonholers, Inc., uses demographic maps.
In the salutation of a friendly letter and the closing of any letter	Dear Joe, How's the market research business? Your friend, Dana
Between the day of the month and the year (and after the year in a date within a sentence)	The results of this poll were published on June 18, 1999, and analyzed for months afterward.
To separate the street, city, and state in addresses and place names	Did you know that the address of the White House is 1600 Pennsylvania Avenue, Washington, D.C. 20502?
In numbers of more than three digits to denote thousands (except calendar years)	In 1999, the population of Eureka, California, was more than 150,000.
To set off a direct quotation from the rest of a sentence	"The real America is a nation of consumer states," explains author Michael J. Weiss.

For more about using punctuation with quotation marks, see p. 248.

Notice how commas are used in the invitation below.

STUDENT MODEL

Dear Irma, **SALUTATION**

When someone suggests, "Let's order a pizza," **DIRECT QUOTE**
what kind of pie comes to mind? Our
demographics class is conducting a taste test on
August 15, 2001, at 501 Bowman Drive, **DATE**
Allensburg, Ohio, from 11:00 A.M. to 1:00 P.M. **ADDRESS**

Gobble all the pizza you can eat, supplied by
Thatza Pizza, Inc., and 1,000 Pies in the **BUSINESS ABBREVIATION**
Sky, Ltd. Vote for your favorite! Matt Green, **NUMBER**
recorder of the class, will tally the votes. **PERSONAL TITLE**

Please let us know if you'll be there.

Sincerely, **CLOSING**
Mai Ngo

❷ Practice and Apply

A. CONCEPT CHECK: Other Comma Rules

Correct comma errors in the sentences below by writing the words that come before and after the mistake and including a correctly used comma.

Do Statistics Lie?

1. Imagine the headlines "Get Mad, Have Attack" "Stay Cool to Keep Heart True," and "Aggravated Heart."
2. These headlines appeared in papers from Baltimore Maryland to Seattle Washington.
3. This nationwide story ran between March 1 1994 and March 31 1994.
4. Anger "can double the chance for heart attack" according to the report.
5. Researchers from Harvard Medical School interviewed 1 500 people who had suffered heart attacks.
6. So many subjects said that they were intensely angry before the attack that researchers concluded that anger increased the risk of heart attack, 2.3 times.
7. Arnold Barnett professor of operations research at MIT noted the conclusion was incorrect.
8. "The only contributors to the data analysis were people who had suffered heart attacks—and survived" said Barnett.
9. "People who had freely expressed anger . . . without a heart attack" continued Barnett, "could never make it into the researchers' sample."
10. This study would be biased even if the research sample were 15 000 instead of 1 500 people.

➡ For a SELF-CHECK and more practice, see the EXERCISE BANK, p. 315.

B. WRITING: Statistical Correspondence

Imagine that you participated in the pizza-tasting party described in the letter on page 228. Write a letter to a friend or relative telling about the experience. Explain how many people were present, what types of pizzas were sampled, how many slices of each type of pie were consumed, and which pizza won the taste test. Remember to follow the comma rules that you learned in this lesson. When you have finished your letter, exchange papers with a partner and proofread each other's work.

Real World Grammar

A Research Summary

The ability to summarize facts and figures with clarity is a useful skill. Commas are essential tools for accurate writing. They enable a writer to embed complicated information clearly and efficiently into a report such as the student model below.

States Producing the Most Garbage: 2004

State	Millions of tons	Population (in 2004)
1. California	77.9	35,893,000
2. Texas	45.9	22,490,000
3. Illinois	40.4	12,713,000
4. New York	36.5	19,227,000
5. Florida	29.2	17,397,000
6. New Jersey	19.8	8,698,000
7. Ohio	15.8	11,459,000
8. Tennessee	12.9	5,900,000

Research Summary (DRAFT)

According to *BioCycle*, a magazine about recycling and waste management, the top garbage-producing state, California, generated 77.9 million tons of garbage in 2004. That's 32 million tons more than its nearest competitor, Texas, which dumped 45.9 million tons of refuse in its landfills. Other top "honors" go to Illinois, New York, Florida, New Jersey, Ohio, and Tennessee, in that order. Still, California generates more than six times the garbage of Tennessee, which has about one-sixth the population of the Golden State.

Before you start wagging your finger at California, however, take a closer look at the statistics. Study the table above and ask yourself if individual Californians, on the average, actually toss the most garbage away. Compare the amount of garbage with each state's population, and you'll find that the people of Illinois win the refuse prize. They produce an average of 3.18 tons of garbage per man, woman, and child. Californians, on the other hand, generate a "mere" 2.17 tons per resident. Sixth-ranked New Jersey actually generates more tons of garbage per person (2.28) than does New York, which ranks fourth in the list above but has more than twice as many people as New Jersey. New York tosses "only" 1.89 tons of trash per person.

Remember, a comma goes after an appositive phrase as well as before it.

Commas set off nonessential clauses.

Use a period at the end of an indirect question, not a question mark

Commas set off parenthetical expressions.

CHAPTER 9

Using Grammar in Writing

Use end marks and commas

For clarity	Use a comma to separate words that might be misread. Use the appropriate end mark to signal whether the sentence should be read as a question, statement, or command.
For efficiency	Use a comma to set off nonessential clauses.
To embed information	Use a comma to set off nonessential appositives and phrases, parenthetical expressions, and nouns of direct address.

PRACTICE AND APPLY

Percentage of college freshman who rated themselves above average in the following categories:

Academic ability: 57.9%   Self-confidence (intellectual): 53.6%
Artistic ability: 26.1%   Leadership ability: 53.6%
Mathematical ability: 39.0%   Competitiveness: 53.7%
Writing ability: 41.7%   Drive to achieve: 65.2%

A. Write a research summary based on the data presented here. Use the research summary on the facing page as a general guide.

B. Exchange your summary with a partner. As you evaluate each other's work, look carefully for errors in end-mark and comma usage. Also, look for ways to embed information to achieve structural variety in your writing (set off by appropriate commas, of course). Watch out for spelling errors, too. Correct any errors you find, and discuss them with your partner.

A. Commas Read the passage. Then write the answers to the questions.

Is one survey method better than **(1)** <u>another or</u> do they all have advantages and disadvantages? **(2)** <u>Consider, for example the</u> face-to-face interview. **(3)** <u>To collect information census takers</u> and pollsters used to go from home to **(4)** <u>home knocking</u> on doors and politely **(5)** <u>asking,</u> "May I take a few minutes of your time?" That worked well in the days when many homes had no telephone, many women did not work outside the **(6)** <u>home and</u> people were more willing to open their doors to strangers. The Census Bureau and private pollsters still conduct some in-home interviews. However, most census forms travel through the **(7)** <u>mail, and most</u> public-opinion polling is done by telephone.

Today, interviews at the mall and focus-group **(8)** <u>gatherings, two methods of face-to-face interviews, have</u> become popular forms of research. **(9)** <u>By observing researchers can see</u> a person's reactions, facial expressions, and gestures, as well as hear opinions. That's why a focus group **(10)** <u>in Miami, Florida, or</u> any other city may be held in a room with a one-way mirror.

1. Is a comma needed? Explain.
2. Is there anything wrong with the comma usage here? Explain.
3. A comma needs to be added here. Where should it go, and why?
4. Is a comma needed? Explain.
5. Is the use of commas correct? Explain.
6. Is a comma needed here? Explain.
7. Is a comma needed here? Explain.
8. Why are commas used here?
9. A comma needs to be added here. Tell where and explain why.
10. Why are there two commas here?

B. End Marks Identify each underlined item as showing either a correct use of end marks or an incorrect use of end marks. For items that are correct, tell why they are correct. For items that are incorrect, tell how to correct them.

Did you know advances in technology have had a huge impact on market **(1)** <u>research. For</u> example, at any time of day, Sunday through Saturday, you can log on to the Internet and respond to a marketing **(2)** <u>survey.</u> **(3)** <u>Talk about convenience?</u> Other innovations—value cards and scanners—were designed to find out what **(4)** <u>John and Jane Q Public are buying.</u> Here's how the system works:

  A. You present your card to receive discounts on specific items.

  B. The cashier scans the card and the products being purchased.

(5) <u>C Store</u> managers and marketers use the purchase information to make marketing and inventory decisions.

For each underlined group of words, choose the correct revision.

Is the President's popularity <u>rising or falling.</u> To answer <u>that question you</u>
(1)   (2)
might consult an opinion poll. Some polls may say yes; <u>and others no.</u> Often,
(3)
when people learn about conflicting <u>survey results they</u> doubt the validity of
(4)
all polls. You might ask how polls can produce <u>such varied results.</u> Results
(5)
may be skewed, a term <u>meaning "biased"</u> by <u>small seemingly insignificant</u>
(6)   (7)
differences in the wording of questions. Poll results also can be skewed when
respondents <u>have no opinion, but</u> offer one anyway.
(8)
The results of polls also can be affected by a high "nonresponse rate."
For example, some people refuse to participate in telephone surveys for
many reasons, including annoyance with phone solicitors, <u>lack of time and</u>
(9)
desire for privacy. In fact, mistrust of information-gathering efforts may
be on the rise. This may cause many <u>people to decline, when</u> they are
(10)
asked to participate in a survey.

---

1. A. rising or falling!
   B. rising or falling?
   C. rising, or falling.
   D. Correct as is

2. A. that question, you
   B. that question. You
   C. that, question you
   D. Correct as is

3. A. and others, no.
   B. and others no?
   C. and others, no?
   D. Correct as is

4. A. survey, results they
   B. survey results, they
   C. survey results they,
   D. Correct as is

5. A. such varied results,
   B. such varied results!
   C. such varied results?
   D. Correct as is

6. A. meaning "biased,"
   B. meaning "biased",
   C. meaning, "biased,"
   D. Correct as is

7. A. small seemingly, insignificant
   B. small seemingly insignificant,
   C. small, seemingly insignificant
   D. Correct as is

8. A. have no opinion but
   B. have no opinion but,
   C. have, no opinion but,
   D. Correct as is

9. A. lack, of time, and
   B. lack of time, and
   C. lack of time and,
   D. Correct as is

10. A. people to decline when,
    B. people to decline when
    C. people, to decline, when
    D. Correct as is

Student Help Desk

End Marks and Commas at a Glance

 Periods end statements or indirect questions.

Exclamation points end exclamatory sentences.

Question marks end direct questions.

Commas set off or separate
- Introductory elements
- Interrupters
- Nonessential clauses and phrases
- Independent clauses in compound sentences
- Items in series or lists

Commas clarify otherwise confusing sentences.

Clarify with Punctuation

What a Difference a Mark Makes!

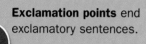

Clarify with Punctuation	What a Difference a Mark Makes!
There's that cartoon character, Donald Duck.	There's that cartoon character, Donald! Duck!
Do not fold, spindle, or mutilate.	Do not fold. Spindle or mutilate!
People who live in glass houses shouldn't throw stones.	People who live in glass houses shouldn't. Throw stones!
What's for dinner, Mom?	What's for dinner? Mom?

Peanuts by Charles Schulz

This is my report on Halley's comma.

HALLEY'S COMMA?

IT'S A VERY FAMOUS COMMA

HE PROBABLY WROTE HOME A LOT

Common Comma Errors

Don't use a comma	Example Error and Correction
to separate a verb from its subject	The Lüscher Color Test⌇measures personality by assessing subjects' color preferences.
to separate a verb from its object or complement	The test shade linked with aggression and autonomy is⌇orange-red.
before the second part of a compound structure that is not an independent clause	Those who prefer the test's blue-green color desire positive self-esteem⌇and resist change.
after a coordinating conjunction that links two independent clauses	Lüscher's shade of dark blue denotes tranquility⌇and⌇those who choose it value calm and contentment.
to connect two independent clauses if there is no conjunction also connecting them	A spontaneous nature characterizes those who prefer bright yellow⌇such people also tend to value selflessness and originality.
to separate an independent clause from a following dependent clause that begins with *after, before, because, if, since, unless, until,* or *when*.	The test is complicated⌇because of its four additional "auxiliary colors" to rank, as well.
to set off essential clauses, phrases, or appositives	The auxiliary color⌇brown⌇was the color most preferred by people⌇who had been displaced after World War II.

The Bottom Line

Checklist for End Marks and Commas

Have I . . .

____ used the correct end mark?

____ made sure I haven't used too many exclamation points?

____ placed a comma after an introductory element?

____ set off nonessential clauses, phrases, and appositives with commas?

____ used a comma before the conjunction that joins the clauses of a compound sentence?

____ added commas when they are needed for clarity?

____ checked for and corrected comma splices?

Other Punctuation Marks

Emoticons	Help
:-)	Smile
;-]	Smile with wink
:-(	Sad
:'-(	Crying
>:-<	Mad
:-O	Surprised
:-|	Grim
:-/	Perplexed
:-}	Embarrassed
O:-)	Angel
:O)	Clown
:-P	Tongue out
:-*	Kiss

Who knew? ;-]
Your pal,
Sandy O:-)

Theme: Computers in the Information Age

Useful Punctuation Marks

Have you ever included an emoticon in an e-mail message? Adding an emotion is a quick and easy way to signal that your message is meant to be funny or sarcastic or tongue-in-cheek. The colons, semicolons, hyphens, parentheses, and brackets that are used to make emoticons are also signals in everyday writing—of quoted material, breaks in thought, omitted words, and more.

Write Away: Keeping in Touch

How do you like to keep in touch with out-of-town friends? Would you rather send e-mail, log on to an online chat, make a phone call, or write a letter? Jot a brief note now to one of those friends. Save a copy of your writing in your 🗁 **Working Portfolio.**

For each underlined group of words, choose the best revision.

Just like you, computers can catch an infectious <u>virus, these</u> computer
(1)
infections can be spread by software, e-mail, or networks. Most people

think of harmful viruses—the Melissa virus spread in the <u>mid 1990's</u>, for
(2)
<u>example, and</u> dread them. Today, however, there are <u>user friendly</u>
(3)   (4)
<u>computer viruses</u>. According to the article <u>The Friendly Virus</u> in
                                              (5)
<u>Newsweek [April 12, 1999]</u>, these viruses are part of a trend called viral
(6)
marketing. *Newsweek* says, "It's the trick of getting customers to

propagate <u>[spread] a product. . . ."</u> One e-mail service attaches an
(7)
advertising blurb to every e-mail message that <u>it's users send</u>. Another
(8)
company's program lets users make cards to send to friends. (The friends

can then make and send <u>their own cards).</u> Some computer viruses are
(9)
things to <u>enjoy, not dread!</u>
(10)

---

1. A. virus: these
   B. virus. these
   C. virus; These
   D. Correct as is

2. A. mid-1990's
   B. mid 1990s
   C. mid-1990s
   D. Correct as is

3. A. example—and
   B. example; and
   C. example) and
   D. Correct as is

4. A. user friendly computer-viruses
   B. user-friendly computer viruses
   C. user-friendly computer-viruses
   D. Correct as is

5. A. *The Friendly Virus*
   B. (The Friendly Virus)
   C. "The Friendly Virus"
   D. Correct as is

6. A. *Newsweek* [April 12, 1999]
   B. *Newsweek* (April 12, 1999)
   C. "Newsweek" (April 12, 1999)
   D. Correct as is

7. A. (spread) a product. . . ."
   B. [spread] a product . . ."
   C. (spread) a product" . . .
   D. Correct as is

8. A. its users send
   B. it's user's send
   C. its user's send
   D. Correct as is

9. A. their own cards)
   B. their own cards.)
   C. their own cards.
   D. Correct as is

10. A. enjoy, not "dread"!
    B. enjoy, not "dread!"
    C. enjoy, (not dread)!
    D. Correct as is

Semicolons and Colons

❶ Here's the Idea

A **semicolon,** like a comma, separates elements in a sentence. A semicolon, however, indicates a stronger break than a comma does. A **colon** signals that an example, a summation, a quotation, or some other form of explanation follows.

Semicolons in Compound Sentences

▶ **Use a semicolon to join the parts of a compound sentence if no coordinating conjunction, such as *and* or *but,* is used.**

I provide information about computer animation technology on my Web site**, and** I post links to other animation sites too.

I provide information about computer animation technology on my Web site**;** I post links to other animation sites too.

▶ **Use a semicolon before a conjunctive adverb or transitional expression that joins the clauses of a compound sentence.**

Note that a conjunctive adverb such as *however* or *therefore* is followed by a comma.

I like to find Web sites with lots of links**; however,** I get frustrated when links don't work.

I check the links on my Web site often**; in fact,** I check them at least once a month to make sure they are still "live."

Don't use a semicolon to separate a phrase or dependent clause from an independent clause, even if the phrase or dependent clause is long.

Incorrect: Conlon likes to search the Web for travel stories about old Route 66**; a route he'd like to travel himself one day.**

Correct: Conlon likes to search the Web for travel stories about old Route 66**, a route he'd like to travel himself one day.**

HISTORIC
U S
66

▶ **Use a semicolon between independent clauses joined by a conjunction if either clause contains commas.**

Julie found a great Web site about desert hiking in Arizona, Utah, and Nevada; and now she plans to hike the Grand Canyon.

Semicolons in Series

▶ **Use semicolons to separate items in a series if one or more of the items contain commas.**

Ben bookmarked writers' Web sites; state travel sites for Louisiana, California, and New Mexico; and National Park Service sites for Yosemite, Grand Teton, and Yellowstone.

Colons with Independent Clauses

▶ **Use a colon after an independent clause to introduce a list of items.**

Kiyo searches the Web for information on three of her interests: current movies, vintage clothing, and soccer.

▶ **Use a colon between two independent clauses when the second explains or elaborates on the first.**

Ben was pleasantly surprised at the computer club meeting: his Web site won an award.

Do not use a colon directly after a verb or a preposition.

Megan likes to chat online with: her sister at college, her cousin in Paris, and her friend in New York.

Emilio's favorite online activities are: playing games, downloading sound files, and chatting with friends.

Other Uses of Colons

▶ **Use a colon to introduce a long quotation.**

Douglas Adams had this to say about computers: "First we thought the PC was a calculator. . . . Then we discovered graphics, and we thought it was a television. With the World Wide Web, we've realized it's a brochure."

▶ **Use a colon after the salutation of a formal business letter.**

Dear Ms. Saunders: To whom it may concern:

> **Use a colon between numerals indicating hours and minutes.**
>
> 10:20 A.M.   5:30 P.M.

> **Use colons to separate numerals in reference to certain religious works, such as the Bible, the Qur'an (Koran), and the Talmud.**
>
> Job 3:2–4   Qur'an 75:22   Mishnah Bikkurim 3:6–7

❷ Practice and Apply

A. CONCEPT CHECK: Semicolons and Colons

Write the words before and after every punctuation mistake in the sentences below, inserting the correct punctuation.

Example: Journey through cyberspace for a variety of travel services; virtual tours, instant reservations, and on-line schedules.
Answer: services: virtual

> **What's on the Web**
>
> **1.** Use the Web to find out about tourist attractions, their sites may include coupons, pictures, and maps.
> **2.** Shop for anything from books to cars on the Web, take the time to compare prices before you buy.
> **3.** Visit a newspaper's Web edition, you'll find timely reports, updated frequently.
> **4.** You'll also find: academic journals, government documents, and other reference sources on the Web.
> **5.** You can skim college catalogs for information about courses, housing, and activities; fill out application forms, and apply for student aid on-line.

➜ For a SELF-CHECK and more practice, see the EXERCISE BANK, p. 316.

B. PROOFREADING: Business Letter

Read this portion of a business letter. Correct errors in the use of colons and semicolons as you did in exercise A above. If there are no errors in a sentence, write *Correct*.

(1) Dear Sales Representative;

(2) What's the wish of every high school student? **(3)** It's probably a homework buddy; or a tutor who could work 24 hours a day! **(4)** As the hands of the clock race past 11;00 P.M., I often find myself at my desk, trying to solve that last math equation. **(5)** Well, *Learning Partner* has made my wish a reality, now with this software program I can get tutorial help in most of my subjects.

Hyphens, Dashes, and Ellipses

❶ Here's the Idea

Hyphens

▶ **Use a hyphen if part of a word must be carried over from one line to the next.** When in doubt about syllabification, consult a dictionary.

Use the following guidelines to avoid hyphenation errors at the ends of lines.

- Do not break words of one syllable:
  pearl, *not* pe-arl.

- Break a word only at syllable breaks:
  croc-odile, *not* cro-codile.

- Do not leave a single letter at the end or beginning of a line:
  ici-cle and pi-ano, *not* i-cicle and pian-o.

- Break a hyphenated word only at the hyphen:
  well-wisher, *not* well-wish-er.

HOT TIP

You can command a computer to break words automatically at the end of lines. This is especially helpful if your work has an extremely uneven right margin. Check your word-processing manual for details.

▶ **Use hyphens in compound numbers from twenty-one to ninety-nine.**

thirty-three   forty-eight   sixty-five

▶ **Use hyphens when writing out fractions.**

My modem is only one-third as fast as my dad's.

▶ **Use hyphens in certain compound nouns.**

great-grandmother   brother-in-law

▶ **Use hyphens between words serving as compound adjectives before nouns.** Usually, a compound adjective that follows the noun it modifies is not hyphenated.

Kofi gave a **well-attended** presentation on the basics of Usenet.

Kofi's presentation on the basics of Usenet was **well attended.**

There are exceptions to this rule, however. For example, do not use a hyphen between an *-ly* adverb and an adjective.

This is an **exceedingly slow** connection.

In their never-ending search for creative social events, the prom committee at Muldoon High devised the come-as-your-favorite-major-appliance dinner and dance.

▶ **Use hyphens when adding certain prefixes and suffixes.**

When to Use a Hyphen		
Prefix or Suffix	**Use a Hyphen?**	**Example**
ex-, quasi-, -elect	yes	The senator-elect is the ex-president of a software company.
pre-, pro-, re-	no	The professional troubleshooter took the precaution of reconfiguring our computer network.
Any prefix or suffix added to a proper noun or proper adjective	yes	We found a Web site about education funding in the post-Reagan administrations.
Any prefix or suffix that creates a word with a double vowel or triple consonant	yes	Victor was ultra-agitated by the bell-like error sound his system made.

If a word would be liable to misinterpretation without a hyphen, use one even with a prefix like *pre-, pro-,* or *re-.*

I don't know how my uncle **recovered** his composure after my aunt **re-covered** his recliner in purple vinyl.

Dashes

▶ **Use dashes to set off explanatory, supplementary, or parenthetical material in sentences.** Parentheses may be used for the same purpose. (See Lesson 5.)

> She had clicked on the bane of every Web surfer—a dead link.

> Before e-mail—way back around the dawn of time—people had to rely on telephones and the postal service to stay in touch.

Many word-processing programs allow you to insert dashes. Check the character maps or help file for inserting an *em dash*. If you can't find a dash, type two hyphens (–) with no space before or after.

Ellipses

▶ **Use an ellipsis (also called ellipsis points) to indicate the omission of part of a quotation.** An ellipses is three spaced periods (. . ., not ...) preceded and followed by spaces. If an ellipsis is used at the end of a sentence, include a period before the ellipsis.

PROFESSIONAL MODELS

> Where a calculator on the ENIAC . . . weighs 30 tons, computers in the future may . . . perhaps weigh 1½ tons.
>
> —*Popular Mechanics*, 1949

> This is why I'm worried about this Millennium Bug. . . . It's a glitch in computer software that, when transmitted via the bite of a mosquito, can cause severe chills and death.
>
> No, sorry, that's malaria.
>
> —Dave Barry, "Come the Millennium, Use the Stairs"

In fiction or informal writing, an ellipsis can also be used to indicate that a thought trails off.

> Evan could have kicked himself. If only he hadn't pressed DELETE . . .

PUNCTUATION

❷ Practice and Apply

A. CONCEPT CHECK: Hyphens, Dashes, and Ellipses

Write the words before and after every punctuation mistake in these sentences, inserting the correct punctuation.

Simply Delicious

1. Urban legends sensational stories that seem plausible but cannot be proved are a part of modern life.
2. These stories spread rapidly by word of mouth, but increas ingly they now appear on the Internet.
3. One well known legend is about a $250 cookie recipe.
4. When a server at a store's café told a patron that the recipe for the great tasting cookies she'd just eaten was only "two-fifty," the diner charged it to her credit card.
5. She was surprised when she received a bill for $250-she thought the server had meant $2.50!
6. The store's credit department refused to remove the charge, so the expatron decided to take revenge.
7. She e-mailed the story and the recipe to her friends, and now they're posted on many Web-sites.
8. Researchers say that this urban legend has been "traced back as far as 1948. . . . [and] shows no sign of waning."
9. No-one knows how this very popular story got started, but the recipe makes a huge batch of tasty cookies.
10. Half a batch will yield about fifty six cookies.

➡ **For a SELF-CHECK and more practice, see the EXERCISE BANK, p. 317.**

B. PROOFREADING: Paragraph

Proofread the following paragraph, correcting the use of hyphens, dashes, and ellipses as you did in exercise A above.

Chains of Letters

Chain letters—letters that each receiver is supposed to copy and send to others are no longer some-thing you receive just by snail mail. Now you can receive these ever annoying letters via e-mail too. One letter now making the rounds promises that if you send the letter to 11 people, you will automatically receive a funny video-clip. Of course, this is ridic-ulous. One researcher reacted with this tongue in cheek comment: "I can't say enough in appreciation of. . . . technology that makes it possible for a vide-o clip to appear . . . simply by forwarding an email."

Apostrophes

❶ Here's the Idea

Possessives

▶ **Use an apostrophe in the possessive form of a noun.**

Where to Put the Apostrophe	
Type of Possessive	**Examples**
Singular noun	author's book, Tess's journal
Plural noun ending in _s_	senators' votes, the Smiths' house
Plural noun not ending in _s_	people's choice, children's toys
Compound noun (singular or plural)	**Singular:** brother-in-law's **Plural:** brothers-in-law's
Two nouns, joint possession	**Singular:** Gilbert and Sullivan's operettas **Plural:** mothers and sons' picnic
Two nouns, individual possession	**Singular:** Doug's and Delia's desks **Plural:** mothers' and sons' meetings
Indefinite pronoun	everyone's business, another's problem
Indefinite pronoun with _else_	someone else's turn, no one else's story

There is one major exception to the rule for forming possessives of singular nouns. The possessive form of a classical or biblical name that ends in s is often made by adding only an apostrophe.

Mars'   Xerxes'   Jesus'   Moses'

Never use an apostrophe in a possessive personal pronoun (_hers, his, theirs, yours, ours, its_). Remember that _it's_ is a contraction meaning "it is."

▶ **Use the possessive forms of nouns expressing measures of time or amount when they precede other nouns.**

one month**'s** delay   two month**s'** delay
one dollar**'s** worth   ten dollar**s'** worth

Contractions and Other Omissions

▶ **Use apostrophes in contractions to show the omission of letters.**

    didn*'*t = did not   she*'*ll = she will   it*'*s = it is

▶ **Use apostrophes to show where sounds are omitted in poetry or in dialects.**

> **LITERARY MODELS**
>
> Make the best o' things the way you find 'em, says I—
> that's my motto.
>
>   —Mark Twain, *The Adventures of Huckleberry Finn*
>
> Time, thou anticipat'st my dread exploits.
> The flighty purpose never is o'ertook
> Unless the deed go with it.
>
>   —William Shakespeare, *Macbeth*

▶ **Use an apostrophe to indicate missing digits in a year number.**

    the class of *'*09   way back in *'*49

Special Plurals

▶ **Use an apostrophe and s to form the plural of an individual letter, numeral, word referred to as a word, or an abbreviation containing periods.**

    He'd better mind his *p***'s** and *q***'s.**

    So what if they hold Ph.D.**'s** in math? Their 4**'s** look like 9**'s.**

▶ **Any punctuation that follows a word that ends with an apostrophe should be placed after the apostrophe.**

    The software was the **girls'**, but the computer was their **parents'.**

Don't use an apostrophe in the plural form of a year number; the correct usage is "the 1990s," not "the 1990's."

❷ Practice and Apply

A. CONCEPT CHECK: Apostrophes

Find the words in which apostrophes are omitted or incorrectly used. Rewrite the words correctly. If a sentence contains no errors in the use of apostrophes, write *Correct*.

A Web Site in Mind

1. Every decade seems to have a name, and the 00s may well become known as the Internet decade.

2. Youre probably aware that there are thousands of Web sites on a wide variety of topics.

3. You can tag along on Lewis's and Clark's expedition to the Pacific Northwest.

4. You can learn about Homer's tales of Odysseus' journeys.

5. After enjoying other peoples sites, you might decide to create one of your own.

6. Of course, you don't want your site to be like everybody elses'.

7. First, decide on your site's theme and purpose.

8. Will you give advice, suggest strategies for turning C grades into As, or challenge visitors to games?

9. Think of a catchy title that will grab a browsers attention.

10. Update your site frequently; don't be caught offering last years news!

➜ For a SELF-CHECK and more practice, see the EXERCISE BANK, p. 317.

B. PROOFREADING: Apostrophe Errors

Check the use of apostrophes in possessives and contractions in the following paragraph. Make any necessary corrections.

Want to Make a Splash?

(1) Whats your goal for your Web site? **(2)** Its probably to entice visitors to your site rather than someone's else. **(3)** If that's the case, you might try to draw peoples attention to your site with a splash page. **(4)** A site's splash page is like it's home page, but the splash page has less information, only one link, and a lot more pizzazz. **(5)** A splash page catches a browsers eye with spectacular graphics and a short, interesting message.

PUNCTUATION

Quotation Marks and Italics

❶ Here's the Idea

Direct Quotations

▶ **Use quotation marks to mark the beginning and end of a direct quotation.** The first word of a quotation introduced by words such as *she said* is usually capitalized. In a divided quotation the first word of the second part is capitalized only if it begins a new *sentence*.

"How can we find our way through all these booths?" fretted the anxious game developer at her first trade show.

Her business partner calmly said, "Don't worry. I have a map."

"But there are so many booths," she worried, "and so little time."

According to the brochure, the show featured "more than 10,001 great game and consumer software titles."

Quotation Marks with Other Punctuation		
Mark	**Where Does It Go?**	**Example**
Period or comma	inside quotation marks	"Let's see," Elena said. "Let's try to do it this way."
Colon or semicolon	outside quotation marks	Forget that list of "must-sees"; Allan has deemed only the following places "tourist-worthy": Meteor Crater, Monument Valley, and the Grand Canyon.
Question mark or exclamation point	inside quotation marks if the quotation is a question or exclamatory sentence	"You're going where?" my mom steamed. "I don't think so!"
	outside quotation marks if the sentence is a question or exclamatory sentence	Did D. H. Lawrence write the story "Araby"? No! James Joyce wrote "Araby"!

Don't set off an indirect quotation with quotation marks.

Ben said that the trade show was the best one he'd ever attended.

► **To set off a quotation within another quotation, use single quotation marks.**

"He said, 'I'll be back in two minutes,' so I'm going to wait for him," Tasha insisted.

If the inside quotation ends or begins the main quotation, the double quotation marks should be placed outside the single quotation marks.

"You can expect him in two hours if he said 'I'll be back in two minutes,'" laughed Dmitry.

► **If a quotation consists of more than one paragraph, each paragraph should begin with a quotation mark. However, a closing quotation mark should not be used until the end of the entire quotation.**

LITERARY MODEL

"My good uncle, it was my pride and my stubbornness that brought all this about, for had I not urged you to war with Sir Launcelot your subjects would not now be in revolt. Alas, that Sir Launcelot is not here, for he would soon drive them out! And it is at Sir Launcelot's hands that I suffer my own death: the wound which he dealt me has reopened. I would not wish it otherwise, because is he not the greatest and gentlest of knights?

"I know that by noon I shall be dead, and I repent bitterly that I may not be reconciled to Sir Launcelot; therefore I pray you, good uncle, give me pen, paper, and ink so that I may write to him."

—Sir Thomas Malory, *Le Morte d'Arthur*

launcelot@camelot.uk.gov

Titles and Names

Quotation Marks or Italics?	
Use quotation marks for these titles.	
Short story	"A Sunrise on the Veld" by Doris Lessing
Chapter	Chapter 10: "Other Punctuation Marks"
Article or essay	"Writing as an Act of Hope" by Isabel Allende
TV episode	"The Trouble with Tribbles" (*Star Trek*)
Short poem	"1996" by Rabindranath Tagore
Use italics for these titles and names.	
Book	*The Waves* by Virginia Woolf
Newspaper	*New York Times*
Magazine	*Wired*
TV series	*Star Trek*
Film or play	*Romeo and Juliet* by William Shakespeare
Vehicle (ship, train, aircraft, spacecraft)	*Titanic, 20th Century Limited, Air Force One, Apollo 11*

If you're using a typewriter or writing in longhand, the correct way to indicate italicized words is to underline them.

Other Uses

▶ **Use quotation marks to enclose slang words, unusual expressions, technical terms, and definitions of words.**

Most people know that *RAM* stands for **"random access memory."**

A **"bitstorm,"** the digital equivalent of gridlock, occurs when there is too much on-line traffic.

Writers sometimes place quotation marks around words to show sarcasm or disagreement.

These **"antiques"** were manufactured last month and **"aged"** with dirt and wood stain.

Since quotation marks can indicate sarcasm, don't use them to emphasize words. Would you want to get your hair done at a shop with this sign?

"BEAUTY" PARLOUR

► **Italicize an unfamiliar foreign word or phrase or a word referred to as a word.**

I know he thinks it's true, but it's just a *conte de fée*—a fairy tale.

Bridal and *bridle* are homophones.

❷ Practice and Apply

A. CONCEPT CHECK: Quotation Marks and Italics

Write the words affected by each error in the use of quotation marks or italics, correcting the mistake. Also correct any capitalization errors you find.

Great Job!

1. According to the article Meet a Real Game Boy in *Time for Kids,* Shannon O'Neil may have the perfect job.
2. As a game counselor for a video-game company, he helps find *bugs,* or program errors, in new games.
3. After I read the article, I asked a friend, "don't you wish you had a job like that?"
4. She said, "There are all kinds of computer jobs. Just read the book Careers in Computing."
5. She said that "she wanted to work with computers."
6. "Well," I said, "I want a job like O'Neil's because he gets paid to play games. What could be better"?

➜ For a SELF-CHECK and more practice, see the EXERCISE BANK, p. 318.

B. REVISION: Using Italics or Quotation Marks

Rewrite the sentences in this paragraph, revising the punctuation and the use of italics as needed.

Home, Sweet Home Office!

(1) "Does the word homework mean only "after-school assignments' to you"? Ms. Barnes, my counselor, asked me. **(2)** "The idea of homework could take on a whole new meaning if you enter the work force as a telecommuter, she said. **(3)** "Think about it, she continued. **(4)** "Telecommuters manage their own time, wear what they want, and, best of all, can live wherever they want"! **(5)** However, in his book Silicon Snake Oil, Clifford Stoll reports that "the lack of meetings and personal interaction isolates workers and reduces loyalty". **(6)** I told Ms. Barnes, I'll have to wait and see if telecommuting is for me. Right now I have some other homework to do."

Parentheses and Brackets

❶ Here's the Idea

Parentheses

▶ **Use parentheses to set off supplementary or explanatory material that is added to a sentence.**

> Tech support asked the customer to bring his CPU **(central processing unit)** in to be repaired.

A complete sentence enclosed in parentheses within another sentence does not begin with a capital letter or end with a period. A parenthetical sentence that stands alone is punctuated and capitalized like any other sentence.

> Instead, the customer brought in a packing box **(tech support had told him the CPU was the box that held the disk drive).**

> Esme compiled a list of Web sites that feature job-hunting tips. **(See Appendix B.)**

▶ **Use parentheses to set off certain references and numerical information.**

Parentheses: Other Uses	
Use	**Example**
To identify a source of information	The South African writer Nadine Gordimer was 15 when she published her first short story (*Language of Literature* 1301).
To enclose figures or letters that identify items in a series	Before you call tech support, be sure that (1) your computer is plugged in, (2) your computer is turned on, and (3) your power supply is functioning.
To set off numerical information such as area codes and dates	To learn more about the Software Swapmeet (Nov. 3–5), call (800) 555–3333.

Brackets

▶ **Use brackets to enclose an explanation or comment added to quoted material.**

> In 1981 Bill Gates said, "640K **[of RAM]** ought to be enough for anybody."

▶ **Use brackets to enclose parenthetical material that appears within parentheses.**

> The number of job listings on the Web is growing each month. (See page 35 [figure 3] for a detailed chart.)

❷ Practice and Apply

A. CONCEPT CHECK: Parentheses and Brackets

Write these sentences, adding parentheses and brackets where needed.

> **Job Hunt**
> **1.** If you are looking for a high-tech job either a summer job or full-time employment, you may find it on the Internet.
> **2.** You can research job opportunities online. (Think of the Internet as a global employment agency.
> **3.** You can also use high-tech strategies to find work (Freeman and Hart, "Internet Job Searching".
> **4.** If you post your résumé on the Net, be sure it is Internet compatible (with no italics, boldface, or fancy typefaces.
> **5.** You might post your résumé in data banks. (Some résumé banks charge a small fee [$20 to $50 will keep your résumé active for a year; others are free.)

➡ **For a SELF-CHECK and more practice, see the EXERCISE BANK, p. 319.**

B. REVISING: Using Parentheses and Brackets

Rewrite this paragraph, using brackets and parentheses where needed to make the meaning clearer. Correct any other errors.

> **Giving Help to Those Who Need It Most!**
> Ann Lewis staffs the help desk at a computer firm, where (you can imagine she gets a lot of unusual calls. Once she received a frantic call from a father who thought his son's pet mouse ironically named Internet was nesting inside the CPU. (the family later found Internet snuggled in a laundry basket.) Then there was the Chicago coffee lover who thought her CD-ROM drive was a cup holder. (the drive is probably still drying out, but what an aroma)! Every shift promises a few callers who want to share news about the latest Elvis e-sighting (last week, on-line, from Poughkeepsie.

Grammar in Literature

Effective Punctuation

Writers use a variety of punctuation marks to

- control the rhythm of their sentences
- show relationships between phrases
- emphasize words and phrases

Notice how Isabel Allende used semicolons, quotation marks, and dashes to clarify and enhance her account of the writing and publication of her novel *The House of the Spirits.*

FROM Writing ISABEL ALLENDE
as an Act of Hope

For a year I wrote every night with no hesitation or plan. Words came out like a violent torrent. I had thousands of untold words stuck in my chest, threatening to choke me. The long silence of exile was turning me to stone; I needed to open a valve and let the river of secret words find a way out. At the end of that year there were five hundred pages on my table; it didn't look like a letter anymore. On the other hand, my grandfather had died long before, so the spiritual message had already reached him. So I thought, "Well, maybe in this way I can tell some other people about him, and about my country, and about my family and myself." So I just organized it a little bit, tied the manuscript with a pink ribbon for luck, and took it to some publishers.

The spirit of my grandmother was protecting the book from the very beginning, so it was refused everywhere in Venezuela. Nobody wanted it—it was too long; I was a woman; nobody knew me. So I sent it by mail to Spain, and the book was published there. It had reviews, and it was translated and distributed in other countries.

In the process of writing the anecdotes of the past, and recalling the emotions and pains of my fate, and telling part of the history of my country, I found that life became more comprehensible and the world more tolerable. I felt that my roots had been recovered and that during that patient exercise of daily writing I had also recovered my own soul. I felt at that time that writing was unavoidable—that I couldn't keep away from it.

Semicolons join related independent clauses, establishing the rhythm of the two sentences.

Quotation marks set Allende's words to herself off from the words addressed to her readers.

Dash introduces a series of rhythmic independent clauses separated by **semicolons.**

Dash introduces a subtle but important clarification of the preceding clause.

Using Punctuation to Vary Your Writing	
Semicolons	Use them to join independent clauses. Semicolons convey a less emphatic rhythm than periods.
Quotation marks	Use them to indicate dialogue. Note how Allende used quotation marks to set off her inner dialogue.
Dashes	Use them to signal diversions in thought and to set off explanatory material.

PRACTICE AND APPLY: Revising with Punctuation

The following paragraph contains a lot of short, choppy sentences. Use punctuation to revise and improve it, following the directions below. You may want to make slight changes in wording as well.

(1) Every night my brother yells at the computer as if it can hear him. (2) It's not that the computer doesn't work properly. (3) After all, it's brand-new and state-of-the-art. (4) The problem is simple. (5) My brother is the most impatient person on the planet. (6) He wants to download a huge sound file. (7) He doesn't want to wait five minutes to hear it. (8) He decides to watch a long video clip, but halfway through the download he decides he's got better things to do. (9) Then he fumes when the computer takes a while to stop the process! (10) He thinks he needs a new computer. (11) I think I need something else, namely, a new brother.

1. In sentence 1, add a direct quotation from the brother's tirade at the computer.
2. Combine sentences 2 and 3.
3. Combine sentences 4 and 5.
4. Combine sentences 6 and 7.
5. In sentence 8, delete the conjunction and join the independent clauses with a semicolon.
6. Rewrite sentence 11 to include a dash.

When you have revised the paragraph, read the two versions aloud with a partner and discuss the differences between them.

Working Portfolio Choose a piece of writing from your portfolio and revise it by varying the punctuation. Use the punctuation marks mentioned in the table above, as well as others discussed in this chapter.

A. Other Punctuation Read the following paragraphs. Then answer the questions below.

You Are Not Alone—Computers Must Pass Tests Too!

As a high school student, you have lots of **(1)** <u>test taking</u> experience **(2)** <u>you</u> may even have taken a test or quiz today. You've probably used some of these techniques to prepare for a **(3)** <u>test</u> studying notes, reviewing textbooks, and listening to **(4)** <u>tape recorded lectures</u>.

(5) <u>Students arent the only ones taking tests</u>; computers have to pass **(6)** <u>"benchmarks"</u> **(7)** <u>rigorous performance tests</u>. Benchmarks measure computer **(8)** <u>software's and hardware's</u> performance. A benchmark for hardware tests a machine's speed and capabilities; a benchmark for software gauges task-oriented performance. According to the *Microsoft Encarta Encyclopedia,* "The design of fair benchmarks is something of an art **(9)** <u>because. . . .</u> hardware and software can exhibit widely variable performance under different **(10)** <u>conditions"</u>.

1. What kind of punctuation should be inserted between the two underlined words?
2. What kind of punctuation is needed before the word *you?*
3. What kind of punctuation is needed after the word *test?*
4. Where is punctuation needed?
5. Where is punctuation needed?
6. Why is the word enclosed in quotation marks?
7. What punctuation should be used to separate the underlined words from the rest of the sentence?
8. Why does each of the underlined nouns contain an apostrophe and s?
9. Is this punctuation correct? Explain.
10. Is the end of the sentence punctuated correctly? Explain.

B. Quotation Marks and Italics, Parentheses and Brackets Proofread the paragraph below. Write the words before and after each punctuation error, correcting the error.

STUDENT MODEL

Computers seem to be everywhere (in homes, businesses, and even TV shows and movies.) Yet with the increased use of the Internet, many people (even those without computers [perhaps even you) fear that their privacy is being violated. In his book Web Psychos, Stalkers, and Pranksters [Coriolis Group, 1997], Michael Banks discusses ways to protect oneself. In Chapter 4, *Where Do They Get My Information?,* he lists types of personal data you may not wish to reveal, including (1) name, age, and address; (2) employer; (3) account numbers; and 4 medical history. He says, "People are too free with their personal information (they reveal too much about themselves) online. His advice can help you protect your anonymity (yes, it is possible.) and enjoy the Web.

For each underscored group of words, choose the best revisions.

There were fewer than <u>twenty six students</u> in Professor Domto's
(1)
Japanese <u>class however</u>, they were scattered among four schools. Distance
(2)
education—one teacher but many <u>locations) is made</u> possible by
(3)
<u>technology: interactive video,</u> computers, satellites, e-mail, <u>Internet-access</u>
(4)   (5)
<u>and fax</u> machines.

Technology plays an important role in <u>young peoples education</u>. In his
(6)
article <u>Distance Education,</u> Michael Moore explains, "Reaching a large
(7)
number of students with relatively few <u>teachers. . . . provides</u> a cost-
(8)
effective way of using limited academic <u>resources."</u>
(9)
Years ago, in the educational journal *Electronic Learning* <u>[May/June</u>
(10)
<u>1994],</u> Alan November predicted that teachers would one day connect
students in networks throughout the world. That prediction has come
true. Who knows what the future holds?

1. A. twentysix students
   B. twenty-six students
   C. twenty-six-students
   D. Correct as is

2. A. class; however
   B. class: however
   C. class, however
   D. Correct as is

3. A. locations is made
   B. locations—is made
   C. locations, is made
   D. Correct as is

4. A. technology; interactive video;
   B. technology: interactive video:
   C. technology; interactive video:
   D. Correct as is

5. A. Internet access, and fax
   B. Internet-access; and fax
   C. Internet access—and fax
   D. Correct as is

6. A. young peoples' education
   B. young people's education
   C. young peoples" education
   D. Correct as is

7. A. *Distance Education,*
   B. (Distance Education),
   C. "Distance Education,"
   D. Correct as is

8. A. teachers . . . provides
   B. teachers...provides
   C. teachers—provides
   D. Correct as is

9. A. resources".
   B. resources:"
   C. resources"
   D. Correct as is

10. A. May/June 1994,
    B. —May/June 1994—
    C. (May/June 1994),
    D. Correct as is

Student Help Desk

Other Punctuation Marks at a Glance

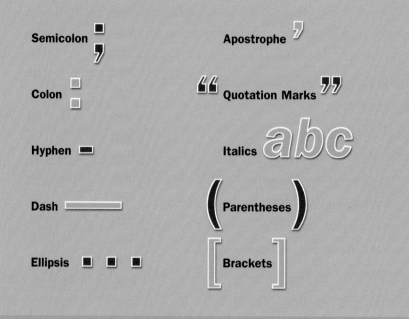

Semicolon

Apostrophe

Colon

Quotation Marks

Hyphen

Italics *abc*

Dash

(Parentheses)

Ellipsis

[Brackets]

Avoid Common Errors Punctuate Properly

For punctuation perfection . . .	Correction
Don't substitute a comma for a semicolon.	You edit the sports page, I'll tackle the advice column. *;*
Don't overuse dashes.	*thought she* Paula knew—at least she thought she knew—how Tameo—the subject of her story—a sympathetic story, really—thought, but she never asked.
Don't set off an indirect quotation with quotation marks.	Trudy told Ramon that he "would have to review the school play."
Don't use parentheses and brackets interchangeably.	Winston Churchill said, "Our task is not only to win the battle [for the Maginot Line]—but to win the War [World War II]."

Title-Sorting Machine

Quotation Marks or Italics?

Quotation Marks

Short story
Chapter of a book
Article
Essay
TV episode
Short poem
Song

Italics

Book
Newspaper
Magazine
TV series
Film
Play
Long musical work
Vehicle (ship, train, etc.)

The Bottom Line

Checklist for Other Punctuation Marks

Have I . . .

____ used appropriate punctuation marks?

____ used a variety of punctuation marks?

____ made sure that clauses joined by semicolons are independent clauses?

____ used a dictionary to double-check hyphenated words?

____ spaced ellipsis points properly?

____ placed apostrophes correctly in possessives?

____ placed other punctuation correctly in relation to quotation marks?

____ included a closing quotation mark at the end of each quotation?

____ included closing parentheses and brackets where needed?

Quick-Fix Editing Machine

You've worked diligently on your assignment. Don't let misplaced commas, sentence fragments, and missing details lower your grade. Use this Quick-Fix Editing Guide to help you detect grammatical errors and make your writing more precise.

Fixing Errors

Improving Style

QUICK FIX

1 Sentence Fragments

What's the problem? Part of a sentence has been left out.
Why does it matter? A fragment doesn't convey a complete thought.
What should you do about it? Find out what's missing and add it.

What's the Problem?

Quick Fix

What's the Problem?	Quick Fix
A. The subject is missing. Has a dance recital tonight.	Add a subject. **My little sister** has a dance recital tonight.
B. A verb is missing. My mother up all night sewing her costume.	Add a verb. My mother **sat** up all night sewing her costume.
C. A helping verb is missing. My sister dance the part of the leading ladybug.	Add a helping verb. My sister **will** dance the part of the leading ladybug.
D. Both a subject and a verb are missing. At the end of the recital.	Add a subject and a verb to make an independent clause. **She is scheduled** to perform at the end of the recital.
E. A subordinate clause is treated as if it were a sentence. Since she goes to all my soccer games.	Combine the sentence fragment with an independent clause. **I feel I ought to go,** since she goes to all my soccer games. <div align="center">OR</div>Delete the conjunction. ~~Since~~ **She** goes to all my soccer games.

For more help, see Chapter 3, pp. 89–91.

QUICK FIX

② Run-On Sentences

What's the problem? Two or more sentences have been run together.

Why does it matter? A run-on sentence doesn't show clearly where one idea ends and another begins.

What should you do about it? Find the best way to separate the ideas or to show the proper relationship between them.

What's the Problem?

A. The end mark separating two distinct thoughts is missing.

In 1972, a company called Atari created the first video game it was called Pong.

B. Two complete thoughts are separated only by a comma.

By modern standards it was a very simple game, it quickly achieved great popularity.

Quick Fix

Add an end mark to divide the run-on sentence and start a new sentence.

In 1972, a company called Atari created the first video game. **It** was called Pong.

Add a conjunction.

By modern standards it was a very simple game, **but** it quickly achieved great popularity.

OR

Change the comma to a semicolon.

By modern standards it was a very simple game**;** it quickly achieved great popularity.

OR

Replace the comma with an end mark, and start a new sentence.

By modern standards it was a very simple game. **It** quickly achieved great popularity.

OR

Change one of the independent clauses into a subordinate clause.

Although it was a very simple game by modern standards, it quickly achieved great popularity.

For more help, see Chapter 3, pp. 90–91.

3 Subject-Verb Agreement

What's the problem? A verb does not agree with its subject in number.

Why does it matter? The reader may regard your work as careless.

What should you do about it? Identify the subject and use a verb that matches it in number.

What's the Problem?

Quick Fix

What's the Problem?	Quick Fix
A. A verb agrees with the object of a preposition rather than with its subject.	Mentally block out the prepositional phrase, and make the verb agree with the true subject.
That house with the **shutters have stood** empty for 40 years.	That **house** with the shutters **has stood** empty for 40 years.
B. A verb agrees with a phrase that comes between the subject and the verb.	Mentally block out the phrase, and make the verb agree with the true subject.
The shutters, like the **porch, is crying** out for repair.	The **shutters,** like the porch, **are crying** out for repair.
C. A verb doesn't agree with an indefinite-pronoun subject.	Decide whether the pronoun is singular or plural, and make the verb agree with it.
One of the doors **are hanging** from a single lonely hinge.	**One** of the doors **is hanging** from a single lonely hinge.
D. A verb in a contraction doesn't agree with its subject.	Use a contraction that agrees with the subject.
It **don't** look as if anyone minds the bats flying in and out of the attic.	It **doesn't** look as if anyone minds the bats flying in and out of the attic.
E. A singular verb is used with a compound subject that contains *and*.	Use a plural verb.
My **sister and I gets** a kick out of watching them fly around.	My **sister and I get** a kick out of watching them fly around.

For more help, see Chapter 5, pp. 130–137.

What's the Problem?

F. A verb doesn't agree with the nearest part of a compound subject containing *or* or *nor*.

Neither the windows nor the **door keep** the rain out.

G. A verb doesn't agree with the true subject in a sentence beginning with *here* or *there*.

There **is possums living** under the front porch.

H. A singular subject ending in *s*, *es*, or *ics* is mistaken for a plural.

The good **news are** that someone is planning to fix the house soon.

I. A collective noun referring to a single unit is treated as plural (or one referring to individuals is treated as singular).

The whole possum **family go** for a walk every evening.

J. A period of time isn't treated as a single unit when it should be.

Forty years are a long time.

For more help, see Chapter 5, pp. 136–143.

Quick Fix

Use a verb that agrees with the part of the compound subject closest to the verb.

Neither the windows nor the **door keeps** the rain out.

Mentally turn the sentence around so that the true subject comes first, and make the verb agree with it.

There **are possums living** under the front porch.

Watch out for these nouns and use a singular verb with them.

The good **news is** that someone is planning to fix the house soon.

If the collective noun refers to a single unit, use a singular verb.

The whole possum **family goes** for a walk every evening.

Use a singular verb whenever the subject refers to a period of time as a single unit.

Forty years is a long time.

QUICK FIX

④ Pronoun Reference Problems

What's the problem? A pronoun does not agree in number or gender with its antecedent, or the antecedent is unclear.

Why does it matter? Lack of agreement or unclear antecedents can cause confusion.

What should you do about it? Find the antecedent and make the pronoun agree with it, or rewrite the sentence to make the antecedent clear.

What's the Problem?

Quick Fix

A. A pronoun doesn't agree with an indefinite-pronoun antecedent.

Soon, **all** television sets will be made so thin that you'll be able to hang **it** on a wall.

Decide whether the indefinite pronoun is singular or plural, and make the pronoun agree with it.

Soon, **all** television sets will be made so thin that you'll be able to hang **them** on a wall.

B. A pronoun doesn't agree with the nearest part of a compound subject joined by *nor* or *or*.

Neither my mother nor my **grandparents** want to give up **her** old TV set just yet.

Find the nearest noun and make the pronoun agree with it.

Neither my mother nor my **grandparents** want to give up **their** old TV set just yet.

C. A pronoun doesn't have an antecedent.

In an article on the future of television, **it** predicted mirror-thin televisions in every living room.

Rewrite the sentence to eliminate the pronoun.

An **article** on the future of television predicted mirror-thin televisions in every living room.

D. A pronoun's antecedent is vague or misleading.

It seems **they** see changes happening soon.

Change the pronoun to a specific noun.

It seems that the **authors** see changes happening soon.

E. A pronoun could refer to more than one noun.

I told my **brother** and my **cousin** about the article, and **he** is eager to buy one of these televisions.

Substitute a noun for the pronoun to make the reference specific.

I told my brother and my cousin about the article, and my **brother** is eager to buy one of these televisions.

For more help, see Chapter 6, pp. 160–163.

5 Incorrect Pronoun Case

What's the problem? A pronoun is in the wrong case.

Why does it matter? Readers may regard your writing, especially in formal situations, as sloppy and careless.

What should you do about it? Identify how the pronoun is being used and replace it with the correct form.

What's the Problem?	Quick Fix
A. A pronoun that follows a linking verb is in the wrong case. I think my mysterious admirer **is him.**	Always use the nominative case after a linking verb. I think my mysterious admirer **is he.** **OR** Reword the sentence. I think **he is** my mysterious admirer.
B. A pronoun used as the object of a preposition is not in the objective case. On Valentine's Day, several people sent cards **to** my brother and **I.**	Always use the objective case for a word used as the object of a preposition. On Valentine's Day, several people sent cards **to** my brother and **me.**
C. The wrong case is used in a comparison. None of my friends were as surprised as **me** to see the flowers on the porch.	Complete the comparison with the appropriate case. None of my friends were as surprised as **I [was]** to see the flowers outside.
D. *Who* or *whom* is used incorrectly. I asked myself **whom could have sent** me a bathtub full of flowers.	Figure out whether the pronoun is used as a subject (*who*) or as an object (*whom*). I asked myself **who could have sent** me a bathtub full of flowers.
E. A pronoun followed by an appositive is in the wrong case. **Us girls** like to get valentines, but I was a little embarrassed.	Mentally eliminate the appositive to test for the correct case. **We** ~~girls~~ like to get valentines, but I was a little embarrassed.

For more help, see Chapter 6, pp. 152–159.

6 *Who* and *Whom*

What's the problem? A form of the pronoun *who* or *whoever* is used incorrectly.

Why does it matter? The correct use of *who, whom, whoever,* and *whomever* in formal situations gives the impression that the speaker or the writer is careful and knowledgeable.

What should you do about it? Decide how the pronoun functions in the sentence to determine which form to use.

What's the Problem?

Quick Fix

What's the Problem?	Quick Fix
A. *Whom* is incorrectly used as a subject. **Whom is running** for mayor?	Use *who* as the subject of a sentence. **Who is running** for mayor?
B. *Who* is incorrectly used as the object of a preposition. **For who** will you vote?	Use *whom* as the object of a preposition. **For whom** will you vote?
C. *Who* is incorrectly used as a direct object. **Who do** you **like** better?	Use *whom* as a direct object. **Whom do** you **like** better?
D. *Whomever* is incorrectly used as the subject of a sentence or a clause. **Whomever wins** the election will take office in the fall.	*Whomever* is used only as an object. Use *whoever* as a subject. **Whoever wins** the election will take office in the fall.
E. *Who's* is incorrectly used as the possessive form of *who*. **Who's job** is it to bake the welcome cake?	Always use *whose* to show possession. **Whose job** is it to bake the welcome cake?

For more help, see Chapter 6, pp. 157–159.

⑦ Confusing Comparisons

What's the problem? The wrong form of a modifier is used in making a comparision.

Why does it matter? Incorrectly worded comparisons can create confusion and may be illogical.

What should you do about it? Delete or add words to make the comparison clear.

What's the Problem?

Quick Fix

QUICK FIX

What's the Problem?	Quick Fix
A. Both -er and more or -est and most were used in making a comparison.	**Eliminate the double comparison.**
It was a very old movie, and it was **more funnier** than I expected it to be.	It was a very old movie, and it was ~~more~~ funnier than I expected it to be.
The other night, I saw the **most funniest** movie I've seen in months.	The other night, I saw the ~~most~~ funniest movie I've seen in months.
B. The word other is missing in a comparison where it is logically needed.	**Add the missing word.**
The star, Buster Keaton, was better than any movie actor I'd ever seen.	The star, Buster Keaton, was better than any **other** movie actor I'd ever seen.
C. A superlative form is used where a comparative form is needed.	**When comparing two things, use the comparative form.**
Film fans argue about what is **funniest:** silent comedy or comedy with sound.	Film fans argue about what is **funnier:** silent comedy or comedy with sound.
D. A comparative form is used where a superlative form is needed.	**When comparing more than two things, use the superlative form.**
I think that Buster Keaton is the **better** of all the great old-time comics.	I think that Buster Keaton is the **best** of all the great old-time comics.

For more help, see Chapter 7, pp. 180–185.

8 Verb Forms and Tenses

What's the problem? The wrong form or tense of a verb is used.

Why does it matter? Readers may regard your work as careless or find it confusing.

What should you do about it? Replace the incorrect verb with the correct form or tense.

What's the Problem?

Quick Fix

What's the Problem?	Quick Fix
A. The wrong form of a verb is used with a helping verb. Last winter, some birds **had flew** up into our air conditioner.	Use a participle form with a helping verb. Last winter, some birds **had flown** up into our air conditioner.
B. A helping verb is missing. They **gone** into the vents while the machine was turned off.	Add a helping verb. They **had gone** into the vents while the machine was turned off.
C. An irregular verb form is spelled incorrectly. This summer we realized that the mother **had builded** a nest in there.	Look up the correct spelling and use it. This summer we realized that the mother **had built** a nest in there.
D. A past participle is used incorrectly. We **gone** outside to get a closer look at the nest and found three eggs.	To show the past, use the past form of the verb. We **went** outside to get a closer look at the nest and found three eggs. **OR** Change the verb to the past perfect form by adding a helping verb. We **had gone** to get a closer look at the nest and found three eggs.
E. Different tenses are used in the same sentence without a valid reason. We **discussed** it and **decide** not to turn on the air conditioner this year.	Use the same tense throughout the sentence. We **discussed** it and **decided** not to turn on the air conditioner this year.

For more help, see Chapter 4, pp. 104–110, 118.

⑨ Misplaced and Dangling Modifiers

What's the problem? A modifying word or phrase is in the wrong place, or it doesn't modify any other word in the sentence.

Why does it matter? The sentence can be confusing or unintentionally funny.

What should you do about it? Move the modifying word or phrase closer to the word it modifies, or add a word for it to modify.

What's the Problem?

What's the Problem?	Quick Fix
A. The adverb *even* or *only* is not placed close to the word it modifies.	Move the adverb to make your meaning clear.
Plants and animals can survive on the edge of **only** Antarctica.	Plant and animal life can exist **only** on the edge of Antarctica.
The climate is **even** too harsh a little distance inland.	The climate is too harsh **even** a little distance inland.
B. A prepositional phrase is too far from the word it modifies.	Move the prepositional phrase closer to the word it modifies.
During the summer **in Antarctica** about 2,000 people **live.**	During the summer about 2,000 people **live in Antarctica.**
C. A participial phrase is too far from the word it modifies.	Move the participial phrase closer to the word or phrase it modifies.
Waddling on the shore and plunging into the water, zoologists study flocks of **penguins.**	Zoologists study flocks of **penguins waddling on the shore and plunging into the water.**
D. A participial phrase does not relate to anything in the sentence.	Reword the sentence by adding a word or phrase for the participial phrase to refer to.
Recording their activity on videotape, the **penguins'** activities are analyzed.	**Recording the penguins' activity on videotape,** the **scientists** analyze what they see.

For more help, see Chapter 7, pp. 187–188.

10 Missing or Misplaced Commas

What's the problem? Commas are missing or are used incorrectly.

Why does it matter? Incorrect use of commas can make sentences difficult to follow.

What should you do about it? Determine where commas are needed and add or delete them wherever it is necessary.

What's the Problem?

Quick Fix

What's the Problem?	Quick Fix
A. A comma is missing before the conjunction in a series. My vegetable garden is wild, weedy and full of bugs.	Add a comma. My vegetable garden is wild, weedy, and full of bugs.
B. A comma is incorrectly placed after a closing quotation mark. "You need to get out there and weed", said my father.	Always put a comma before a closing quotation mark. "You need to get out there and weed," said my father.
C. A comma is missing after an introductory phrase or clause. Even if he's right I just hate to get my hands muddy.	Find the end of the phrase or clause, and add a comma. Even if he's right, I just hate to get my hands muddy.
D. Commas are missing around a nonessential phrase or clause. The aphids which are vicious little creatures are threatening to take over the spinach.	Add commas to set off the nonessential phrase or clause. The aphids, which are vicious little creatures, are threatening to take over the spinach.
E. A comma is missing from a compound sentence. The tomatoes never ripen and the beans have brown spots all over.	Add a comma before the conjunction. The tomatoes never ripen, and the beans have brown spots all over.

For more help, see Chapter 9, pp. 222–229.

(11) Using Active and Passive Voice

What's the problem? The overuse of a verb in the passive voice makes a written piece dull.

Why does it matter? The active voice engages readers' attention better than the passive voice does.

What should you do about it? Rewrite the sentence, and use the active voice rather than the passive voice.

What's the Problem?

Quick Fix

A. The passive voice makes a sentence dull.

Snowboarding **is tried** by more people every year.

Revise the sentence to use the active voice.

Every year, more people **try** snowboarding.

B. The passive voice takes the emphasis away from the performer of an action.

Terrific stunts **are** regularly **performed** by professional snowboarders.

Revise the sentence to change the voice from passive to active.

Professional snowboarders regularly **perform** terrific stunts.

C. A passive voice makes a sentence wordy.

These stunts **should** not **be attempted** by inexperienced snowboarders.

Revise the sentence to change the voice from passive to active.

Inexperienced snowboarders **should** not **attempt** these stunts.

Note: The passive voice can be used effectively when you want to . . .

emphasize the receiver of an action or the action itself

Awards **are given** for the most daring snowboarder.

make a statement about an action whose performer need not be specified or is not known

Unfortunately, the trophy **was stolen** last year.

12 Improving Weak Sentences

What's the problem? A sentence contains too many ideas or repeats ideas.

Why does it matter? Overloaded or empty sentences can bore readers or weaken the message.

What should you do about it? Make sure that every sentence contains one substantial, clearly focused idea.

What's the Problem?

Quick Fix

A. An idea is repeated.

Last year, my uncle bought a very expensive stereo system **that cost a lot of money.**

Eliminate the repeated idea.

Last year, my uncle bought a very expensive stereo system. ~~that cost a lot of money~~

B. One long sentence contains too many weakly linked ideas.

He has a lot of extra equipment that he uses to keep the stereo working perfectly and won't let anyone else touch it because he says it's very delicate and other people might break it, but it seems to me that he spends more time taking care of the stereo than listening to it.

Divide the sentence into two or more sentences while using subordinate clauses to show relationships between ideas.

He has a lot of extra equipment to keep the stereo working perfectly and won't let anyone else touch it. Because it's so delicate, he's afraid that someone will break it. It seems to me that he spends much more time taking care of the stereo than listening to it.

C. Too much information about a topic is crammed into one sentence.

I got my stereo at a discount store and it sounds great, and the only thing I have to do is keep my little brother and his friends away from it because they're too young to use it properly.

Divide the sentence into two or more sentences, and use subordinate clauses to show relationships between ideas.

I got my stereo at a discount store; it sounds great. I just have to keep my little brother and his friends away from it because they're too young to use it properly.

13 Avoiding Wordiness

What's the problem? A sentence contains unnecessary words.

Why does it matter? The meaning of wordy sentences may be unclear to readers.

What should you do about it? Use concise language and eliminate extra words.

What's the Problem?

Quick Fix

A. A single idea is unnecessarily expressed in two ways.

On New Year's Eve, **December 31,** we like to celebrate with a special dinner.

Delete the unnecessary words.

On New Year's Eve, ~~December 31,~~ we like to celebrate with a special dinner.

B. A sentence contains words that do not add to its meaning.

The idea is that we like to make the last night of the year a big family event.

Delete the unnecessary words.

~~The idea is that~~ We like to make the last night of the year a big family event.

C. A simple idea is expressed in too many words.

We stop and **sit there and remember and recall** the **happy and enjoyable** times of the past 12 months.

Simplify the expression.

We stop ~~and sit there and remember~~ and recall the happy ~~and enjoyable~~ times of the past 12 months.

D. A clause is used when a phrase would do.

Mom, **who is** the unofficial master of ceremonies, invites each of us to share our favorite memories of the past year.

Reduce the clause to a phrase.

Mom, ~~who is~~ the unofficial master of ceremonies, invites each of us to share our favorite memories of the past year.

14 Varying Sentence Beginnings

What's the problem? Too many sentences begin in the same way.

Why does it matter? Lack of variety in sentence beginnings makes writing dull and choppy.

What should you do about it? Reword some sentences so that they begin with prepositional phrases, verbal phrases, or subordinate clauses.

What's the Problem?

Too many sentences in a paragraph start with the same word.

Benjamin Franklin was a remarkable man. **He** was a scientist. **He** was a writer. **He** was an ambassador. **He** was an inventor.

Franklin wrote *Poor Richard's Almanac.* **He** helped to write the Declaration of Independence. **He** invented bifocal eyeglasses and the Franklin stove.

Franklin served as minister to France. **He** was very popular with the French people. **He** saw to it that France remained an ally of the United States during the Revolutionary War.

Quick Fix

Start the sentence with a prepositional phrase.

Benjamin Franklin was a remarkable man. **At different times,** he was a writer, an ambassador, a scientist, and an inventor.

OR

Start the sentence with a verbal phrase.

Finding various outlets for his genius, Franklin wrote *Poor Richard's Almanac,* helped to write the Declaration of Independence, and invented bifocal eyeglasses and the Franklin stove.

OR

Start the sentence with a subordinate clause.

When Franklin served as minister to France, he was very popular with the French people and saw to it that France remained an ally of the United States during the Revolutionary War.

What's the problem? A piece of writing contains too many simple sentences.

Why does it matter? Monotony in sentence structure makes writing dull and lifeless.

What should you do about it? Combine or reword sentences to create different structures.

What's the Problem?

The use of too many simple sentences leads to dull or choppy writing.

In July 1969, the Apollo 11 lunar module landed on the moon. Two astronauts were aboard. They were the first men to walk on the moon's surface.

The Apollo lunar module landed on the moon six times. Astronauts from all six missions walked on the moon. The program ended after that.

The Apollo moon landings provided worthwhile information. They also thrilled the whole world. They represented striking evidence of how far human beings had progressed.

Quick Fix

Combine the sentences to form a compound sentence.

In July 1969, the Apollo 11 lunar module landed on the moon**, and** the two astronauts aboard were the first to walk on its surface.

OR

Combine the sentences to form a complex sentence.

Before the Apollo program ended, astronauts landed a lunar module on the moon six times and walked on the moon's surface each time.

OR

Combine the sentences to form a compound-complex sentence.

While the Apollo moon landings provided worthwhile information, they thrilled the whole world**, and** they represented striking evidence of human progress.

QUICK FIX

16 Adding Supporting Details

What's the problem? Unfamiliar terms aren't defined, and claims aren't supported.

Why does it matter? Undefined terms and unsupported claims weaken explanatory or persuasive writing.

What should you do about it? Add supporting information to clarify statements and reasons.

What's the Problem?

Quick Fix

A. A key term is not defined.

Our downtown has really improved with the **Midas Project.**

Define the term.

Our downtown has really improved with the Midas Project**, a city plan for the development of public spaces.**

B. No reason is given for an opinion.

Everyone will want to come downtown now.

Add a reason.

Everyone will want to come downtown now **to stroll among the lovely new gardens.**

C. No supporting facts are given for an opinion.

The downtown fish and wicker markets are doing well.

Add facts.

The downtown fish and wicker markets **have increased their revenue by 30%, and twice as many pedestrians are in the downtown area every evening.**

D. No supporting examples are given.

It looks as if a number of new businesses will be opening.

Add examples.

It looks as if a number of new businesses will be opening; **we've been told to expect a puppet theater, a Vietnamese restaurant, and several art galleries.**

Avoiding Clichés and Slang

What's the problem? A formal written piece contains clichés or slang expressions.

Why does it matter? Clichés do not convey fresh images to readers; slang is inappropriate in formal writing.

What should you do about it? Reword the sentences to replace the clichés or slang with clear, suitable language.

What's the Problem?

Quick Fix

A. A sentence contains a cliché.

Eliminate the cliché and use a fresh image.

The intricately folded linen napkins on the dining table were **as white as snow.**

The intricately folded linen napkins on the dining table were **as white as hospital sheets.**

B. A sentence contains inappropriate slang.

Get rid of the slang and replace it with more appropriate language.

The table had been exquisitely decorated with **awesome** flowers.

The table had been exquisitely decorated with **profuse sprays of delicate** flowers.

QUICK FIX

18 Using Precise Words

What's the problem? Nouns, pronouns, modifiers, or verbs are not precise.

Why does it matter? When a writer uses vague or general words, readers' interest is not engaged.

What should you do about it? Replace general words with precise and vivid ones.

What's the Problem?

Quick Fix

A. Nouns and pronouns are too general.

The **men** ran onto the **field** while **they** cheered.

Use specific language.

The **football players** ran onto the **stadium turf** while the **fans** cheered.

B. Modifiers are too vague.

The **crowded** bleachers rang with **loud** cheers from the **excited** fans.

Use more precise and vivid adjectives and adverbs.

The **densely packed** bleachers rang with **deafening** cheers from the **deliriously passionate** fans.

C. Verbs tell what is happening rather than show it.

Cheerleaders **urged** the crowd to **yell** even louder.

Revise to show what happens by using precise and vivid verbs and modifiers.

An **energetic** squad of cheerleaders **leaped and tumbled every which way, while they screamed** at the fans to **cheer** and **roar** even louder.

QUICK FIX

19 Using Figurative Language

What's the problem? A piece of writing is lifeless or unimaginative.

Why does it matter? Lifeless writing bores readers because it doesn't help them to form mental pictures of what is being described.

What should you do about it? Add figures of speech to make the writing more lively and to create pictures in readers' minds. Do not, however, combine figures of speech that have no logical connection.

What's the Problem?

A. A description is dull and lifeless.

On the day of my first camping trip, I was **very nervous.**

OR

Nature **was unknown** to me.

B. Figures of speech that have no logical connection have been used together.

I had hoped to look **as tough and seasoned as rawhide** and **as cool as a polar bear sitting on an iceberg,** but my knees were knocking together.

Quick Fix

Add similes or other figures of speech.

On the day of my first camping trip, I was **as nervous as a soldier going off to war.**

OR

Use a metaphor.

As far as I was concerned, **nature was a big minefield, full of unpleasant surprises.**

Delete one of the figures of speech.

I had hoped to look **as tough and seasoned as rawhide, ~~and as cool as a polar bear sitting on an iceberg,~~** but my knees were knocking together.

20 **Paragraphing**

What's the problem? A paragraph contains too many ideas.

Why does it matter? An overlong paragraph doesn't signal the appearance of a new idea and it discourages readers from continuing.

What should you do about it? Break the paragraph into smaller paragraphs, each of which focuses on one main idea. Start a new paragraph whenever the speaker, setting, or focus changes.

What's the Problem?

One paragraph contains too many ideas.

We all know the story of how my grandparents got married. My grandmother used to tell it every year. When my grandfather was a young doctor, he studied with a very famous heart surgeon. The surgeon forbade his interns to be married because he didn't want them to be distracted by family life. My grandfather met my grandmother, who worked in a lab at the hospital. They fell in love and eloped, even though it was against the rules. When the surgeon found out, he confronted my grandfather. "Why did you go and get married? Don't you know the rules?" My grandfather replied, "Yes, sir, I know what I did, but I can promise you—it will never happen again."

Quick Fix

We all know the story of how my grandparents got married. My grandmother used to tell it every year.

Start a new paragraph to introduce a new idea.

When my grandfather was a young doctor, he studied with a famous heart surgeon. The surgeon forbade his interns to marry, because he didn't want them distracted by family life.

Start a new paragraph to change the setting.

My grandfather met my grandmother, who worked in a lab at the hospital. They fell in love and eloped, even though it was against the rules.

Start a new paragraph whenever the speaker changes.

When the surgeon found out, he confronted my grandfather. "Why did you go and get married? Don't you know the rules?"

My grandfather replied, "Yes, sir, I know what I did, but I can promise you—it will never happen again."

QUICK FIX

What's the Problem?

An essay or an article is treated as one long paragraph.

Clara's Clam House is going to be the biggest phenomenon to hit Merrell Beach since Hurricane Al in 1976. The service is warm and charming, and the clams are out of this world. Clara Miller has been developing her shellfish expertise since her early clamming days on the beach with her grandfather; she counts the family clambakes among her most cherished memories. Clara spent her childhood summers on a shrimping boat in the Gulf and gradually came to pull her weight at family picnics by cooking up enough crabs, oysters, and lobsters to feed the entire clan. This summer she has finally realized her lifelong dream of opening a family restaurant, and her 40 years of experience have clearly paid off. Every dish on the widely varied menu, from the succulent lobstertail to the fresh clams ("just like Grandpa used to make, only with more pepper"), shows Clara's inventive touch. So grab your hat and head down to Clara's! Young and old alike are guaranteed to find tasty nourishment for both the belly and the spirit.

Quick Fix

Clara's Clam House is going to be the biggest phenomenon to hit Merrell Beach since Hurricane Al in 1976. The service is warm and charming, and the clams are out of this world.

Start a new paragraph to introduce the first main idea.

Clara Miller has been developing her shellfish expertise since her early clamming days on the beach with her grandfather; she counts the family clambakes among her most cherished memories. Clara spent her childhood summers on a shrimping boat in the Gulf and gradually came to pull her weight at family picnics by cooking up enough crabs, oysters, and lobsters to feed the entire clan.

Start a new paragraph to introduce another main idea.

This summer she has finally realized her lifelong dream of opening a family restaurant, and her 40 years of experience have clearly paid off. Every dish on the widely varied menu, from the succulent lobstertail to the fresh clams ("just like Grandpa used to make, only with more pepper"), shows Clara's inventive touch.

Start a new paragraph to conclude.

So grab your hat and hurry down to Clara's! Young and old alike are guaranteed to find tasty nourishment for both the belly and the spirit.

Student Resources

Review: Parts of Speech

1. Nouns (links to review, p. 8)

Write all of the nouns in the following sentences. Identify each as concrete, abstract, proper, possessive, or compound. (You will use more than one category to identify some nouns.)

1. In the early 20th century, European nationalism created an atmosphere conducive to war.
2. The assassination of Archduke Francis Ferdinand sparked World War I.
3. Gavrilo Princip, the assassin of the Austro-Hungarian archduke, was a member of a Serbian terrorist organization.
4. Certain that the Serbian government was behind Princip's action, Austria-Hungary declared war on Serbia.
5. Although this conflict was relatively small, military alliances and disputes between other European countries soon led to more widespread warfare.
6. The Allies—France, Great Britain, and Russia—supported Serbia against the Central Powers of Austria-Hungary and Germany.
7. Germany won most of the first battles, but France and Britain eventually halted German advances on the western front.
8. German attacks on civilian ships drew the United States into the conflict.
9. After the United States took up the Allied cause, the tide turned against the Central Powers.
10. The Central Powers finally surrendered, but the harsh terms of the peace agreement eventually led to World War II.

2. Pronouns (links to review, p. 12)

Write each pronoun, identifying it as personal, intensive, reflexive, possessive, relative, demonstrative, indefinite, or interrogative.

1. If you find yourself in Oxford, England, visit the Pitt Rivers Museum.
2. Many are fascinated by the exhibits from all over the world.
3. This is an institution that houses a collection of more than half a million artifacts.
4. Augustus Pitt-Rivers himself acquired some of the items on display, but most of his artifacts were given to him by other collectors.

5. Pitt-Rivers, who was a lieutenant general in the British army, devoted much of his own effort to obtaining unusual firearms.
6. Anyone who visits the museum will be awed by its various exhibits.
7. These include a costume that was worn by the chief mourner at Tahitian funerals.
8. Who donated the museum's collection of No masks, which are used in Japanese dramas?
9. In 1884 Pitt-Rivers made history when he gave his collection to Oxford.
10. Today we who enjoy the museum can offer our thanks to him.

3. Verbs (links to review, p. 15)

Write each verb or verb phrase in these sentences and identify it as linking or action. Circle any auxiliary verbs.

1. Today, Kodiak bears are the largest land carnivores.
2. Did you know that an African dinosaur may once have been the largest carnivore on land?
3. Around 90 million years ago *Carcharodontosaurus saharicus* ("shark-toothed reptile from the Sahara") roamed what is now Africa.
4. Although fossils of this monstrous beast were discovered in the early 20th century and housed in a Munich museum, they were destroyed during World War II.
5. Then, in 1995, an expedition led by Dr. Paul Sereno of the University of Chicago excavated an enormous carcharodontosaurus skull in the Moroccan Sahara.
6. This fierce predator had sharp claws that could eviscerate its prey.
7. It sported jagged-edged teeth that grew as long as five inches.
8. The size of the skull suggests that this dinosaur was at least five feet longer than the largest known *Tyrannosaurus rex*.
9. Its brain, however, measured only half the size of the brain of the fearsome tyrannosaurus.
10. If it were alive today, this 45-foot-long dinosaur would dwarf a 9-foot-long brown bear.

4. Adjectives and Adverbs (links to review, p. 18)

Write the adjectives and adverbs in the following sentences. Indicate whether each is an adjective or an adverb, and identify the word or words it modifies. You do not need to include articles.

1. If you seriously plan to climb Mt. Everest, you should hire plenty of hardy Sherpa guides.
2. From the earliest climbing expeditions, robust, skillful Sherpas have played an essential role.
3. The first humans to reach the summit of the world's highest mountain were the New Zealander Edmund Hillary and Tenzing Norgay, a Sherpa.
4. The Sherpa Ang Rita proudly holds the extraordinary record of ten successful summit attempts.
5. Initially, the Sherpa were simple herders who migrated from eastern Tibet to Nepal about 600 years ago.
6. Their villages are among the loftiest human habitations, and they breathe easily at extremely high elevations.
7. Puzzled biologists theorize that the Sherpa's ability to live high in the Himalayas is genetic.
8. Apparently, the Sherpa's blood carries oxygen more efficiently than that of most people.
9. Sherpa have paid a high price for their undaunted courage in accompanying adventure treks up Everest.
10. In the last 70 years, more than one-third of the lives the perilous mountain has claimed have been unlucky Sherpa climbers.

5. Prepositions (links to review, p. 20)

Write the prepositional phrases in the following sentences. Circle each preposition.

1. St. James's Park, acquired by Henry VIII in the 1500s as a deer park, is the oldest park in London.
2. A hospital built in the 13th century once stood on the site.
3. Henry erected a palace in the park, and since 1702 it has been the official home of the monarch of England.
4. Although the queen actually lives in Buckingham Palace, St. James's Palace still serves as her official residence.
5. St. James's Palace is where the Prince of Wales lives when he is in London.

6. St. James's Park has been open to the public since the reign of Charles II.
7. During the early 18th century, milk from cows in the park was sold to people strolling the paths of St. James's.
8. Today the park is famous for its wealth of famous monuments and the beauty of its scenery.
9. Although pelicans are not native to Britain, a flock of them live on Duck Island in the midst of the park's lake.
10. A 17th-century Russian ambassador gave some pelicans to the park, and it has become a tradition for foreign diplomats to follow suit.

6. Conjunctions (links to review, p. 23)

Write the conjunctions and conjunctive adverbs in the following sentences.

1. The first dictionaries were produced by the ancient Greeks and Romans.
2. Although they are called dictionaries, most of these works were not like the general dictionaries used today.
3. Most early dictionaries were either catalogs of hard words or lists of specialized words.
4. When Robert Cawdrey prepared *A Table Alphabeticall of Hard Wordes* in 1604, he produced the first English dictionary.
5. Nathan Bailey's dictionary was the first to define most English words and not just the difficult ones.
6. Early in the 18th century a group of esteemed writers wanted to compile a complete dictionary so that English usage and spelling could be standardized.
7. Samuel Johnson not only undertook this task but also spent years choosing literary quotations to illustrate definitions.
8. After it was published in 1755, Johnson's *A Dictionary of the English Language* remained a principal reference book for nearly a century.
9. In 1828 Noah Webster published a dictionary with 70,000 entries; indeed, his goal was to produce an American reference comparable to Johnson's.
10. Since that first publication, Webster's dictionaries have been regularly updated, and they are still popular today.

1 | Parts of the Sentence

1. Subjects and Predicates (links to exercise A, p. 28)

➡ **1.** Jekyll's <u>butler</u> / <u>alerted</u> the doctor's friends.
3. <u>Mr. Utterson</u>, an attorney and long-time friend of Dr. Jekyll's, / <u>suspected</u> Hyde of blackmail.

Copy each sentence. Draw a line between the complete subject and the complete predicate. Underline the simple subject once and underline the simple predicate twice.

1. Edgar Allan Poe lived a double life in many ways.
2. The writer struggled throughout his life for respectability and financial stability.
3. Poe rarely received more than $100 for his most brilliant stories.
4. Poe was adopted by John Allan, a Richmond merchant, after the death of his itinerant actor parents.
5. As a young, ambitious man, Poe enrolled in the University of Virginia.
6. The brilliant yet unstable university student had incurred many debts before long.
7. Allan was enraged by his talented adopted son's lack of discipline.
8. Unfortunately, Poe never inherited any of the Allan fortune.
9. Poe wrote short stories, poems, and criticism after finishing a stint in the military.
10. The unhappy genius authored such impressive works as "The Fall of the House of Usher" and "The Gold Bug."

2. Compound Sentence Parts (links to exercise A, p. 30)

➡ **3.** compound verb: saw and carried

Write the compound subject or compound verb in each sentence.

1. The beautiful music of Orpheus' lyre calmed and enchanted all who heard it.
2. Apollo and Calliope, both gifted in music, were the parents of Orpheus.
3. Orpheus and his beloved, Eurydice, invited many guests to their wedding ceremony.
4. After the wedding the shepherd Aristaeus desired Eurydice and pursued her.

5. Eurydice quickly fled but fell suddenly.
6. She sickened and died from a snakebite.
7. Orpheus played mournful tunes on his lyre and sought his wife in the underworld.
8. Pluto and Proserpine greeted him in their subterranean palace.
9. Orpheus sang before them and won Eurydice's release from the underworld.
10. Unfortunately, he glanced back at his wife on their journey and thereby lost her forever.

3. Identifying Kinds of Sentences (links to exercise, p. 31)

➡ **2.** interrogative   **5.** declarative

Identify each of the following sentences as declarative, imperative, interrogative, or exclamatory.

1. Most large organizations find that change comes slowly.
2. Take the efforts of the U.S. Army to change attitudes about women soldiers, for instance.
3. The army began recruiting more women in 1973, when the draft ended.
4. The army then, although larger than today's army, contained only 3 percent women.
5. Today, more than one in five of the army's recruits are female!
6. However, according to military sources, "Some Army leaders, mostly male, have probably been slow in adjusting to the concept of having greater numbers of women in the ranks."
7. Brigadier General Evelyn P. Foote rejects complaints about women in the military as "hogwash."
8. Her reaction is blunt, don't you think?
9. General Foote says that female soldiers say the same thing over and over.
10. "Treat us as equals."

4. Subjects in Unusual Positions (links to exercise A, p. 33)

➡ **2.** subject: layer; verb: forms
  4. subject: cells and veins; verb: are obstructed

Write the subject and the verb in each sentence.

1. Right in your own backyard buzzes the commonplace housefly.
2. By what name do scientists know this household pest?

3. There are few insects that multiply faster than the fly.
4. In several clusters are laid about 100 to 150 eggs.
5. There exists a five-day larval stage before the pupa stage.
6. From the pupa case emerges the adult fly.
7. After only a week is this insect ready for egg-laying.
8. In only three weeks is the fly's life cycle complete.
9. Grouped with the most ancient of insects are the flies.
10. In amber can be found fossils of flies.

5. Identifying Subject Complements (links to exercise, p. 35)

➡ 1. remains = predicate nominative
   3. mysterious = predicate adjective

Identify the predicate adjective or predicate nominative in each sentence.

1. Limestone is a rock formed from coral and seashells.
2. This rock, consisting mainly of calcium carbonate, looks very distinctive.
3. Cement is one of the products that contain limestone.
4. Limestone appears gray when it is weathered.
5. Limestone is also a superior building material.
6. Finely ground limestone is a neutralizer of acids in soils.
7. Common classroom chalk is a type of soft white limestone.
8. Most of the stalactites and stalagmites in caves are limestone formations.
9. Marble, a metamorphosed form of limestone, feels smooth.
10. With its many uses, limestone remains valuable.

6. Objects of Verbs (links to exercise, p. 37)

➡ 1. thousands, direct object
   3. trees, indirect object; coating, direct object

Write and identify each direct object, indirect object, and objective complement in these sentences.

1. Last week I was baby-sitting a little boy in my neighborhood.
2. I rented him an old film, *Dr. Jekyll and Mr. Hyde*.
3. It might give us some excitement on a Friday night.
4. Maybe he would find the plot fascinating.
5. Anyway, we made ourselves two bowls of popcorn.
6. I made myself comfortable on the couch.
7. The little boy called himself fearless and moved up.
8. Suddenly, a crash of loud music frightened both him and me.

9. You can call me chicken, but I turned off the VCR.

10. "Wow! I call that movie weird," the little boy said happily.

2 Using Phrases

1. Prepositional Phrases (links to exercise A, p. 52)

➡ **1.** of Michael Palin's 1997 journey (adj)
   2. around the Pacific Rim (adv)

Write each prepositional phrase, indicating whether it is an adjective phrase (Adj.) or an adverb phrase (Adv.).

1. A demolition derby is an unusual form of entertainment.

2. The event takes place on a racetrack.

3. Although cars are driven around the track, a "demo" is not really a race.

4. Smashing and destroying cars is the object of a demolition derby.

5. The derby ends after all cars but one are no longer working.

6. Drivers don't drive new cars in these contests.

7. However, they do add new safety features to old, dilapidated cars.

8. The drivers actually enjoy ramming their cars into other cars.

9. The demolition derby has been called "the lowest thing in auto racing."

10. Yet derbies draw many spectators, so drivers continue competing in them.

2. Appositive Phrases (links to exercise A, p. 54)

➡ **1.** an endangered species

Write the appositives and appositive phrases in these sentences.

1. At the National Zoo in Washington, D.C., visitors perch in a *machan*—a kind of tree platform—and watch for tigers.

2. They also stroll along "Tiger Tracks," a 250-foot elevated wooden trail, as they walk the Great Cats exhibit.

3. One tiger visitors might see is the Sumatran male Rokan.

4. Visitors also enjoy seeing Kerinci, a 13-year-old tigress from Sumatra, who was found as an orphaned cub.

5. They're sure to note that her daughter Soy is bigger than she is.

3. Participial Phrases (links to exercise A, p. 57)

➡ **1.** Launched in 1957 (*Sputnik 1*)

Write the participles and participial phrases in the following sentences. If a participle or participial phrase modifies a noun or pronoun in the sentence, write that word in parentheses.

1. Sailing in the Pacific Ocean west of Chile, Woodes Rogers reached the island of Más a Tierra in February 1709.
2. Having seen a fire on the desolate island, Rogers sent some men ashore to investigate.
3. They found a man clothed in goatskins.
4. The man was Alexander Selkirk, who, joining a band of buccaneers, had run away to sea.
5. The buccaneers' captain, having argued with Selkirk, had put him ashore on the island four years earlier.
6. For shelter, Selkirk had built two huts covered with grass.
7. Building fires from allspice wood, he provided himself with heat and light.
8. He lived on crawfish and goat meat cooked over the fires.
9. The English writer Daniel Defoe created a fictional character based on Selkirk and his experiences.
10. The title of Defoe's novel, published in 1719, is *Robinson Crusoe.*

4. Gerund Phrases (links to exercise A, p. 59)

➡ **1.** Traveling across the country with his poodle, Charley; S

Write each gerund and gerund phrase in these sentences, indicating whether it functions as a subject, a predicate nominative, a direct object, an indirect object, an object of a preposition, or an appositive.

1. In his journal, William Bradford gives an eyewitness account of the colonizing of Plymouth, Massachusetts, in 1620.
2. After sailing across the Atlantic aboard the *Mayflower,* Pilgrim scouts chose Plymouth as the site for colonization.
3. Establishing the first permanent European settlement in New England was the work ahead for the Pilgrims.
4. For them, just finding a spring of fresh water was a great relief.
5. They quickly accomplished their next job, building a fire near the shore so that those still aboard the ship could find them.
6. Another accomplishment was locating decent farmland.
7. The Pilgrims truly appreciated finding animals such as deer.

8. By keeping a written account of the colony's development, William Bradford helped future generations understand the trials and triumphs of the settlement's early years.
9. Publishing the *History of Plymouth Plantation* earned Bradford the title "father of American history."
10. Another of his accomplishments was serving as governor of Plymouth.

5. Infinitive Phrases (links to exercise A, p. 61)

➡ **1.** to seek rare and exotic creatures, Adv.

Write each infinitive or infinitive phrase in these sentences. In the phrases, underline the infinitives. Tell whether each infinitive or phrase functions as a subject, an object, a predicate nominative, an adjective, or an adverb.

1. When Nick Caloyianis visited northern Canada's Baffin Island, his goal was to photograph the Greenland shark.
2. After two weeks he hadn't had an opportunity to see even one.
3. Then, after almost two hours in freezing water, Nick was able to make out a huge shape swimming toward him.
4. To come face to face with a Greenland shark terrified him.
5. He knew that to eat, the shark simply opened its huge mouth and sucked in prey.
6. Yet Caloyianis bravely stayed by a mesh bag filled with bait to lure this predator.
7. The shark was eager to take the bait, sucking it up in one pass.
8. Caloyianis was able to take two pictures, becoming the first photographer of a Greenland shark beneath Arctic ice.
9. Caloyianis thinks the shark was probably unaware of his presence, because Greenland sharks lack the ability to see very well.
10. Because they spend most of their time in darkness, these sharks never even try to use their eyes.

6. Problems with Phrases (links to exercise A, p. 63)

➡ **3.** They jumped into their car without her purse.

Rewrite each sentence to correct a misplaced or dangling modifier, changing words or word order as necessary.

1. Looking for a special night out with my pet, the new restaurant for dogs and their owners seemed a good idea.
2. Sitting on their owners' laps, waiters there serve smaller dogs.
3. Under the tables, most owners keep larger dogs.

4. Serving water and table scraps, both the canine customers and their owners adore the waiters.
5. Provided with special monogrammed bowls, some owners pamper their dogs.
6. Tugging on her leash, I often find myself dragged by Lulu to the nearby outdoor café that welcomes dogs.
7. Serving freshly baked dog biscuits, she considers this place one of her favorites.
8. Tied to chairs or table legs, some owners keep their dogs from begging at other tables.
9. Lying on the floor, one waiter was accidentally tripped by a dog.
10. Licking him on the face, the waiter accepted the dog's apology.

3 Using Clauses

1. Kinds of Clauses (links to exercise A, p. 78)

➔ **1.** subordinate clause   **3.** independent clause

Identify the underlined words in each sentence as an independent clause or a subordinate clause.

1. Planning for travel can be overwhelming.
2. In the old days, people would visit travel agents, who were the main sources of travel information.
3. Now on the Internet alone there is more information than a dozen agents could provide.
4. Fortunately, before novice surfers paddle into the ocean of information, they can consult guides.
5. One guide that is very popular is *Travel Planning Online for Dummies*.
6. The author guides readers through the planning process, although he doesn't list every relevant Web site.
7. Many travel magazines are available on-line, and they update their information regularly.
8. People who want to share their travel experiences can contribute on-line travelogues and diaries.
9. These on-line locations provide personal views and information that can't be found in ordinary sources.
10. As surfers gain confidence, they can check out e-zines, virtual-adventure sites, and on-line bookstores.

2. Adjective and Adverb Clauses (links to exercise A, p. 82)

➡ **2.** <u>because</u> he was making his first dive in *Alvin,* a small research submarine; was

Write the adjective or adverb clause in each sentence, underlining the introductory word or words. If the clause is elliptical, write the omitted word or words in parentheses. Then write the word or words modified by the clause.

1. Robert Ballard is not someone who rests on his laurels.
2. In his career thus far, Ballard has made more discoveries than most other scientists.
3. In 1997 he led an expedition that discovered eight shipwrecks on the bottom of the Mediterranean Sea.
4. While they examined the wrecks, the scientists made a discovery.
5. The discovery was more remarkable than anyone had imagined.
6. Two of the wrecks, which sat upright on the ocean floor, were ancient Roman trading ships.
7. When those ancient sailors journeyed the seas, they had only the stars as a guide.
8. If they followed the shores of the Mediterranean, they would be able to avoid the treacherous deep waters.
9. Some captains, however, must have risked everything when the possibility of riches gleamed in their eyes.
10. Therefore, the expedition searched along a deep-sea route where rough seas and sudden storms were common.

3. Noun Clauses (links to exercise A, p. 85)

➡ **1.** whether time travel is possible; direct object
  3. whoever drives it; indirect object

Write the noun clause in each sentence. Indicate whether it functions as a subject, a direct object, an indirect object, a predicate nominative, an object of a preposition, a direct object of a gerund or an infinitive, or an appositive.

1. Everyone knows that travel can be hazardous.
2. To face what we fear most is a test of courage.
3. What Paul Theroux feared most was the prospect of an annoying seatmate on the train.
4. Theroux's talkative traveler gave whoever was within earshot an endless stream of commentary.
5. That someone would listen to the story of his life encouraged the traveler to continue.

6. Theroux wondered how long this could go on.
7. How the man's marriage ended was of no interest to Theroux.
8. This endless story of his, that his life was such a mess, continued until the train stopped in Puerto Limón.
9. Theroux thought only about how to ditch the talkative man.
10. However, when Theroux found nowhere to stay in Puerto Limón, he discovered that the man was generous to a fault.

4. Sentence Structure (links to exercise A, p. 88)

➡ **2.** compound sentence   **4.** simple

Identify each of the following sentences as simple, compound, complex, or compound-complex.

1. Lions, tigers, and bears may frighten the average traveler, but Tim Flannery has come to fear the mosquito.
2. Flannery, who is an Australian biologist, once studied nocturnal mammals in Papua New Guinea.
3. As bats emerged on their nightly rounds, the fearless biologist was ready to observe them.
4. As he watched the bats, the mosquitoes formed dense clouds and zeroed in on him.
5. Neither clothing nor repellent offered protection.
6. After he completed his work on New Guinea, Flannery returned home to Australia.
7. He contracted malaria because he had been bitten by an anopheles mosquito that carried the disease.
8. The disease can be fatal, but he had contracted the least dangerous strain.
9. Attacks of malaria are often sudden and unexpected.
10. While Flannery was having lunch with friends in Woolloomooloo, his "souvenir" of New Guinea attacked; he turned pale, shook violently, and began to sweat.

5. Fragments and Run-Ons (links to exercise A, p. 91)

➡ **1.** Kamchadal canoes were precarious because they capsized so easily.

Rewrite each item below, correcting the phrase fragment, clause fragment, or run-on sentence.

1. One winter George Kennan tried to cross the Siberian steppes, they seemed to go on endlessly.
2. Kennan and his companions were traveling on dogsled. When a roaring snowstorm took them by surprise.

3. They took shelter. Among some trees along the banks of a small stream.

4. Blinded by flying snow and unable to breathe. Neither the dogs nor the men dared to continue.

5. It was Christmas far from home, the men were sad and weary.

6. The wind roared so loudly. That they couldn't hear one another speak.

7. Sleeping bags made of fur were the only protection. That they had against the driving wind.

8. When the storm abated. They emerged from their cold cocoons.

9. Because they had spent two days buried in stiff, cold fur bags. Their bodies were sore and exhausted.

10. A new problem arose, they had run out of food for the dogs, it was necessary to find a settlement soon.

4 Using Verbs

1. Correcting Errors in Principal Parts (links to exercise, p. 106)

➜ **4.** changed

Correct errors in the principal parts of verbs in the passage. If a sentence does not contain an error, write *Correct*.

(1) Thomas Edison think too much sleep was unhealthy. **(2)** Yet the need for sleep varys from one person to the next. **(3)** Edison, for example, usually gotten four to six hours of sleep each night. **(4)** Albert Einstein, however, sworn that ten hours were necessary for him. **(5)** Researchers have begin to investigate individual differences. **(6)** In England, a 72-year-old woman drawed pictures all night. **(7)** She needed only one hour of sleep. **(8)** After doctors had putten her through tests, they confirmed her claims. **(9)** Apparently, her body and mind had growed accustomed to little sleep. **(10)** Such an exception to the rule has lead to the need for more research.

2. Verb Tenses (links to exercise A, p. 110)

➜ **1.** discovered, past
 2. had performed, past perfect

Write the verbs in these sentences and identify their tenses.

(1) Before the discovery of REM sleep, scientists thought that sleep was a simple physical process. **(2)** By the age of 60, the average person has spent roughly 20 years asleep. **(3)** Every night a person alternates between REM and non-REM sleep. **(4)** In an effort to understand sleep, scientists have used machines that measure brain waves, eye movement, hormone production, and other physical indicators. **(5)** Others have studied sleep in animals, including guinea pigs and cockroaches. **(6)** During one test, a sleeping hamster's body temperature fell to room temperature. **(7)** Researchers compared this change to hibernation, but they discovered that hibernation caused a need for more sleep. **(8)** Despite all the studies, scientists today still know very little about the purpose of sleep. **(9)** Because their tests have raised even more questions, researchers will continue to conduct experiments. **(10)** Perhaps by the year 2050 they will have found the answer to why we sleep.

3. Progressive and Emphatic Forms (links to exercise A, p. 113)

➜ **1.** are calling, present progressive

3. has been experiencing, present perfect progressive

Write the progressive and emphatic forms in the following sentences. Identify the form and tense of each.

1. Most adults should be sleeping about eight hours a night.
2. Your brain is always keeping track of how much sleep it is owed.
3. If you've been sleeping six hours a night instead of eight, you've incurred two hours of sleep debt each night.
4. Your sleep debt was adding up as the days passed.
5. At the end of the next five days, you'll be missing ten more hours of sleep.
6. Even if you do sleep an extra three hours on the weekend, you won't completely make up for the ten hours you lost.
7. Some scientists have been wondering what happens to sleep debt over the long term.
8. One group did survey the sleep, exercise, nutrition, and other habits of over a million Americans.
9. People who had been sleeping less than seven hours a night did not live as long as those who slept more.
10. When we reach middle age, many of us will have been accumulating years of sleep debt.

4. Active and Passive Voice (links to exercise A, p. 115)

➜ **1.** can be overestimated, passive
2. have embarked, active

Write the main verb in each sentence and identify its voice as active or passive.

1. Few people can name a famous bed.
2. Nevertheless, the Victoria and Albert Museum houses perhaps the most famous bed in England.
3. The bed was first installed in the 1500s at an inn in Ware.
4. This large four-poster Tudor bed has been called the Great Bed of Ware.
5. It measures about 11 feet long and more than 10 feet wide.
6. The date 1460 is carved into the bed's massive oak frame.
7. The museum's experts, however, have dated it between 1575 and 1600.
8. Shakespeare mentioned the great bed in *Twelfth Night.*
9. It was also referred to by Ben Jonson in *Epicoene, or The Silent Woman.*
10. Historical furniture is highly regarded by some people.

5. The Moods of Verbs (links to exercise A, p. 117)

➡ 1. indicative   2. imperative

Identify the mood of the underlined verb in each sentence.

1. Many new writers <u>have been</u> guilty of ending a story by saying that its events were "just a dream."
2. Others <u>have revealed</u> crucial information in a character's dream, leaving readers feeling cheated.
3. The author Nancy Kress <u>advises</u> against these trite, unimaginative devices.
4. Instead, she recommends that a writer <u>include</u> a dream only as a story detail.
5. Never <u>use</u> dreams as character motivation or as the climax or resolution of a story.
6. Some authors write as though they <u>were</u> disciples of Sigmund Freud.
7. Kress says that using Freud's dream symbolism <u>disappoints</u> readers and reveals a writer's lack of imagination.
8. An effective dream in a story <u>stems</u> naturally from the conflict that a character is facing.
9. <u>Tell</u> a character's dream only if it will help the reader understand the character better.
10. <u>Remember</u> that dreams as plot devices are taboo, but dreams as ways of providing insight into characters can be effective.

6. Problems with Verbs (links to exercise A, p. 121)

➜ **1.** are lying　　　　　**2.** flash

Correct the verb errors in the following sentences.

1. Unless we describe our dreams and hypnagogic hallucinations, they were lost forever.
2. Solutions to many problems have laid in people's dreams.
3. Elias Howe, for example, had been trying to invent a sewing machine but is frustrated by a problem in its design.
4. In a dream he was captured by savages who were rising their spears and shouting.
5. The spears had eye-shaped holes near their points, and these give him the solution to his problem.
6. As it wrestled with a problem, his brain makes a creative connection during sleep.
7. If he would have relied only on his waking insights, he would not have found a solution.
8. The answer set in a corner of his brain, waiting to be discovered.
9. By saying "Leave me sleep on it," we sometimes surrender a problem to our brain.
10. Howe might of solved his problem much sooner if he'd only taken a nap right away.

⑤ Subject-Verb Agreement

1. Agreement in Person and Number (links to exercise A, p. 132)

➜ **2.** have　　　　　**3.** does rely

Identify the sentences in which subjects and verbs don't agree. In each case, write the correct verb. If a sentence is correct, write *Correct.*

1. Tai chi, a martial art from China, have both health and relaxation benefits.
2. Opposing yet complementary forces known as yin and yang governs the practice of tai chi.
3. According to legend, Zhang Sanfeng, a Chinese monk, was the developer of tai chi.
4. In China, this martial art, with its emphasis on controlled movements, date back to the 13th century.

5. Students of tai chi practices series of exercises known as forms.
6. With names such as The White Crane Spreads Its Wings, the movements of tai chi are graceful and expressive.
7. Students involved in ballet or modern dance applauds the discipline and beauty of tai chi.
8. Tai chi, when practiced as one of the martial arts, is a very powerful form of self-defense.
9. Today, the Yang style of this martial art is taught more often than other styles.
10. This style of the art were named for a legendary tai chi master.

2. Indefinite Pronouns as Subjects (links to exercise A, p. 134)

➡ **2.** consider   **3.** excels

Identify the sentences in which subjects and verbs don't agree. In each case, write the correct verb. If a sentence is correct, write *Correct*.

1. One of the most inexpensive yet effective exercise tools are a jump rope.
2. Many of the world's top athletes uses this simple exercise device.
3. Few deny that jumping rope promotes a healthy heart, lean muscles, and strong bones.
4. Even some of the instructors in military boot camps incorporates rope jumping in their recruits' classes.
5. When jumping rope, someone burn about 200 calories every 15 minutes.

3. Agreement Between Compound Subjects and Verbs (links to exercise, p. 137)

➡ **2.** are   **4.** are

Choose the correct verb form in parentheses for each of the following sentences.

1. Sprints and longer runs (is, are) among track and field's most popular events for many teenagers.
2. Young women and men (gains, gain) a strong work ethic and pride through participation in track.
3. Neither novices nor experienced runners (questions, question) the physical and emotional challenges of running.

4. When one runner fell in the 10,000-meter race at the Indiana state championships, his teammates and opponents (was, were) amazed at his determination to finish the race.

5. Neither scrapes nor bleeding (was, were) going to stop him from competing.

4. Other Confusing Subjects (links to exercise A, p. 140)

➡ **1.** combines   **2.** was

Choose the correct verb form in parentheses for each of the following sentences.

1. Having a simple rubber ball (enables, enable) you to participate in many sports and games.
2. In the early 1900s the youth of America (was, were) introduced to a pink rubber ball known as the Spalding.
3. What a few may remember (is, are) that children nicknamed the ball Spaldeen.
4. With this ball a whole generation (was, were) able to play street games such as stoopball, curb ball, and stickball.
5. Whoever has played stickball (knows, know) that it's a lot like baseball.
6. Organizing a stickball game (means, mean) assembling a group of friends.
7. Every stickball team (begins, begin) a game by marking the bases.
8. Then the group (marks, mark) the boundaries of their stickball field.
9. Catching a fly ball (requires, require) skill and physical agility in this great urban sport.
10. News of a game (spreads, spread) quickly through a neighborhood, and soon others are joining the fun.

5. Special Agreement Problems (links to exercise A, p. 143)

➡ **2.** are   **5.** Correct

Identify the sentences in which subjects and verbs don't agree. In each case, write the correct verb. If a sentence is correct, write *Correct.*

1. Introduced at the 1896 Olympics were the first hurdles race, 110 meters in length.
2. There are a number of hurdling events, all of which requires competitors to clear a series of barriers.
3. The original hurdles were sheep barriers nailed to a track.

4. Today's hurdles have wooden bars that are supported by metal stands.
5. There is several main hurdling events for men and women: the 100 meters for women, the 110 meters for men, and the 400 meters for both sexes.

6 Using Pronouns

1. Nominative and Objective Cases (links to exercise, p. 154)

➡ **1.** he, N   **2.** him, O

Write the correct pronoun in parentheses. Then identify the pronoun as nominative (N) or objective (O).

1. Listen to the jokes in Bill Cosby's early routines, and (they/them) can tell you much about his childhood.
2. To learn more about (he/him) right now, however, just read on.
3. A sixth-grade teacher found Cosby bright but said that (he/him) preferred clowning to doing schoolwork.
4. In high school he had trouble with academic studies, since he devoted more time to sports than (they/them).
5. He might have played football professionally had (he/him) not begun earning money by telling jokes.

2. Possessive Case (links to exercise A, p. 156)

➡ **1.** their

Write the correct pronoun in parentheses.

1. Molly Ivins is a columnist for the *Fort Worth Star-Telegram;* (her/hers) columns mostly focus on politics.
2. She often focuses specifically on the Texas legislature, finding (it's/its) antics hilarious.
3. (My/Mine) vocabulary now contains words like *Bubba* because of Ivins's writing.
4. Some of the best columns come from (her/hers) following political candidates on the campaign trail.
5. She both exposes and laughs at (their/they're) corrupt behavior.

3. *Who* and *Whom* (links to exercise A, p. 159)

→ **2.** who

Write the correct pronoun in parentheses.

1. I like the films of the Marx Brothers, (who/whom) have inspired such later comedians as Mel Brooks and Woody Allen.
2. (Whoever/Whomever) views their films is hard-pressed to keep up with their antics.
3. Groucho, (whose/who's) real name was Julius, was known for his fast talk and bad puns, as well as his mustache and cigar.
4. Adolph, to (whom/who) the name Harpo was given, actually did play the harp.
5. Harpo became a silent performer when a critic by (whom/who) he was reviewed said that he was a wonderful mime but a poor speaker.
6. Zeppo was named after a vaudeville monkey (who's/whose) name was Zippo.
7. (Whoever/Whomever) has seen *Monkey Business, Horse Feathers,* and *Duck Soup* has seen brilliant send-ups of gangster movies, college, and war.
8. The brothers, (who/whom) had a busy life, once filmed *The Cocoanuts* during the day while performing *Animal Crackers* at night on Broadway.
9. After Zeppo left the act, Margaret Dumont, (who/whom) was featured in many Marx Brothers films, was often called the fourth Marx brother.
10. Comedy fans should give thanks to (whomever/whoever) put the Marx Brothers' films on video.

4. Pronoun-Antecedent Agreement (links to exercise A, p. 163)

→ **1.** The show *M*A*S*H* was about a U.S. Army medical unit during the Korean War and its comic and tragic moments.
2. Hardly anyone wanted to risk his or her neck on a dark comedy.

Rewrite each sentence so that every pronoun agrees with its antecedent. Write *Correct* if a sentence contains no agreement errors.

1. One all-time favorite *M*A*S*H* episode is the one in which Colonel Henry Blake takes his leave of Korea.
2. Everyone who really served in Korea counted the hours until their homecoming.
3. In this episode each of the characters has their own reasons to be pleased about Colonel Blake's departure.

4. Margaret is happy because now she will put an end to Hawkeye's and Trapper's pranks.
5. Trapper and Hawkeye are happy that his friend gets to go home.
6. However, nobody in the unit wants their daily life controlled by Frank Burns.
7. The unit say goodbye to Henry in its own different ways, some sad, some funny.
8. Neither Hawkeye nor Radar can believe their ears when the message about Henry's plane comes in.
9. Henry Blake's plane has been shot down, and its plunge into the ocean has left no survivors.
10. Most of the cast had tears in its eyes after filming this scene.

5. Other Pronoun Problems (links to exercise A, p. 166)

→ **1.** We   **2.** they

Write the correct pronoun in parentheses.

1. Whoopi Goldberg is in a class by herself; few comics are as versatile as (she/her).
2. (We/Us) fans can enjoy her in films, on television, in recordings, and even in print.
3. The success of Comic Relief's fundraising is largely due to the show's hosts: Billy Crystal, Robin Williams, and (she/her).
4. In addition to hosting the show, Crystal, Williams, and (she/herself) perform on it.
5. Her career took off in 1983, when Mike Nichols (him/himself) saw her perform and decided to produce a one-woman show on Broadway.
6. Seeing this show on cable TV, Steven Spielberg was as impressed as (he/him) and cast her in a featured role in *The Color Purple*.
7. Since that film debut (we/us) moviegoers have seen her in both comedies and dramas.
8. Some actors play the same kind of character repeatedly; Goldberg has a wider range than (they/them).
9. What's more, the job of hosting the Oscars often goes to one of two comics, Billy Crystal or (she/her).
10. Few performers are as adept at acting, hosting, and making people laugh as (she/her).

6. Pronoun Reference Problems (links to exercise, p. 169)

→ **2.** The book *Saturday Night Live: The First Twenty Years* says that Carlin wore a suit with a T-shirt instead.

3. If you like to watch vintage *Saturday Night Live* on cable TV, read this book about the program.

Rewrite these sentences to correct reference problems. For pronouns with ambiguous reference, there may be more than one correct answer.

1. When comics frequently use a specific kind of humor, the audience comes to expect this from them.

2. A comedian who uses insult humor must understand his target.

3. In some insult humor, you have comics using gender clichés.

4. A male comic might complain about his wife's poor cooking, but this usually doesn't offend the audience.

5. They say that women will almost always laugh at jokes about men watching sports on television.

6. A comic who specializes in slapstick will eventually become known for her clumsy pratfalls.

7. Chevy Chase constantly fell down on *Saturday Night Live,* and this became his trademark.

8. When Steve Martin wore a fake arrow through his head in his act, it soon became wildly popular.

9. If you are unsure about any joke in your comedy act, discard it.

10. If you're joking about politics, be sure to keep it current.

7 Using Modifiers

1. Adjectives and Adverbs (links to exercise, p. 179)

→ **1.** Your, memory (system); different (areas); your (brain)

3. different (portions); varying, memory (functions)

Identify the words that function as modifiers in the following sentences. Do not include articles. What does each word modify?

1. Frequently, people learn tasks that they need to perform on a consistent basis.

2. Engrams—memory traces in the brain—govern the performance of actions that are repeated daily.

3. Sensory areas of the brain's cortex hold engrams that actually control motor skills.

4. The appropriate engram must be activated for a person to simply tie a shoe or drive a car.
5. A great deal of teenagers' learning is the result of repetitive actions, such as faithfully memorizing vocabulary lists or math formulas.
6. Imagine the variety of engrams that your memory utilizes now in your daily life as a high school student.
7. Most students have even tried various techniques to help them recall challenging material for important final exams.
8. A popular and effective technique primarily used to promote memorization and retention of material is the SQ3R method.
9. This study technique, designed to boost school performance, was developed by Francis Robinson in 1970.
10. Students carefully survey, question, read, recite, and review material in steps.

2. Modifiers in Comparisons (links to exercise A, p. 182)

➡ **1.** most mundane   **3.** better

For each sentence below, choose the correct modifier.

1. Many people can relate surprisingly detailed facts about the (dramaticest, most dramatic) experiences in their lives.
2. For example, people (older, oldest) than your grandparents can probably pinpoint exactly what they were doing on D-day.
3. Teenagers can probably describe the (precisest, most precise) details about getting their driving license or falling in love for the first time.
4. Special memories about the best or (worse, worst) moments of our lives are called flashbulb memories.
5. Theorists believe that they are remembered (better, best) than other memories because of their highly charged emotional content.

3. Problems with Comparisons (links to exercise A, p. 185)

➡ **1.** does   **5.** most vivid

Identify and correct double and illogical comparisons in these sentences.

1. Ekaterina Gordeeva and Sergei Grinkov were among the most famousest pairs skaters of recent time.

2. In her inspirational book *My Sergei,* Gordeeva recounts memories of their good working arrangement and even more better personal relationship.
3. Gordeeva recalls the years that she spent at a sports school that had a more rigorouser physical education program than other schools.
4. She remembers her coach with fondness because he arranged for her, when 11 years old, to skate with the more stronger, 15-year-old Grinkov.
5. She describes Sergei's competing with boys who were as athletic, or even more athletic, as he was.
6. Although she always felt secure with her partner, Gordeeva confesses that the throws were more frightening to her than any move.
7. After their marriage, the couple made a most surprisingest comeback and won a gold medal at Lillehammer.
8. Although Gordeeva had enjoyed a tranquil existence up to this point, she suffered a shock more terrible than anything.
9. Her husband, who had as many career hopes as any young skater, died of a heart attack while training for a Stars on Ice performance.
10. Today, life is more difficulter for Gordeeva, but she is still a formidable competitor as a singles skater.

4. Other Modifier Problems (links to exercise A, p. 189)

➡ 3. Recovering from the trauma of World War I, Graves recorded his reminiscences in his book *Goodbye to All That.*
4. In the first section of the book, Graves says he could never forget his boarding-school days.

Rewrite the following sentences so that modifiers are used correctly.

1. One of the keenest observers of his times, a diary was kept by the amiable English public servant and man of letters Samuel Pepys.
2. Born in 1633, Pepys received at Magdalene College in Cambridge his education.
3. Pepys was a detailed recorder of the comings and goings of people with an extraordinary ear for dialogue.
4. Pepys's career in business and politics couldn't hardly have been more colorful.
5. For nine years, the diary Pepys kept gives modern readers a window into his century.

6. The diary entries shortly after the events occurred were written at irregular intervals.
7. The diary hardly doesn't hold back even the most minute details of Pepys's life—even his arguments with his wife appear!
8. Behind the diary, historians suggest was Pepys's vanity.
9. Pepys loved life, and he always celebrated the anniversary of his recovery from a dangerous operation with a banquet.
10. Pepys never expected millions of people to read his diary, writing in his own secret code.

8 Capitalization

1. Names (links to exercise A, p. 200)

➡ **1.** Roy Rowan

Rewrite the words that contain capitalization errors, using correct capitalization. If a sentence contains no errors, write *Correct.*

1. In 1513 the Political theorist niccolò machiavelli wrote a book called *The Prince,* in which he advocated the use of unethical methods to get and wield power.
2. The prince in the book was modeled on Cesare Borgia, the son of pope Alexander VI.
3. Borgia was named archbishop, then cardinal, and finally commander of the papal army.
4. His enemies accused him of murdering his Brother juan, but no proof was ever provided.
5. Juan, duke of Gandía, had many enemies at the time.

2. Other Names and Places (links to exercise A, p. 203)

➡ **1.** Buddhists, Buddhas   **3.** Kosala, Ganges River, Nepal

Rewrite the words that contain capitalization errors, using correct capitalization.

1. Mother Teresa was born in 1910 in what is now skopje, macedonia.
2. She was the daughter of an albanian grocer.
3. At 17 she joined the Institute of the Blessed Virgin Mary in ireland, then went to calcutta, india, where she taught in a school for well-to-do girls.
4. In 1946 she felt called to tend the sick and dying and asked for permission from rome to leave her order to do so.
5. Soon thereafter she founded the roman catholic Order of the Missionaries of Charity.

3. Organizations and Other Subjects (links to exercise, p. 207)

➜ **1.** Seneca Falls Convention   **3.** junior

Rewrite the words that contain capitalization errors, using correct capitalization. If a sentence contains no errors, write *Correct*.

1. Jane Addams, an American social worker, is probably best known for establishing the social welfare center hull house.
2. She was apparently inspired to establish this center by conditions in the slums of Chicago, Illinois, as well as by toynbee hall, a settlement house she had visited in England.
3. Addams had graduated from Rockford college—then Rockford seminary—in 1881.
4. She traveled in Europe both after her graduation and during world war I.
5. In fact, when the War broke out, she became chairperson of the woman's peace party.
6. She also served as chairperson of the international congress of women.
7. She continued to take the lead in social reform movements.
8. Even before the War, she had campaigned for the Progressive party and had campaigned for woman suffrage.
9. In 1931 she was awarded the nobel peace prize.
10. She did, however, have to share the Award with another winner, Nicholas Murray Butler.

4. First Words and Titles (links to exercise, p. 209)

➜ The first correction in the passage should be *Suffragist*.

Rewrite the words that are incorrectly capitalized in this e-mail message.

hey Samantha,

I just got a book that will really help us with our report on Tennyson. For example, it says that Alfred, Lord Tennyson, was appointed poet laureate in 1850. also, he was the one who wrote that poem "The Charge of The Light Brigade," which has the famous lines "Theirs not to make reply, / theirs not to reason why, / theirs but to do and die." The author explains that this poem deals with a "suicidal" and "Completely useless" cavalry attack in some war.

Based on what I've read so far, we may want to break up our section on Tennyson's writings as follows:

II. Writings of Tennyson
   A. Poetry
   b. famous quotations

Anyway, you and i can talk about this more on Monday.

See You soon,

Jamie

5. Abbreviations (links to exercise A, p. 211)

➡ **1.** NFL, NBA, WCW

Rewrite the words that contain capitalization errors, using correct capitalization. If a sentence contains no errors, write *Correct*.

   1. Whether you're in st. Paul, minn., or st. Petersburg, Russia, your success in the business world will depend on the training and information you get.
   2. In the u.s. a person can learn how to start a business by attending a Small Business Administration (sba) workshop.
   3. Another agency that's helpful to young women and men is the Young Entrepreneurs' Organization (Yeo).
   4. Anyone can find out about federal programs and services from the Federal Information Center (FIC).
   5. The FIC offers information through a toll-free number from 9:00 a.m. to 5:00 p.m. Est or Edt on workdays.

9 End Marks and Commas

1. Periods and Other End Marks (links to exercise A, p. 221)

➡ **1.** change.   **3.** Yuck!; packaging.

Write each word that should be followed by an end mark, adding the correct mark (period, question mark, or exclamation point).

   1. Did you know that color trends run in cycles
   2. Avocado green and harvest gold were popular colors in 1970s kitchens
   3. By the 1980s these colors were passé
   4. Designers looked at '70s kitchens and thought, "Ugh How tacky can you get"
   5. In the late 1990s, however, kitchens were again sporting those colors

6. You may wonder why few food packages are blue
7. Choosing colors that appeal to consumers is complicated
8. Mr or Ms J Q Public expects a food's package color to reflect what is inside
9. How many blue foods can you name
10. Not many, I'm willing to bet

2. Commas in Sentence Parts (links to exercise A, p. 225)

➜ **1.** popular, well-respected   **2.** Inventory, also

Each sentence below is missing at least one comma. Write the words before and after each missing comma, adding the comma between them.

1. Students are you looking for a tool to help you assess your career interests?
2. Many practical understandable assessment tools are based on John Holland's theory of vocational interests.
3. If you take a Holland-based test you will receive a three-letter code identifying your vocational interests.
4. A code of RIS for example means that you have traits of the Realistic Investigative and Social personality types.
5. The letter order indicates that you fit the Realistic type most the Investigative type less and the Social type even less.
6. You can conclude that you resemble the Artistic Enterprising and Conventional types—the other three Holland personality types—very little.
7. Each Holland type is associated with specific career preferences and you can use your code to guide you to a job you will enjoy.
8. Social people for example share interests with teachers so certain people classified as Social might enjoy a career in front of a classroom.
9. Armed with your Holland code you can consult reference materials to help you identify potential careers.
10. One such reference is the *Dictionary of Holland Occupational Codes* a book coauthored by John Holland which you can probably find at the library.

3. Fixing Comma Problems (links to exercise A, p. 227)

➜ **1.** Research confirms that different groups of people communicate differently.
2. Often, body language, not spoken language, causes problems among people from different cultures.

Rewrite the sentences below, correcting errors in comma usage. In some cases, there may be more than one way to correct an error. If a sentence needs no corrections, write *Correct.*

1. Everyone knows that people from different cultures speak different languages, some people think that body language is universal.
2. Smiling Americans traveling abroad should learn has different meanings in different cultures.
3. When they are happy Americans smile.
4. By smiling a Japanese person might be showing happiness, sadness, or even anger.
5. Koreans view a stranger's smile as a sign of shallowness; the French as a sign of rudeness.
6. Here's a tip for moviegoers in Russia, if you need to pass seated patrons to get to your seat, face them, don't turn your back to them.
7. In many nations although not in the United States and Canada crossing your ankle over your knee is considered an insulting gesture.
8. By doing so you show the sole of your shoe a sign of great disrespect in many cultures.
9. In many cultures direct eye contact is considered a sign of honesty and interest; in others a sign of defiance or flirtation.
10. Don't put your hands in your pockets when talking to a Belgian, doing so is considered the height of rudeness.

4. Other Comma Rules (links to exercise A, p. 229)

➜ **1.** Attack," "Stay **2.** Baltimore, Maryland, to Seattle, Washington

Correct each comma error in the sentences below by writing the words that come before and after the mistake, adding the comma between them.

1. Public-opinion polls predicted that the presidential election on November 2 1948 would be a landslide.
2. Responses indicated that Thomas E. Dewey would defeat Harry S. Truman the incumbent president.
3. "As the election approached, opinion polls gave the Republican candidate, . . . Thomas E. Dewey, a comfortable lead" states one U.S. history textbook.
4. Many Americans were sure that Dewey the governor of New York would be the next president.
5. However, straight-talking Harry Truman from Independence Missouri surprised the pollsters.

6. On the morning of November 3 1948 a smiling President Truman held up a copy of the *Chicago Daily Tribune*.
7. Its headline was "Dewey Defeats Truman" but the headline was wrong.
8. Truman garnered 24104030 popular votes, while Dewey trailed behind with 21971004.
9. To learn more about Harry S. Truman, contact the Harry S. Truman Library and Museum, 500 West U.S. Highway 24 Independence MO 64050.
10. Today pollsters such as the Gallup Organization and Yankelovich Partners Inc. still predict how Americans will react to important issues.

10 Other Punctuation

1. Semicolons and Colons (links to exercise A, p. 240)

➡ **1.** attractions: their OR attractions; their

Write the words before and after every punctuation mistake in the sentences below, and correct the error.

1. E-mail, or electronic mail, works in this way; a message is transmitted from one computer to another over the Internet.
2. E-mail enables you to send a friend an urgent message at 4;00 in the morning.
3. You can use e-mail if you have the following, a computer with a modem, Internet access, and a destination address.
4. An e-mail address should include the user's name, a domain name, and a suffix that tells the domain's classification, for example, the suffix *edu* indicates an educational domain.
5. An e-mail address may also reveal where a user lives; for example, *uk* indicates that the addressee is located in the United Kingdom; *au,* in Australia, and *ke,* in Kenya.
6. E-mail users send: important business information, electronic greeting cards, and friendly messages.
7. An e-mail user can send the same message to a number of different addresses, this is called broadcasting.
8. For example, you can broadcast the same holiday greeting to friends in New York, New York; Boston, Massachusetts, San Francisco, California; and Chicago, Illinois.
9. The use of e-mail is growing quickly, many billions of messages were sent last year.

10. Most e-mail programs allow senders to attach digitized photos, long, complicated text files; and sound bites to an e-mail message.

2. Hyphens, Dashes, and Ellipses (links to exercise A, p. 244)

→ **1.** legends—sensational, proved—are; **2.** increas-ingly

Write the words before and after every punctuation mistake in the sentences below, and correct the error.

1. In today's high tech world, any mechanic who doesn't understand computerized car functions will quickly become an exmechanic.

2. Most automotive operations from opening windows to controlling exhaust emissions are now handled by microchips.

3. A microchip monitors and controls a car's essential systems— engine speed, oxygen level in the exhaust, and temperature and averts potential problems.

4. Dangerous situations wheel lock and transmission problems, for example—can be detected by the car's computer.

5. Whether a motorist is nineteen or ninety nine, the computer can analyze the driver's style and routine.

6. Some cars are equipped with highly re-active sensors that alert unsuspecting drivers when other automobiles are approaching in a blind spot.

7. Often a computer prevents an accident by activating dashboard lights; this micro-miracle can really save the day!

8. In addition to ensuring driving safety, a computer can even fine tune your radio and lock in your favorite station.

9. In some cars a computer remembers the seat position preferr- ed by each regular driver and adjusts the driver's seat accordingly.

10. According to Mr. Jenkins, our business instructor, "Future automobile computer systems will enable a driver to obtain stock information over the Internet. . . . during an average daily commute."

3. Apostrophes (links to exercise A, p. 247)

→ **1.** '00s   **2.** You're

In the sentences below, find the words in which apostrophes are omitted or incorrectly used. Rewrite the words correctly. If a sentence contains no errors, write *Correct*.

1. Dont you think it would be fun to test exciting new software and get paid for it?

2. To insure that it's operating standards are met, the software industrys instituted a process called beta testing.
3. A good way to get a job in software development in the 2000's is to begin as a beta tester.
4. Beta testings' function is to determine whether a program is free of "bugs", or programming errors.
5. Beta testing puts the power where it belongs—in consumers's hands.
6. Software companies solicit prominent end users' and customers opinions about programs.
7. Beta testers are regular computer users'; they don't have to have Ph.D.s.
8. The key is to make sure everyone's programs run smoothly.
9. If beta tester's report a problem, the software is usually repaired and retested.
10. A software developer usually wont release a product to the public if it hasnt passed beta tests.

4. Quotation Marks and Italics (links to exercise A, p. 251)

➡ 1. "Meet a Real Game Boy"

Write the words affected by each error in the use of quotation marks or italics, correcting the mistake.

1. As our computer-science class wrapped up for the term, Ms. Nguyen asked, "What trends do you envision for the World Wide Web"?
2. I had just read some predictions in a book called "The Age of Computers."
3. "It seems to me that new technology will make it easier to search the Web", I responded.
4. "Yes", Ms. Nguyen agreed. "There must be some new search-engine concepts in development right now!"
5. My friend Thomas added, "In today's newspaper the analyst Jane Hintin predicts, 'In a few years, there will be new copyright laws designed for increased protection of intellectual property."
6. "I also saw that article in the 'Daily Post,' Thomas, and I think that Hintin makes some excellent points," agreed Ms. Nguyen.
7. Jill interjected, "I think business on the Web will just keep increasing.
8. Jamal told us about a magazine article entitled The New Web.

9. The article was about Webbers, or computers used only to access the Internet.
10. Later I read our textbook's final chapter, The Future's Closer Than You Think, and I couldn't agree more with the title!

5. Parentheses and Brackets (links to exercise A, p. 253)

➜ **1.** If you are looking for a high-tech job (either a summer job or full-time employment), you may find it on the Internet.

Rewrite each sentence, adding or correcting parentheses or brackets where needed and correcting any misplaced commas or end marks.

1. A robot is a program that searches the WWW World Wide Web.
2. Robots are known by many other names, including (1) wanderers, (2) softbots, (3) spiders, 4 crawlers, and 5) fish.
3. Resourceful little devices that they are, robots often retain the address (also known as the URL [Uniform Resource Locator) of every Web page they have searched.
4. A type of robot known as an index spider performs even more specialized functions. (it saves page titles and even whole Web pages for users).
5. The reference librarian, Mrs. Shields, wrote in a memo, "In order to save time, [some) robots delete invalid addresses."

Forming Plural Nouns

To form the plural of most nouns, just add -s.

prizes   dreams   circles   stations

For most singular nouns ending in o, add -s.

solos   halos   studios   photos   pianos

For a few nouns ending in o, add -es.

heroes   tomatoes   potatoes   echoes

When the singular noun ends in s, sh, ch, x, or z, add -es.

waitresses   brushes   ditches   axes   buzzes

When a singular noun ends in y with a consonant before it, change the y to i and add -es.

army—armies   candy—candies   baby—babies
diary—diaries   ferry—ferries   conspiracy—conspiracies

When a vowel (a, e, i, o, u) comes before the y, just add -s.

boy—boys   way—ways   array—arrays
alloy—alloys   weekday—weekdays   jockey—jockeys

For most nouns ending in f or fe, change the f to v and add -es or -s. Since there is no rule, you must memorize such words.

life—lives   calf—calves   knife—knives
thief—thieves   shelf—shelves   loaf—loaves

For some nouns ending in f, add -s to make the plural.

roofs   chiefs   reefs   beliefs

Some nouns have the same form for both singular and plural.

deer   sheep   moose   salmon   trout

For some nouns, the plural is formed in a special way.

man—men   goose—geese   ox—oxen
woman—women   mouse—mice   child—children

For a compound noun written as one word, form the plural by changing the last word in the compound to its plural form.

stepchild—stepchildren   firefly—fireflies

If a compound noun is written as a hyphenated word or as two separate words, change the most important word to the plural form.

brother-in-law—brothers-in-law   life jacket—life jackets

Forming Possessives

If a noun is singular, add 's.

   mother—my mother's car   Ross—Ross's desk

Exception: the s after the apostrophe is dropped after *Jesus'*, *Moses'*, and certain names in classical mythology (*Zeus'*). These possessive forms, therefore, can be pronounced easily.

If a noun is plural and ends with **s**, just add an apostrophe.

   parents—my parents' car   the Santinis—the Santinis' house

If a noun is plural but does not end in **s**, add 's.

   people—the people's choice women—the women's coats

Spelling Rules

Words Ending in a Silent *e*

Before adding a suffix beginning with a vowel or **y** to a word ending in a silent **e**, drop the **e** (with some exceptions).

   amaze + -ing = amazing   love + -able = lovable
   create + -ed = created   nerve + -ous = nervous

Exceptions: *change + -able = changeable; courage + -ous = courageous*

When adding a suffix beginning with a consonant to a word ending in a silent **e**, keep the **e** (with some exceptions).

   late + -ly = lately   spite + -ful = spiteful
   noise + -less = noiseless   state + -ment = statement

Exceptions include *truly, argument, ninth, wholly,* and *awful.*

When a suffix beginning with **a** or **o** is added to a word with a final silent **e**, the final **e** is usually retained if it is preceded by a soft **c** or a soft **g**.

   bridge + -able = bridgeable   peace + -able = peaceable
   outrage + -ous = outrageous advantage + -ous = advantageous

When a suffix beginning with a vowel is added to words ending in **ee** or **oe**, the final silent **e** is retained.

   agree + -ing = agreeing   free + -ing = freeing
   hoe + -ing = hoeing   see + -ing = seeing

Words Ending in y

Before adding a suffix to a word that ends in **y** preceded by a consonant, change the **y** to **i**.

easy + -est = easiest	crazy + -est = craziest
silly + -ness = silliness	marry + -age = marriage

Exceptions include *dryness, shyness,* and *slyness.*

However, when you add *-ing,* the **y** does not change.

empty + -ed = emptied   but   empty + -ing = emptying

When adding a suffix to a word that ends in **y** and is preceded by a vowel, the **y** usually does not change.

play + -er = player	employ + -ed = employed
coy + -ness = coyness	pay + -able = payable

Exceptions include *daily* and *gaily.*

Words Ending in a Consonant

In one-syllable words that end in one consonant preceded by one vowel, double the final consonant before adding a suffix beginning with a vowel, such as *-ed* or *-ing.* These are sometimes called 1+1+1 words.

dip + -ed = dipped	set + -ing = setting
slim + -est = slimmest	fit + -er = fitter

The rule does not apply to words of one syllable that end in a consonant preceded by two vowels.

feel + -ing = feeling	peel + -ed = peeled
reap + -ed = reaped	loot + -ed = looted

In words of more than one syllable, double the final consonant **(1)** when the word ends with one consonant preceded by one vowel and **(2)** when the word is accented on the last syllable.

be•gin´   per•mit´   re•fer´

In the following examples, note that in the new words formed with suffixes, the accent remains on the same syllable.

be•gin´ + -ing = be•gin´ning = beginning
per•mit´ + -ed = per•mit´ted = permitted

In the following examples, the accent does not remain on the same syllable; thus, the final consonant is not doubled.

re•fer´ + -ence = ref´er•ence = reference
con•fer´ + -ence = con´fer•ence = conference

Prefixes and Suffixes

When adding a prefix to a word, do not change the spelling of the base word. When a prefix creates a double letter, keep both letters.

dis- + approve = disapprove re- + build = rebuild
ir- + regular = irregular   mis- + spell = misspell
anti- + trust = antitrust   il- + logical = illogical

When adding *-ly* to a word ending in *l,* keep both *l*'s. When adding *-ness* to a word ending in *n,* keep both *n*'s.

careful + -ly = carefully   sudden + -ness = suddenness
final + -ly = finally   thin + -ness = thinness

Special Spelling Problems

Only one English word ends in *-sede: supersede.* Three words end in *-ceed: exceed, proceed,* and *succeed.* All other verbs ending in the sound *-seed* are spelled with *-cede.*

concede precede recede secede

In words with *ie* and *ei* when the sound is long *e* ($\bar{e}$), the word is spelled *ie* except after *c* (with some exceptions).

i before *e*	thief	relieve	piece	field	grieve	pier
except after *c*	conceit	perceive	ceiling	receive	receipt
Exceptions:	either	neither	weird	leisure	seize

Commonly Misspelled Words

abbreviate	development	lightning	rehearse
accidentally	dictionary	literature	repetition
achievement	different	loneliness	restaurant
amateur	disappear	marriage	rhythm
analyze	disappoint	mathematics	ridiculous
anonymous	discipline	minimum	sandwich
answer	dissatisfied	mischievous	schedule
apologize	efficient	mortgage	scissors
appearance	eighth	necessary	seize
appreciate	eligible	nickel	separate
appropriate	eliminate	ninety	sergeant
argument	embarrass	noticeable	similar
associate	enthusiastic	nuclear	sincerely
awkward	especially	nuisance	sophomore
beginning	exaggerate	obstacle	souvenir
believe	exceed	occasionally	specifically
bicycle	existence	occurrence	strategy
brief	experience	opinion	success
bulletin	familiar	opportunity	surprise
bureau	fascinating	outrageous	syllable
business	February	parallel	sympathy
calendar	financial	particularly	symptom
campaign	foreign	permanent	temperature
candidate	fourth	permissible	thorough
certain	fragile	persuade	throughout
changeable	generally	pleasant	tomorrow
characteristic	government	pneumonia	traffic
column	grammar	possess	tragedy
committee	guarantee	possibility	transferred
courageous	guard	prejudice	truly
courteous	height	privilege	Tuesday
criticize	humorous	probably	twelfth
curiosity	immediately	pursue	undoubtedly
decision	independent	psychology	unnecessary
definitely	indispensable	realize	usable
dependent	irritable	receipt	vacuum
description	judgment	receive	vicinity
desirable	knowledge	recognize	village
despair	laboratory	recommend	weird
desperate	license	reference	yield

Good writers master words that are easy to misuse and misspell. Study the following words, noting how their meanings differ.

accept, except	*Accept* means "to agree to something" or "to receive something willingly." *Except* usually means "not including." **Did the teacher** *accept* **your report?** **Everyone smiled for the photographer** *except* **Jody.**
adapt, adopt	*Adapt* means "to make apt or suitable; to adjust." *Adopt* means "to opt or choose as one's own; to accept." **The writer** *adapted* **the play for the screen.** **After years of living in Japan, she had** *adopted* **its culture.**
advice, advise	*Advice* is a noun that means "counsel given to someone." *Advise* is a verb that means "to give counsel." **Jim should take some of his own** *advice.* **The mechanic** *advised* **me to get new brakes for my car.**
affect, effect	*Affect* means "to move or influence" or "to wear or to pretend to have." *Effect* as a verb means "to bring about." As a noun, *effect* means "the result of an action." **The news from South Africa** *affected* **him deeply.** **The band's singer** *affects* **a British accent.** **The students tried to** *effect* **a change in school policy.** **What** *effect* **did the acidic soil produce in the plants?**
all ready, already	*All ready* means "all are ready" or "completely prepared." *Already* means "previously." **The students were** *all ready* **for the field trip.** **We had** *already* **pitched our tent before it started raining.**
all right	*All right* is the correct spelling. *Alright* is nonstandard and should not be used.
a lot	*A lot* may be used in informal writing. *Alot* is incorrect.
all together altogether	are adverbs that mean "entirely" or "on the whole." **The news story is** *altogether* **false.** **Let's sing a song** *all together.*

among, between	are prepositions. *Between* refers to two people or things. The object of *between* is never singular. *Among* refers to a group of three or more. **Texas lies** *between* **Louisiana and New Mexico.** **What are the differences** *among* **the four candidates?**
anywhere, nowhere, somewhere, anyway	are all correct. *Anywheres, nowheres, somewheres,* and *anyways* are incorrect. **I don't see geometry mentioned** *anywhere.* *Somewhere* **in this book is a map of ancient Sumer.** *Anyway,* **this street map is out of date.**
borrow, lend	*Borrow* means "to receive something on loan." *Lend* means "to give out temporarily." **Please** *lend* **me your book.** **He** *borrowed* **five dollars from his sister.**
bring, take	*Bring* refers to movement toward or with. *Take* refers to movement away from. **I'll** *bring* **you a glass of water.** **Would you please** *take* **these apples to Pam and John?**
can, may	*Can* means "to be able; to have the power to do something." *May* means "to have permission to do something." *May* can also mean "possibly will." **We** *may* **not use pesticides on our community garden.** **Pesticides** *may* **not be necessary, anyway.** **Vegetables** *can* **grow nicely without pesticides.**
capital, capitol, the Capitol	*Capital* means "excellent," "most serious," or "most important." It also means "seat of government." *Capitol* is a "building in which a state legislature meets." The *Capitol* is "the building in Washington, D.C., in which the U.S. Congress meets." **Proper nouns begin with** *capital* **letters.** **Is Madison the** *capital* **of Wisconsin?** **Protesters rallied at the state** *capitol.* **A subway connects the Senate and the House in** *the Capitol.*
choose, chose	*Choose* is a verb that means "to decide or prefer." *Chose* is the past tense form of *choose.* **He had to** *choose* **between art and band.** **She** *chose* **to write for the school newspaper.**

desert, dessert	*Desert* (des´ ert) means "a dry, sandy, barren region." *Desert* (de sert´) means "to abandon." *Dessert* (des sert´) is a sweet, such as cake. **The Sahara in North Africa is the world's largest *desert*.** **The night guard did not *desert* his post.** **Alison's favorite *dessert* is chocolate cake.**
differ from, differ with	*Differ from* means "to be dissimilar." *Differ with* means "to disagree with." **The racing bike *differs* greatly *from* the mountain bike.** **I *differ with* her as to the meaning of Hamlet's speech.**
different from	is used to compare dissimilar items. *Different than* is nonstandard. **The hot sauce is much *different from* the yogurt sauce.**
farther, further	*Farther* refers to distance. *Further* refers to something additional. **We traveled two hundred miles *farther* that afternoon.** **This idea needs *further* discussion.**
fewer, less	*Fewer* refers to numbers of things that can be counted. *Less* refers to amount, degree, or value. ***Fewer* than ten students camped out.** **We made *less* money this year on the walkathon than last year.**
good, well	*Good* is always an adjective. *Well* is usually an adverb that modifies an action verb. *Well* can also be an adjective meaning "in good health." **Dana felt *good* when she finished painting her room.** **Angela ran *well* in yesterday's race.** **I felt *well* when I left my house.**
imply, infer	*Imply* means "to suggest something in an indirect way." *Infer* means "to come to a conclusion based on something that has been read or heard." **Josh *implied* that he would be taking the bus.** **From what you said, I *inferred* that the book would be difficult.**
its, it's	*Its* is a possessive pronoun. *It's* is a contraction for *it is* or *it has*. **Sanibel Island is known for *its* beautiful beaches.** ***It's* great weather for a picnic.**

kind of, sort of	Neither of these two expressions should be followed by the word *a*. **What *kind of* horse is Scout?** **What *sorts of* animals live in swamps?** The use of these two expressions as adverbs, as in "It's kind of hot today," is informal.
lay, lie	*Lay* is a verb that means "to place." It takes a direct object. *Lie* is a verb that means "to be in a certain place." *Lie,* or its past form *lay,* never takes a direct object. **The carpenter will *lay* the planks on the bench.** **My cat likes to *lie* under the bed.**
lead, led	*Lead* can be a noun that means "a heavy metal" or a verb that means "to show the way." *Led* is the past tense form of the verb. ***Lead* is used in nuclear reactors.** **Raul always *leads* his team onto the field.** **She *led* the class as president of the student council.**
learn, teach	*Learn* means "to gain knowledge." *Teach* means "to instruct." **Enrique is *learning* about black holes in space.** **Marva *teaches* astronomy at a college in the city.**
leave, let	*Leave* means "to go away from." *Leave* can be transitive or intransitive. *Let* is usually used with another verb. It means "to allow to." **Don't *leave* the refrigerator open.** **She *leaves* for Scotland tomorrow.** **Cyclops wouldn't *let* Odysseus' men *leave* the cave.**
like	as a conjunction before a clause is incorrect. Use *as* or *as if*. **Ramon talked *as if* he had a cold.**
loan, lone	*Loan* refers to "something given for temporary use." *Lone* refers to "the condition of being by oneself, alone." **I gave that shirt to Max as a gift, not a *loan*.** **The *lone* plant in our yard turned out to be a weed.**
lose, loose	*Lose* means "to mislay or suffer the loss of something." *Loose* means "free" or "not fastened." **That tire will *lose* air unless you patch it.** **My little brother has three *loose* teeth.**

majority	means more than half of a group of things or people that can be counted. It is incorrect to use *majority* in referring to time or distance, as in "The majority of our time there was wasted." **Most of our time there was wasted.** **The *majority* of the students study a foreign language.**
most, almost	*Most* can be a pronoun, an adjective, or an adverb, but it should never be used in place of *almost,* an adverb that means "nearly." *Most* **of the students enjoy writing in their journals.** (pronoun) *Most* **mammals give birth to live young.** (adjective) **You missed the** *most* **exciting part of the trip.** (adverb) *Almost* **every mammal gives live birth.** (adverb)
of	is incorrectly used in a phrase such as *could of.* Examples of correct wordings are *could have, should have,* and *must have.* **I** *must have* **missed the phone call.** **If you had played, we** *would have* **won.**
principal, principle	*Principal* means "of chief or central importance" and refers to the head of a school. *Principle* is a "basic truth, standard, or rule of behavior." **Lack of customers is the** *principal* **reason for closing the store.** **The** *principal* **of our school awarded the trophy.** **One of my** *principles* **is to be honest with others.**
quiet, quite	*Quiet* refers to "freedom from noise or disturbance." *Quite* means "truly" or "almost completely." **Observers must be** *quiet* **during the recording session.** **We were** *quite* **worried about the results of the test.**
raise, rise	*Raise* means "to lift" or "to make something go up." It takes a direct object. *Rise* means "to go upward." It does not take a direct object. **The maintenance workers** *raise* **the flag each morning.** **The city's population is expected to** *rise* **steadily.**
real, really	*Real* is an adjective meaning "actual; true." Really is an adverb meaning "in reality; in fact." *Real* **skill comes from concentration and practice.** **She doesn't** *really* **know all the facts.**

seldom	should not be followed by *ever,* as in "We seldom ever run more than a mile." *Seldom, rarely, very seldom,* and *hardly ever* all are correct. **I** *seldom* **hear traditional jazz.**
set, sit	*Set* means "to place" and takes a direct object. *Sit* means "to occupy a seat or a place" and does not take a direct object. **He** *set* **the box down outside the shed.** **We** *sit* **in the last row of the upper balcony.**
stationary, stationery	*Stationary* means "fixed or unmoving." *Stationery* means "fine paper for writing letters." **The wheel pivots, but the seat is** *stationary.* **Rex wrote on special** *stationery* **imprinted with his name.**
than, then	*Than* is used to introduce the second part of a comparison. *Then* means "next in order." **Ramon is stronger** *than* **Mark.** **Cut the grass and** *then* **trim the hedges.**
their, there, they're	*Their* means "belonging to them." *There* means "in that place." *They're* is the contraction for *they are.* **All the campers returned to** *their* **cabins.** **I keep my card collection** *there* **in those folders.** **Lisa and Beth run daily;** *they're* **on the track team.**
way	refers to distance; *ways* is nonstandard and should not be used in writing. **The subway was a long** *way* **from the stadium.**
whose, who's	*Whose* is the possessive form of *who. Who's* is a contraction for *who is* or *who has.* ***Whose* parents will drive us to the movies?** ***Who's* going to the recycling center?**
your, you're	*Your* is the possessive form of *you. You're* is a contraction for *you are.* **What was** *your* **record in the fifty-yard dash?** ***You're* one of the winners of the essay contest.**

Index

A

semicolons in, 238
Compound subjects, 29, 46, 136–137
  joined by *and*, 136, 148
  joined by *nor*, 136, 148
  joined by *or*, 136, 148
Compound verbs, 29, 46
Computers. *See* Internet.
Concrete nouns, 7
Conjunctions, 21–22, 23. *See also*
  Conjunctive adverbs; Run-on
  sentences.
  commas in compound sentences,
  224
  coordinating, 21, 76
  correlative, 21
  semicolon between independent
  clauses, 239
  subordinating, 22, 77, 84
Conjunctive adverbs, 21
Constellation, capitalization of, 206
Continent names, capitalization of, 202
Coordinating conjunctions, 21, 76
Correlative conjunctions, 21
Correspondence. *See* Letters
  (documents).
Could of, might of, would of, and *should
  of,* 120
Country names, capitalization of, 202

D

Dangling modifiers, 187–188
Dashes, 243, 255, 258
Dates
  capitalization of, 213
  commas with, 228
Days, capitalization of, 213
Definitions
  quotation marks for, 250
Degrees (educational), capitalization of,
  217
Degrees of comparison, 194, 195
  negative superlative, 194
  superlative, 180–185, 194
Deities, capitalization of, 201
Demonstrative pronouns, 11
  as adjectives, 178
Denominations (religious), capitalization
  of, 201
Dependent clauses, 76
  separating from independent clause,
  238

Desert and *dessert,* 328
Dessert and *desert,* 326
Diagramming sentences, 38–41
  adjectives and adverbs, 39
  complex sentences, 92
  compound-complex sentences, 95
  compound sentences, 92
  compound subjects and verbs,
  38–39
  direct objects, 40
  indirect objects, 40–41
  objective complements, 41
  phrases, 64–67
  simple subjects and verbs, 38
  subject complements, 39–40
Different from, 328
Differ from and *differ with,* 328
Direct address
  capitalization of titles, 199
  nouns of, 222
Directions (geographical), capitalization
  of, 202
Direct objects, 36, 46
  diagramming, 40
  transitive verb and, 13
Direct quotations
  capitalization in, 208
  punctuating, 248
Divided quotations, capitalization in,
  208
Double negatives, 188, 195
Drafting,
  rough draft, 170

E

Educational degrees, capitalization of,
  217
Effect and *affect,* 326
Ellipses, 243, 258
Elliptical clauses, 81
  pronoun in, 175
Else, possessive of, 245
Emphatic verb forms, 112
End marks, 218–221, 234–235. *See
  also* Exclamation points; Periods;
  Question marks.
-er, in comparison, 194
Essays
  quotation marks for titles, 250
Essential (restrictive) adjective clauses,
  80

100
colons with, 239
joining with commas, 224
separating from dependent clause, 238
Indicative mood (of a verb), 116
Indirect objects, 36, 46
diagramming, 40–41
Infer and *imply*, 326
Infinitive, 55, 60
Infinitive phrases, 60–61, 72
commas after, 222
diagramming, 66–67
Initials, capitalization of, 198
Institutional names, capitalization of, 205
Intensive pronouns, 10, 165
Interjections, 22
commas with, 222
Internet.
capitalization etiquette for, 217
case in, 217
Interrogative pronouns, 10
Interrogative sentences, 31. *See also* Questions.
Interrupters, commas with, 222–223
Intransitive verbs, 13
Introductory elements, commas with, 222
Inverted sentences
subject of sentence in, 32, 47
subject-verb agreement in, 141, 149
Irregular comparisons, 181
Irregular verbs, 105, 126
Italics, 250, 258, 259
for foreign words or phrases, 251
for titles (literary), 250
for words referred to as words, 251
Its and *it's,* 328

J, K

Jr., capitalization of, 199
Junior (as school term), capitalization of, 206
Kind of and *sort of,* 329
Knowledge, capitalization of tests of, 217

L

Land features, capitalization of, 202

Landmarks, capitalization of, 206
Language names, capitalization of, 201
Lay and *lie,* 119, 329
Lead and *led,* 329
Learn and *teach,* 329
Least, in comparison, 194
Leave and *let,* 119, 329
Led and *lead,* 329
Lend and *borrow,* 327
Less
in comparison, 194
and *fewer,* 328
Let and *leave,* 119, 329
Letters (alphabet), plurals of, 246
Letters (documents).
business letters, 228, 239
capitalization in, 208
colons in business letters, 239
commas in salutations and closings, 228
cover letters, 228
Levels of language
technical terms, 250
Lie and *lay,* 119, 329
Like, 329
Linking verbs, 13–14, 104
be as, 14
Lists
colons to introduce, 239
commas with, 224
in compositions, 314
Literary works, capitalization of titles, 209, 213
Loan and *lone,* 329
Lone and *loan,* 329
Loose and *lose,* 329

M

Magazines,
italics for titles, 250
Main clauses. *See* Independent (main) clauses.
Majority, 330
May and *can,* 327
Mechanics. *See* Capitalization; Punctuation.
Might of, would of, should of, and *could of,* 120
Misplaced modifiers, 62, 187–188, 195
Modifiers, 176–195. *See also*

for slang terms, 250
for technical terms, 250
for titles (literary), 250
for unusual words, 250

Quotations
brackets in, 252
capitalization in, 208
colons to introduce, 239
commas with, 228
of more than one paragraph, 249
omissions from, 243
within quotation, 248

R

Races, capitalization of, 201
Raise and *rise,* 119, 330
Real and *really,* 330
Reference problems, of pronouns,
167–169
Reference works,
parentheses for, 252
Reflexive pronouns, 10, 165
Regions, capitalization of, 202
Regular verbs, 104
Relative adverbs, 79
adjective clause introduced by, 93
Relative clauses, 79
Relative pronouns, 11, 79, 84
subject-verb agreement with, 142
Religious terms, capitalization of, 201
Religious works, colons in, 240
Research summary, commas in,
230–233
Restrictive (essential) adjective
clauses, 80
Restrictive (essential) appositives, 53,
72
Revising,
of feature article, 43
of speech, 171
Rise and *raise,* 119, 330
Rough draft, of speech, 170
Run-on sentences, 90
comma splice as, 224
correcting, 101

S

-s
forming possessives, 322
plurals with singular nouns ending

in, 245, 321
subject-verb agreement with singular
nouns ending in, 138–139
as word ending, 131
Sacred days, capitalization of, 201
Sacred writings, capitalization of, 201
Salutations
commas in, 228
of formal business letters, 239
School subjects and terms,
capitalization of, 206
Seasons, capitalization of, 202
Second-person pronouns, 130, 152
Seldom, 331
Semicolons, 238–240, 255, 258
in compound sentences, 238
quotation marks with, 248
in series, 239
Senior (as school term), capitalization
of, 206
Sentence combining. *See* Compound
sentences.
Sentence fragments, 89. *See also*
Sentences.
correcting, 101
subject or predicate missing from
sentence, 27
Sentence parts, commas in, 222–225
Sentences. *See also* Compound
sentences; Imperative
sentences, subject-verb
agreement in; Inverted
sentences; Sentence structure.
agreement with predicate
nominatives, 142
beginning with here and there, 32,
47
complex, 87, 93
declarative, 31
diagramming, 38–41, 64–67, 92–96
exclamatory, 31
fragments of, 27
imperative, 31
interrogative, 31
parts of, 24–47
run-on, 90, 101
subject complements in, 34–35
subject in, 32
subjects in unusual positions in,
32–33
subject-verb agreement in inverted,
141
types of, 31

with titles, 139, 148
in writing yearbook captions, 144–145
Subjunctive mood (of a verb), 116
Subordinate clauses, 76, 97, 100
adjective clauses as, 79
adverb clauses as, 80–81
noun clauses as, 83–85
who and *whom* in, 158
Subordinating conjunctions, 22, 77, 84
Suffixes, 322, 323, 324
hyphens with, 242
Superlative degree, adjectives and, 180–185, 194
Supplementary material, dashes for, 243

T

Take and *bring,* 119, 327
Teach and *learn,* 329
Technical terms, quotation marks for, 250
Television
italics for series titles, 250
quotation marks for episode titles, 250
Tenses of verbs, 122, 123, 127
forming and using, 107–109
future, 107, 127
future perfect, 107, 109, 127
future perfect progressive, 111, 127
future progressive, 111, 127
future tense, 108
improper shift in, 118
past, 107, 108, 127
past perfect, 107, 109, 127
past perfect progressive, 111, 127
past progressive, 111, 127
perfect, 107
present, 107, 127
present perfect, 107, 108, 127
present perfect progressive, 111, 127
present progressive, 111, 127
progressive, 111, 127
simple, 107
Tests
of knowledge, 217
Than and *then,* 331
That, rules for adjectival use of, 186
Their, there, and *they're,* 331
Them, rules for adjectival use of, 186

There
subject in sentence beginning with, 32, 47
subject-verb agreement with, 141, 149
their, and *they're,* 331
These, rules for adjectival use of, 186
Third-person pronouns, 130, 152
This, rules for adjectival use of, 186
Those, rules for adjectival use of, 186
Time
capitalization of, 210
colons in, 240
possessives as measures of, 245
Titles (literary), 209, 213
of compositions, 314
italics with, 250
quotation marks with, 250
subject-verb agreement with, 139
Titles (personal), 199, 213
Train names
capitalization of, 206
italics for, 250
Transitive verb, 13
Transportation vehicles. *See* Vehicle names.

U, V

Universe, capitalization of objects in, 206
Us, with appositives, 164
Vehicle names
capitalization of, 206
italics for, 250
Verbal phrases, 55
Verbals, 55
gerund phrases, 58–59
gerunds, 55
infinitive phrases, 60–61
infinitives, 55
participles, 55
Verb phrases, 14
Verbs, 13–15, 102–127. *See also* Adverbs; Objects of verbs; Subject-verb agreement; Verbals.
action, 13, 104
auxiliary, 14
commonly confused verbs, 119–120, 326, 327, 328, 329, 330, 331
compound, 29

W, Y, Z

Acknowledgments

CHAPTER 8   196 © David Burnett/Contact Press Images/PNI; 199 IBM Corporation; 200 © Shelley Gazin/Corbis; 203 © Charles & Josette Lenars/Corbis; 205 Paul Schutzer/Life Magazine © Time Inc. 206 NASA; 207 © Corbis-Bettmann; 208 © Corbis/Hulton-Deutsch Collection; 210 © Rainbird/Robert Harding Picture Library; 212, 212–213 bottom © Henry Horenstein/Getty Images; 213 center left, bottom right © Getty Images

CHAPTER 9   218 background © Steven Weinberg/Getty Images; foreground Illustration by Daniel Guidera; 221 © Robert Bone/Words & Pictures/PNI; 225 Arne Hodalic/Corbis; 231 © Michael S. Yamashita/Corbis; 234 bottom, Peanuts reprinted by permission of United Feature Syndicate, Inc.

CHAPTER 10   236 background Photo by Sharon Hoogstraten; 238 © Elizabeth Sumners/Nonstock/PNI; 242 Close to Home copyright © 1993. John McPherson. Reprinted with permission of Universal Press Syndicate. All rights reserved; 247 © Getty Images; 250 © Richard Bickel/Corbis; 259 top left to right © Getty Images.

For Literature and Text

Agencia Literaria Carmen Balcells S. A.: Excerpt from "Writing as an Act of Hope" by Isabel Allende in *Paths of Resistance,* edited by William Zinsser. Copyright © 1989 by Isabel Allende. Reprinted by permission of the author's agent.

The Beacon News: Excerpt from "Fame Sets the Stage for a Showcase of Talent" by Dan Zeff, from *The Beacon News,* January 31, 1999.

Chicago Tribune: Excerpts from "City's Residency Probers Under Attack" by Gary Washburn, from *Chicago Tribune,* March 11, 1999. Copyright © 1999 Chicago Tribune Company. All rights reserved. Used with permission.

Grove/Atlantic and Random House Canada: Excerpt from "At the Pitt-Rivers," from *Pack of Cards and Other Stories* by Penelope Lively. Copyright © 1978 by Penelope Lively. Used by permission of Grove/Atlantic, Inc. and Random House Canada.

New York Times: Excerpt from "A Blue Oasis, Seen from Space" by Dennis Overbye, from *New York Times,* December 22, 1998. Copyright © 1998 by the New York Times Co. Reprinted by permission.

Northwest Regional Educational Laboratory: "Six Traits of Good Writing" used by permission of Northwest Regional Educational Laboratory, Portland, Oregon.

Random House: From *Dave Barry Does Japan* by Dave Barry. Copyright © 1992 by Dave Barry. Used by permission of Random House, Inc.
      Excerpt from "Civil Peace," from *Girls at War and Other Stories* by Chinua Achebe. Copyright © 1972, 1973 by Chinua Achebe. Published by Doubleday, a division of Random House, Inc.
      Excerpt from "A Cup of Tea," from *The Short Stories of Katherine Mansfield* by Katherine Mansfield. Published by Random House, Inc.

Scovil Chichak Galen Literary Agency: Excerpt from "We'll Never Conquer Space" by Arthur C. Clarke. Copyright © Arthur C. Clarke. Reprinted by permission of the author and the author's agents, Scovil Chichak Galen Literary Agency, Inc.

The editors have made every effort to trace the ownership of all copyrighted material found in this book and to make full acknowledgment for its use. Omissions brought to our attention will be corrected in a subsequent edition.